James J. Wesley Johnston

Dwellers in Gotham

A Romance of New York

James J. Wesley Johnston

Dwellers in Gotham
A Romance of New York

ISBN/EAN: 9783744673655

Printed in Europe, USA, Canada, Australia, Japan

Cover: Foto ©Thomas Meinert / pixelio.de

More available books at **www.hansebooks.com**

DWELLERS IN GOTHAM

A Romance of New York

By ANNAN DALE

NEW YORK: EATON & MAINS
CINCINNATI: CURTS & JENNINGS

To those who have adopted the Motto,

"For the wrong that needs resistance,
For the right that needs assistance,
For the future in the distance,
And the good that I can do,"

This book is gratefully dedicated.

New York. 1898.

CONTENTS.

v

BOOK I.—BREAD

Dwellers in Gotham.

CHAPTER I.

College Cronies.

"THERE is nothing about books that to me is so dull, so dreary, and so useless as a preface. If an author has anything to say, why not say it in the book itself, and not weary one with prologues and announcements?" and with an impatient gesture the speaker shut the book which he held in his hand; but, finding that this did not quite meet the necessities of the case, he began pacing up and down the room with considerable vigor.

"What you say is true, but why waste so much energy upon such a trifle? Here you are striding around and consuming yourself generally, simply because your author invited you to enter his house by a graceful, winding path instead of the common, prosaic door," was the answer of a young man who was languidly smoking a "bull-dog" briar, and with the same languor was watching the tiny smoke rings floating over his head and beyond the couch upon which he was comfortably stretched.

"I don't object to winding paths, or even driveways and avenues, if they are necessary, but when a man's house is on the street, and that street a public

thoroughfare, why the way in should be through a
series of vestibules all posters and placards is not
quite clear to my mind;" and the eyes still glowed,
though with less fire, and the striding was not quite
so vehement.

"Ah! my dear boy, the number of things which
are not quite clear to your mind reach out beyond
the limits of even my comprehension. It grieves
me to think that the cloudiness and general obscura-
tion of which you complain are natural; but you are
young, and your case is by no means hopeless.
'Don't give up the ship,' and remember I am your
friend;" and with an indolence worthy of an Oriental
he allowed his eyes listlessly to follow the rings of
smoke in the direction of the open window.

"Well, if it pleases you to think that I am dense
and sublimely stupid, you will be sufficiently just to
make proper allowance for my associations. One
thing, however, you have not done, and that is, made
me as easy and indifferent as you are. I still take
an interest in things and in people, and the concerns
of this world are matters of concern to me; but you
look on and smile on, like a graven cherub in some
cathedral;" and the tone, though of good-humored
banter, was edged with delicate reproof.

"I thought it was coming! Now bring on your
'Macedonian cry,' also the 'sad undertone of life,'
and don't forget 'the pitiful and pathetic struggle.'
It is fully three days since you aired the 'woes and
wrongs' and the 'sacred rights trampled.' Meantime
let me so arrange these pillows that the body of my
flesh may not impede the high movement of your

soul;" and, so saying, he assumed an air of patient endurance.

"O, thou well-fed, well-clad, well-formed Gallio! Little dost thou care for the riot in the market place, or the angry mob shouting and struggling. For Gallio fares sumptuously every day. He has a handsome allowance from his father; he can fit up his apartments as he pleases; upon him no burden or obligation rests. Then why should he trouble or vex his complacent soul with the 'woes and wrongs' which sit so lightly on his tongue, or with the 'Macedonian cry' which he has never heard?"

"Capital! You have struck a new lead, old fellow. That Gallio idea is fine; but now, as a worthy Roman who had the good sense to mind his own business, he commends himself most refreshingly. I am glad you brought him with you this afternoon. Bring him again, and I would suggest him as something of an example for yourself. As between Paul, the iconoclast, and Demetrius, the labor agitator, I would do just as Gallio did—drive the whole raft of wranglers away and let them settle their dispute elsewhere;" and the smoke rings curled as gracefully as ever, and were followed with the same languid interest.

"Yes, but wasn't it cowardly—a mean evasion of responsibility? It was his place to give judgment; he was there to settle just such disputes, and for a man arbitrarily to dispose of the whole business as he did shows an utter indifference to the claims of justice;" and the eyes had now regained their former glow, and the face was full of earnestness.

" Now, Vaughen, as your ' guide, philosopher, and friend,' let me give you some good advice. It is very evident that you don't understand Gallio ; this, however, is only natural, as he was before your time. It is a disadvantage to be either behind or before your age. David, Israel's favorite king, had the good sense to ' serve his own generation,' which accounts for his general success. These Utopian men who insist upon climbing the hills of futurity and planning for the interests of unborn millions are exceedingly tiresome. It is true that Solomon did not say, ' Make hay while the sun shines,' but he did say, ' The churning of milk bringeth forth butter,' which means practically the same thing. Take my advice, and churn milk. Improve the breed and condition of the cows; see that the pasturage is good; get the latest and most improved churn ; let butter be your objective point. The world insists upon your making butter, and the more of it you can make and market the better for yourself and all concerned."

The place was a New England college town ; the speakers were Edward Vaughen and John Disney; the time was the month of June, and the year was early in the nineties. The room was Disney's, but the close companionship of four years had given Vaughen a sense of ownership little less, if, indeed, anything, than that of the legal occupant. Entering college at the same time, both fairly studious and having many things in common, the young men became fast friends, and now that they were to separate within a few weeks much of their last days were spent together.

When Vaughen spoke of Disney as a well-fed, well-clad, and well-formed Gallio he was justified in large measure, for there was in Disney's bearing and appearance every indication of ample means and luxurious tastes. His room was richly furnished, though the effect was thoroughly masculine. True, no imposing pugilists in warlike attitudes, with hands about the size of a huge dumpling and very much in the foreground, occupied the place of honor over the mantelpiece; neither was there the usual group of celebrities whose fields of distinction varied all the way from dime museums to Metropolitan Opera Houses; nor was there any pretentious display of Indian clubs and golf sticks and fishing rods so arranged as to suggest the athlete and the sportsman, an arrangement, by the way, often only a delusion and a snare. Still, despite its daintiness and color and the absence of anything suggestive of the "sport," the room had a virility distinctively its own, and which no one could call in question.

The same was true of Disney himself; for he could pull an oar, swing a bat, don the gloves—in short, do anything that was expected of a strong, active young fellow.

Among certain of the college men he was very popular, for though he could say sharp things, yet he was never ungenerous nor hurtful, and his keen weapon rarely flashed save for amusement.

Vaughen afforded him rare enjoyment, for Vaughen was ardent, full of sympathy, easily aroused, rather inclined, however, to heroics, and upon his favorite themes he would declaim and orate

in a dramatic but somewhat tragic way. Then
Vaughen had tendencies toward socialism which he
aired with much freedom and fluency, but as he knew
even less of socialism than of the Northwest Passage
these tendencies were fairly vague and indefinite.
But, like all young men of his temperament, he was
shy of definitions, and as for cold, rigorous logic, he
treated it much as the priest and the Levite did the
poor fellow who lay on the roadside between Jerusalem and Jericho.   Nevertheless it was really pleasant to hear him so earnestly espouse the cause of the
common people, and the fact that he knew nothing
whatever concerning the real merits of the question
added, if anything, to the satisfaction of listening to
him.   But orators have no right to be held down to
the dead level of plain facts and common statistics.
An imagination which was intended to fly at will in
the upper heavens should not be treated as a barn-
yard fowl.   At least so John Disney reasoned, and,
knowing that Edward Vaughen was not seriously
embarrassed by either the extent or the accuracy
of his information, he could not but enjoy his
oratory.

   "You started in by saying something concerning
a preface," said Disney, "but with characteristic and
becoming consistency you have wandered from your
theme like the sheep from the fold, and unless some
kind shepherd goes after you and brings you back
you will be lost among the mountains."

   "I may have wandered from the preface, but I
tell you, Disney, it is not the one sheep which is
hungry and homeless on the desolate hills; the ninety

and nine are there. Think of the want, the poverty, the hopeless misery— "

" O, Vaughen ! It is only a day or two since you went all over this, and with these same sheep too. Now, I don't like sheep. A sheep never had the same attraction for me that a goat has. There is something positively funny about a goat. A goat's eye has a twinkle as though there were mischief behind it, and the way in which a goat will stand up and face a frowning world is simply heroic. But a sheep is altogether too saintly. Don't, therefore, make such harrowing and distressful appeals to me. I didn't make this world ; it was here before I came, and will be here when I am gone, and if you spend your time declaiming about ' woes ' and ' wrongs,' just remember, my dear boy, that no butter will come from your churn, and as I have often urged upon you, butter, the right kind of butter, is a decided addition to bread. To get bread is comparatively easy, but to get bread and butter in harmonious and abundant relations is the problem of life. The bread board apart from the churn means barrenness, if not barbarism. Hobbs, who lives down in the town in a small tenement, and who can hardly make ends meet, he has bread, but no butter ; Dobbs, who lives up here on the hill in his big house and with every comfort, he has both bread and butter. See ? But my pipe has gone out ; let us do the same."

CHAPTER II.

A Family Council.

JOHN DISNEY was not provokingly and a, gressively rich, as Edward Vaughen migl seem to suggest, for while he had a genero1 college allowance, still his father was neither a ra1 road magnate nor a cotton king, and not even a cor mon millionaire. Dr. Disney, however, was on i: timate terms with many of these magnates ar kings, for he was a physician of extensive practi(among some of the most wealthy and influential fan ilies in New York, and enjoyed in consequence very handsome revenue.

When it is said that Dr. Disney's services were : the most urgent demand by a certain class who: ailments are not obtrusive nor alarming no reflectic is intended, for Dr. Disney was skillful, and in son respects a master in his profession ; but he had di covered that there were those who enjoyed the visi of a doctor, provided he maintained an irreproac able brougham, and whose coming to a house co duced to its importance and dignity. His broughar therefore, was a model of its kind ; and seemed partake of the bearing and character of its occupan It was not somber, neither was it pretentious, yet was essentially dignified and suggestive, and peop instinctively looked from it to the house befo which it stood, the one somehow reflecting upon tl other. His horses, though full-blooded and capable of good work when required, behaved with a due sense of the proprieties; hence there was no jerky switching of tails, no impatient pawing and stamping of feet, no restless twitching and shaking of heads, such as other horses indulge in when the call has been unreasonably prolonged. With a keen sense of the rank and dignity which they were required to maintain they pointedly refused to recognize any of their kin save those who could claim perfect equality, and the contempt with which they received advances from a hired hack or a dry-goods wagon was in the highest form of equine etiquette.

As for the coachman, he was a Personage. His livery was sedate and impressive; his face was both proud and profound. With a bearing which nothing human could disturb he occupied his exalted position, scarcely deigning by a glance to notice the unhappy creatures who were compelled to use the sidewalk.

But, while Dr. Disney's appointments met the demands of the most exacting, they were also in perfect accord with his own gracious and imposing personality. Besides being dignified, Dr. Disney was of stalwart proportions, of handsome countenance, of stately figure, while, in addition, there was an air of conscious superiority which potently diffused itself, so that the very atmosphere in which he lived and moved and had his being seemed charged with mysterious suggestions of greatness and skill. No man in New York knew better the value of appearances, and no man knew better how to maintain them—with seem-

2

ingly no intention of doing so. He was never affected, but always careful; never excited, but always calm and deliberate; and the quiet, dignified way in which he entered the home of a patient was a study in the art of deportment.

"And how is our friend this morning?" was a favorite salutation, and by judicious use of emphasis and intonation he contrived to make "our friend" feel fairly comfortable, particularly if the sickness was largely imaginative—a circumstance by no means rare. Being a man, he could not well possess the "low, sweet voice" which is a woman's peculiar gift, but the masculinity of his tones was tempered with a nicety of shading that was simply exquisite.

At the proper time many of his patients went to Newport, to the Berkshires, and to Europe for just that peculiar tonic or change of air which was essential in each case, and, as a proof of his undoubted skill in diagnosis and interpretation of symptoms, in every instance the patient was sent to the very place which had been chosen before even the doctor gave his opinion!

His general methods were both popular and successful, and as his popularity gave him much personal satisfaction, and his success yielded him a handsome income, he had no special cause for complaint. Dr. Disney, however, was not a happy man. No one looking at that face, which now at fifty was almost as ruddy and as free from the marks of care as in his early manhood, would suspect anything of mystery and sorrow, yet behind the open smile, the frank, blue eye, the cheery, cordial greeting, there was something which now and then cast a deep shadow full upon his path, causing an anxiety at times so intense as to banish sleep, and to make him seem but the semblance of his former self. Even on the street, when driving to the homes of his patients, something like a key would unlock the mystic doors; a strained, anxious look would come upon him; for the moment he seemed haunted, startled, but his strong will soon reasserted itself, so that when he left the carriage and went up the steps of the house to which he had been summoned there was no trace of agitation whatever, and he was the same calm, suave physician as before.

"John's letters have given me some concern of late," he said to Mrs. Disney, as they sat in the library in the rare enjoyment of an evening free from any professional or social engagement, and when at such times family councils usually were held.

"In what way?" replied Mrs. Disney, though the reply was in the form of a question, and accompanied by a look of serious inquiry.

"Well, I hardly know, but somehow a feeling of uneasiness is associated with almost every letter of his, more especially during the past few months."

"He has not been overexerting himself, I hope?" and this time it was the mother voice which gave accent and emphasis to the inquiry.

"O, no! John has neither overworked himself in study nor abused himself in play, for he is too idle for the one and too lazy for the other;" this, however, in a tone which had more of approval than reproof.

"What, then, gives you concern? Has John fallen into bad habits or taken up with objectionable people?" and by this time Mrs. Disney had finished her coffee and was leaning over that she might see her husband's face.

"No; there is no trouble of that sort. John does not return heavily burdened with honors and medals, but his college life generally has been all right."

"Then the only thing is money, and that need not astonish you, for John never was a brilliant economist. Still"—giving a look around, taking in the luxurious library, with its big easy chairs, its rare old engravings, its book shelves filled with the choicest and richest literature, its varied and costly bric-a-brac—"we are really not so poor after all, and if John has been a little bit extravagant we must only put up with it."

"It isn't exactly money, and yet it relates to money, for, if I understand the case, John has got hold of some socialistic notions and is beginning to pose as an advanced reformer."

"What! John a socialist! O, that is impossible!" exclaimed Mrs. Disney, whose ideas of socialism were of the fierce, lurid type made familiar by Carlyle's *French Revolution*, and still more recently in the Paris Commune; hence the possibility of her son being of that uncouth, unsavory multitude, with matted hair, ragged beard, generally unkempt and disreputable, was anything but pleasant to one so refined and sensitive.

"That is Edward Vaughen's work," broke in Madge Disney, John's only sister and his junior by some three years, a young lady with whom we are likely to have a more intimate acquaintance. "Last season at Newport Edward Vaughen, John's particular crony, spent part of the vacation with us, and he had all sorts of notions and fancies. I saw quite a little of him, and, indeed, I rather enjoyed his pet phrases about 'the seriousness of life,' 'the evasion of responsibility,' and all that kind of thing—a rather good-looking fellow, but perfectly harmless."

"What do you mean by 'harmless?'" said Dr. Disney, rising from his chair and going over to the mantelpiece, upon which he rested his hand, meanwhile smiling pleasantly at his daughter.

"Just this: the socialism that John will acquire from Mr. Vaughen is not at all dangerous. The fact is"—and here Madge allowed the bright laugh which had been accumulating for some minutes to ripple out in her speech until every word tinkled and chimed with girlish merriment—"Mr. Vaughen is merely a faddist; he has taken this up as a means of gaining some little distinction which was not otherwise possible to him; he likes to warm himself at the fire of his own eloquence. He has two or three pet theories which he rubs together as Robinson Crusoe did his bits of wood, and the tiny flame seen through the eyes of his self-conceit appears a positive conflagration."

"Still he has inoculated John with some of the virus," said the doctor, lapsing for the moment into professional phrase.

"Yes; but the virus, as you call it, won't 'take' in any alarming way. 'Take' is the proper term, is

it not ?   I have heard Mr. Vaughen talk in the most
deliciously bewildering way of the 'unearned increment' and 'grinding monopolies,' but the poor fellow hadn't the faintest idea of either the one or the
other.   There was no particular harm in my appear-
ing to be interested, and so I asked him to tell me
just what he meant, when he blushed and stam-
mered and floundered around in the most delightful
way.   Mr. Vaughen is a social theosophist, a soap-
bubble reformer, a cloud-dweller and substitute
philanthropist, who will probably get some sense
later on."

   " You seem to have made the most of your opportunities," laughed Dr. Disney.

   "He was genuinely interesting, I admit.   He was
both pathetic and bathetic.   He brought in ' the toiling millions' and 'life's sad undertone' most dra-
matically ; but better than all, the young man took
himself seriously, which added by so much to the
occasion."

   " It would distress me exceedingly to have John
take any part in such follies and theories," said Mrs.
Disney, " for few young men have better prospects
and opportunities."

   "There is no cause for anxiety," answered Madge.
" We all know John ; with him the horny-handed
son of toil may be both a man and a brother, but
John, as he says himself, 'likes his bread well buttered,' and unless all signs fail he will have his bread
well buttered from now on."

CHAPTER III.

Sister and Brother.

WHEN Madge Disney in her eager, characteristic way said, "We all know John," she
used a common, everyday phrase, yet a
more misleading or deceptive form of speech it
would be difficult to imagine.

There is an inscrutable mystery surrounding every
life, and into that mystery no one ever penetrates.
That mountain in yon distant wilderness, wrapped in
smoke, burning in flame, trembling in thunder, and
out of whose solemnity and grandeur a great voice
sounds as of a mighty trumpet, is more than the
sublime vision of a Hebrew seer; it is a type of the
mystery and awfulness of human life, a life that is
so distinct and solitary as to invest it with a sacred-
ness which must not be profaned.

We know each other's names; we have a general
idea of each other's form and appearance; occasionally we pick up a pebble on the beach of each other's
character and disposition, but beyond this no one
ever goes. Under the soft moss of gentle manner
there are masses of granite of which we do not
dream; under the sloping hills with their vineyards
purpling in the sun a volcano is hidden. The body
which we have thought was a temple enshrining
beauty and purity is often only a lair for a ravenous
beast; and the bosom which we imagined a holy altar

often flames with the most intense and degrading
passion.

The brilliant pupil of Gamaliel never uttered a
more profound truth than when he said, "For what
man knoweth the things of a man, save the spirit of
man which is in him?"

Now here was John—easy, careless, with a vein of
cynicism which gave color and vividness to his conversation; one whom no one suspected of strong conviction or deep feeling; not without principle, but
seemingly without earnestness; outwardly content
with himself and his surroundings; and though by no
means unfeeling or indifferent, yet so far his exer-
tions for the well-being of mankind had been limited
to the promotion of his own comfort. This John
Madge knew; but the real John, the John like some
cathedral inclosed within planken walls and hidden
behind staging and scaffolding, was a being of whom
she knew nothing whatever.

For some time, however, Dr. Disney had suspected that John was not all on the surface, and that
back of his languid, graceful indolence there was a
strong, masterful spirit which in time would assert
itself.

It was the custom of the Disneys to leave town
early in June, but this year as an affectionate com-
pliment to John they remained at home until he had
returned from college. Indeed, it was in the plans
of the family to attend commencement, but the
sudden and serious illness of Mrs. Disney's father
summoned her to his bedside, and though Dr. Disney
was anxious that Madge should share in the college

festivities, still under the circumstances she thought
it best to remain at home.

For a girl just turned twenty years of age, and
who was supposed to be impulsive, Madge possessed
her full share of worldly wisdom. Quick, bright,
keen; with speech as nimble and sure-footed as a
chamois; with a calm assurance which was as pronounced as it was ladylike; with a serene confidence
in herself which, though just a little imperious, was
always attractive; having, besides, a good, sound heart
and a wholesome conscience, she was quite a favorite in her immediate circle. Beyond that circle,
however, Madge was not so definitely popular; as, for
instance, among the Fitz Noodles, the Van Boodles,
the McSwoodles, and certain other members of New
York's proud nobility whose ancestors came over on
the *Mayflower*, though, strange to say, their names
are not found in the roll of that brave ship's passengers.

But what right has anyone to crawl under the
ruins of the centuries looking for " logs " and
" lists," and putting pages of faded handwriting be-
neath a microscope? Such a proceeding is positively
cruel, for it permits no generous use of the imagination. Why not allow Mrs. Fitz Noodle the rewards
and benefits of her illustrious kinship? Anyone
looking at her row of chins, three in number, descend-
ing in elegant curves upon her antique but ample
bosom; her graceful nose, with broad foundations and
celestial terminations; her low, narrow forehead,
sicklied over with the pale cast of a weak digestion,
can see at once her high lineage, and if her great

progenitor happened to be a foretopman on the *May-flower* are not her claims to a lofty descent abundantly verified? These things should not be laughed at, nor even spoken of lightly.

It is true that some most unworthy and irreverent people sit on the benches in Central Park during the early summer afternoons, and when such distinguished persons as the Van Boodles and the Mc-Swoodles in their stately and imposing carriages roll by nudge each other and say, " Soap," " Patent Medicine," " Spades and Shovels," " Beer," and other coarse and unfeeling expressions; but who can tell how much spite and envy have to do with this open contempt of pedigree? The man on the bench may be just as much of a snob as the man in the carriage. That supercilious smile from the benches is often but a flimsy disguise with which disappointment would fain hide itself.

But while Madge affected a certain democracy of air and bearing there was something in the poise of her shapely head, in the set of her well-formed shoulders, in the look of her clear, gray eyes, which could not be mistaken, and which assured for her recognition as of the Gotham aristocracy. She could, therefore, afford to make light of some things which others held in much esteem. Still she was full of tact, and seldom ran counter to the customs and decrees of the august Gothamites. She declined, therefore, to accept her father's proposition to attend the commencement festivities, though in all honesty this declination involved severe disappointment.

" John," she said one morning, several days after

her brother had returned from college and the doctor had started on his round—for, though the season was well on, a number of his patients were yet in town—"what are you going to do with yourself now that you are at home?"

"Do you mean your question for to-day or to-morrow or next day?"

"I think I can answer for to-day or to-morrow, but it is the next day and the day after to which I refer;" going over to the piano, ostensibly to gather up and arrange some music which had been taken from the rack, but in reality to have John's face in a better light, for Madge meant this to be a serious conversation.

John Disney had an open, frank countenance, and Madge was familiar with its every movement and expression; hence her anxiety to note the effect of her words.

"Frankly, Madge, I don't know," said John, playing idly with a birthday charm which hung on his watch chain, but it was evident that the subject was one of special interest.

"But I thought you did know, for was it not understood that you would continue in your studies and in due time take up some of papa's work, and eventually share his practice?"

"Yes, that was the plan, but my thoughts now take a different course."

"Still, a professional life is one of recognized standing, in many respects to be preferred to any other;" and by this time Madge had gathered up the stray music, seated herself at the piano, and was touching the keys lightly yet perceptibly, thus relieving the conversation from overseriousness.

"Very true, my wise and venerable sister, but the matter with me is not altogether one of standing."

"What is it then?"

"I wish you could answer it for me, for I most assuredly cannot answer it for myself."

"But what brought this change about? You know what papa expects and how disappointed he will be."

"Of course I do, and I am sorry for him, but the fact remains that I have no inclination whatever for his profession, and, moreover, I am utterly unfitted for it."

"Why, how can that be? It seems to me that you were 'born in the purple,' and have only to assume your inheritance in due season;" and now Madge had wheeled around from the piano and was looking earnestly at her brother.

"You asked me a moment since, Madge, what I was going to do with myself, and the whole difficulty is just there. It is the 'myself' which embarrasses me. I can do something with my education, particularly if I complete the course which was originally intended. I can do something with my talents, for though I do not claim any remarkable gifts, still I have sense enough not to go into the napkin business, and dig a hole in the earth. I can do something with my opportunities, for there are openings possible to me which I fully appreciate; still the question of 'myself' remains unanswered, and

that is the question which troubles me. In other
words, where can I put my life to the best use, so that
it may tell upon the best life of others? is the problem that I am trying to solve, and I confess that so
far I am baffled."

Madge was startled. She had never seen John
in any such mood as this. Usually he was light,
easy, bantering, not exactly frivolous, still a good
deal of a trifler, and disposed generally to put aside
anything that was serious. But he was serious now;
she could see it in his face, hear it in his voice, and
feel it in his soul. Still, there was a measure of impatience in both her face and tone as she replied :

"I am afraid Mr. Vaughen has had something to
do with this. Last summer I wondered if his influence
was just the right sort for you, and a few weeks
since, when papa was speaking of some notions of
yours, I put the whole blame upon Mr. Vaughen."

"Vaughen!" and here John allowed the grave,
serious look to pass away into a smile; "the dear fellow has his hobbies and theories, but there is
nothing serious in either them or himself. Lots of
college men take up with that sort of thing. Stubbs—
his father is a banker, one of the most careful in
the city—would divide up the whole business, giving share and share alike, after the manner of a
certain time with which the name of Ananias is un-
pleasantly associated. But we take Stubbs with sundry grains of salt. Knobbs is anxious to be at the
head of a 'community,' but Knobbs is at heart one
of the most exclusive fellows you could imagine. He
won't travel in the day coach of a common train, nor

take a meal in a public restaurant, or do anything that will bring him near the average man; nevertheless he airs himself on the community scheme after the manner of an apostle. Jenks is full of cooperation; tap him anywhere, and like maple trees in the season trickling with sap, so he trickles with cooperation. The fact that his father is at the head of a big trust, and that there have been any number of scandals connected with that trust, doesn't affect Jenks. Jenks is immense; I don't mean in size, but in his own opinion, and for an hour now and then he is rare sport."

By this time, John was the gay light-hearted youth of the morning, droll in his own inimitable way, while Madge was laughing heartily.

"Madge," said John, a few minutes later, "what say you to a run to Coney Island? We can get a sniff of the sea, hear some music, see crowds of people, and generally enjoy ourselves."

"Coney Island! What would mamma say, or papa?"

"I have spoken to the pater, and it is all right. You needn't be afraid of meeting anyone. The people of our set are all away. We can take the 'Elevated' to the Battery; there get a boat which goes to the Iron Pier, and see something of a world which will be as new to you as the one discovered by Columbus."

"But, John, has papa really given his consent to my going?"

From the anxious way in which Madge repeated this question it was very evident that she greatly desired the Bohemian outing which John proposed. Yet she was not quite sure that Dr. Disney would fully approve of it.

"If you hurry, we can get the noon boat," was John's reply, consulting the time-table in the newspaper.

Madge hurried, and they were in good time for the boat.

CHAPTER IV.

Mark Brompton's Nephew.

JOHN DISNEY had no intention of being unjust to Edward Vaughen when he spoke of his "notions" in a light and satiric way, and even went so far as to suggest that Vaughen himself was not to be taken seriously. Nevertheless he was unjust, though unintentionally so. A hurt can be both severe and painful, whether through inadvertence or design. That ancient fable of a stone-throwing boy and an expostulating frog has applications of various kinds, and is likely to have for a long time to come. The way in which we misjudge each other is one of life's saddest mysteries. What blunderers we are! How coarse and dull and unfeeling! With heavy, hob-nailed boots we trample upon the delicate threads and lines of each other's hopes and aspirations, and many a noble, beautiful life has been broken and crushed under our pitiless feet.

The trouble with Edward Vaughen was not lack of seriousness. Like another young man whose name and history are not unknown, he was a dreamer; he had a vision of the circling stars and the bending sheaves; his imagination clothed itself with a coat of many colors, and he could easily see a future in which he would not only ride in a chariot, but also be hailed as the friend and champion of suffering mankind. Hence he was vague, deliciously, refreshingly vague. Theories as beautiful as dewdrops sparkled in the morning sun of his eager, hopeful life. The eastern sky of his ambitions was flushing the dull, leaden gray and tinting the somber clouds with a glory all its own.

Ah! we who are older and wiser may have but scant sympathy with the dreams of youth. Yet there are times when some of us would gladly exchange much of our worldly wisdom for the daring, the eagerness, the enthusiasm of those triumphant days when all things were ours and when life, like clay in the hands of the potter, could be molded to our wish.

Vaughen's theories and notions were not, however, as Madge somewhat flippantly suggested, a mere fad taken up for the time being; they were his by inheritance; he was born into them; indeed, so conscious was he of this possession that long before full manhood was attained he had entered upon this estate.

The little town of Eastwich said that Thomas Vaughen, Edward's father, was a very singular man, and Eastwich knew what it was talking about, for Thomas Vaughen had not only been born and brought up there, but had lived there all his life, and was now buried in the little well-kept cemetery with which everyone in Eastwich was so familiar.

"He might have been one of the richest men in the county," remarked Mr. Ragsby, the owner of the Eastwich paper mill and a man of much local prominence, to Lawyer Salvage, as they rode together on the day of Thomas Vaughen's funeral.

"He was one of the kindest and most generous
3

men I ever knew," said Deacon Calvin to his neighbor, Squire Calendar, a vestryman of St. John's, as
they followed in the next carriage.

"He was as brave as a lion and as tender as a
woman," one Grand Army man said to another, as
the little company went to the funeral of their com-
rade.

It was a lovely afternoon, and all Eastwich had
gathered in the cemetery, and under that sky which
seemed as a dome of infinite depth arching into the
uttermost heavens, never were words more impressive
and thrilling—"And I heard a voice from heaven
saying unto me, Write, Blessed are the dead which
die in the Lord."

Mrs. Vaughen was a woman of much strength and
quality of mind, and also of corresponding strength
and quality of heart; hence outwardly she bore her
sorrow and bereavement with such quietness as to
cause some surprise, for her married life had been one
of rare sweetness and peace.

Mrs. Paletot, the chief milliner and dressmaker of
Eastwich, was almost grieved at the simple character
of Mrs. Vaughen's mourning ; still it would be unfair
to Mrs. Paletot to insinuate that this had anything
to do with her remark to Mrs. Cutler, whose husband
kept the grocery and hardware store:

"Mrs. Vaughen may be in deep trouble, but she
doesn't show much of it on either her gown or bonnet."

Mrs. Marble, the wife of the tombstone and epitaph
man, whispered around that it was only the very
plainest tablet, with just the name cut upon it, that

was ordered, "hardly enough to be even respectful to such a man as Thomas Vaughen."

These tender and sympathetic remarks, with others of equal sweetness and beauty, were repeated, passed on, and duly commented upon, but Mrs. Vaughen's sad, sweet face gave no indication of the feelings of her neighbors and friends.

The woman who can command herself in such times as these, who does not bring out her heart so as to exhibit its flutterings, its throbbings, its quiverings; who does not make piteous appeals for sympathy, and with tear-shot voice and tear-stained eye call upon the emotions of her friends—she, poor soul, will be adjudged as lacking in tenderness, and will be harshly pronounced upon, chiefly, however, by those of her own sex.

At the time suggested by the opening of our story Mrs. Vaughen received a letter, the contents of which may help us somewhat:

"NEW YORK, June 20.

"MY DEAR MARY : I was glad to learn through a note from Edward of the completion of his college course and his desire to enter upon a business life.

"Let me suggest his coming to me at as early a date as may be convenient. I wish I could persuade you to come at the same time.

"Augusta and the girls are abroad. Percy is with some friends on a yachting trip. Some things require my attention in the city, and as I am alone your coming with Edward would really be a great favor.   Your affectionate brother,

"MARK BROMPTON."

Mark was Mrs. Vaughen's only brother, and her
senior by several years. When only a lad he had
gone to New York, and by dint of the hardest kind
of hard work gradually made his way, so that now
he was at the head of one of the largest houses in
the city. He was not one of the fortunate boys who
find an Aladdin's lamp or a vizier's ring. He had
no unknown benefactor who secured for him posi-
tions of honor and trust. He was no youthful hero,
who in peril of his life sprang at the reins of the
frightened horses who were tearing madly down the
street and with the strength of a Hercules brought
them to a standstill, thus saving the life of the millionaire and his lovely daughter, completing the
romance by marrying the aforesaid daughter in due
time. There was nothing romantic about Mark
Brompton   He just kept plodding along in the ordinary, common way—messenger boy, office boy, junior
clerk, and so on step by step, always cool, always
shrewd, carefully considering what was best, eminently
practical, rigid in his economies, rendering good
service but expecting full reward, and ever watchful
of his own interests. With him business was business, business all the time, and business with a profit.
He was honest, but he was hard ; he kept his word,
but he insisted upon the other man keeping his; he
paid promptly, but never more than was written in
the bond, nor would he receive less. In his office he
knew neither friendship nor sentiment, and to all
seeming had no more heart than an automatic calcu-
lator. At the proper time he married, and the
proper time with him was not when his heart was

young, but when he had attained such standing as gave him access to homes of solidity and wealth; hence when he asked Augusta Glenville to become his wife he was fully aware that she would not be a portionless bride. And so he went on from prospering to prosper.

When Thomas Vaughen died Mark Brompton went to Eastwich not only to attend the funeral and be present with his sister in her sorrow, but also to arrange her affairs and give her such assistance as was necessary. There was not much, however, to arrange, for Thomas Vaughen had spent his life in laying up treasure "where neither moth nor rust doth corrupt;" still with characteristic unselfishness he had provided against his wife being dependent, so that with the sale of the business her income was enough for her simple needs. Nothing would induce her to leave Eastwich; that pathetic hillock in the little churchyard made the whole place sacred to her and claimed her presence and care.

But while Mark Brompton could not quite understand the fine feeling which prompted the refusal of his sister to leave Eastwich, yet in a measure he was relieved, for her coming to New York would involve certain family embarrassments which he was anxious to avoid. He arranged, however, to send Edward to college, and promised to open his way in the city afterward. With his usual faithfulness he carried out his part of the compact, and while Edward could not speak with enthusiasm of his uncle's generosity, still Mr. Brompton was fairly entitled to respect and consideration for what he had done.

CHAPTER V.

A Bohemian Outing.

THOSE who are not familiar with New York imagine that in the summer the heat is simply intolerable, and that no one remains in the city who can possibly get away. It is true that in certain sections uptown it would seem as if this idea was the correct one, for there are whole blocks of houses and almost blocks of streets where every shutter is closed, every blind is drawn, every door is boarded up, and where it is very evident that a general exodus has taken place. The favored residents of these select and fashionable regions could not dream of exposing themselves to the horrors of a New York summer; hence trunks are packed, boxes are strapped, trains are laden, steamers are filled, and away go the "four hundred," leaving the city desolate and forsaken. Possibly the population of the city is not perceptibly affected, but people should be weighed as well as counted, and what are numbers as compared with quality? East Side Gothamites are not of much account except by census takers; the real dwellers in Gotham are in the uptown regions. According to the standard of the chosen ones, in July New York is simply empty.

Newspapers are published, but what do they chronicle other than reports from the distant resorts— Mrs. McFlimsie's dinner party in honor of the

Marquis Tête de Bois; the engagement of Miss Namby Pam to Count Spaghetti; the fancy ball under the direction of the Von der Plonks, and such other mighty and thrilling events?

The great stores also keep open, but they sell only common things to the common people, of whom there seem as many as ever, which only proves how much plebeianism there is even in Gotham.

It is true also that most of the churches observe regular service, but in the select neighborhoods the ministerial "understudy" meets the full necessities of the case, for why should the eloquent sermons of the regular incumbent be spent upon the few unfortunate ones who cannot escape from the metropolis?

It is very probable that the fact of "everyone being out of town" weighed in Madge Disney's mind when she consented to accompany her brother to Coney Island, for she was morally certain that none of her friends was within even a hundred miles of the city. Still she had certain qualms, though in strict truth they were not of conscience, but rather a fear of the proprieties.

It is singular, but true withal, that there are those with whom propriety is a stronger deterrent than conscience. If the Ten Commandments could only be adopted and accepted as part of the social code, the moral law might secure more generous recognition. For the social code not only demands but insists upon obedience, and one must either be very rich or very handsome who will defy its mandates. With a sway that is absolute it prescribes the length of a horse's tail, the cut of a woman's gown, the shape of a man's hat, and woe betide those who disobey!

No wonder, therefore, that Madge felt anxious and uncomfortable, and if a telegram had come from her mother, or her father unexpectedly returned, she would have gladly put aside her promise to John and inwardly rejoiced at her deliverance.

But no relief came; John was impatient to be off, and so Madge went, but her first sensations were anything but pleasant.

After reaching the boat and being comfortably seated Madge looked cautiously around and discovered, very much to her satisfaction, that her fellow-travelers were not such barbarians as she had feared. Many of them were just as well dressed and as lady-like as she was, and some of the young men would compare favorably with even her own handsome brother. Among the younger groups there was possibly a little more hilarity than some would approve of, and more than once a laugh that might be called boisterous, but when John suggested that to most of these people such an outing as this meant an escape from the stifling store, the cooped-up office, the noise, the din, the heat, and the general restraint under which so much of their lives was spent, she soon found herself not only framing excuses for their rather zealous pleasure-making, but even once or twice she could not forbear a smile at some bright repartee or quaint saying spoken loud enough for her to overhear.

Others impressed her as belonging more particularly to the artisan class, for their clothes sat rather consciously and indicated an unfamiliarity with the daily life of the wearer. A certain swarthy neck undoubtedly resented a stiff collar; the well-shaped, sturdy head felt the strain of a close-fitting hat; the brawny, rugged shoulders chafed under the restraints of a fairly made coat; but the man was genuine; that Madge could see in the care which he took of his little children, and the affection with which he regarded their mother, a pale, sad-faced woman, who looked wistfully upon the sea, thinking, doubtless, of her early home far across the ocean.

One group after the other came within the reach of Madge's clear gray but kindly eyes, and concerning each group she had many wonderings and imaginings.

But who can describe a boatload of passengers on the way to Coney Island? For it surely includes all sorts and conditions of men, women, and children—children with tiny pails and shovels for service in the sand; children with whips and balloons and mouths smeared with colored candy; children who cry and scream until one sighs for the fog horn; children who are sweet and pretty, sleeping most of the way through; then the women with babies and the women without babies; the women with husbands and the women without husbands; the women who have nice frocks and the women who have nice faces; then the men who are out for a frolic and the men who are out with their families; the men to whom the occasion is one which they enjoy with their wives and children; the men who are reckless and selfish, wasting both the day and themselves.

People of varied language and of varied life—men
from the mill, the shop, the foundry, the yard ; men
who have just laid down the hammer, the trowel, the
shears, the pen ; women from the store, the desk, the
sewing machine, the typewriter ; women who have
escaped from the burden, the toil, the care, the
drudgery—what a comfort it is that once in a while
they can get out and see God's sky, look upon God's
sea, and feel something of the light and joy of life!
A very world is a Coney Island steamer ; more of a
world even than an ocean steamship, for it usually
carries but two classes—the saloon and the steerage—
whereas a Coney Island boat is a world in miniature.

Down the harbor, with the Statue of Liberty standing out in all its mighty proportions ; through the
Narrows, with the hills of Staten Island on the one
hand and the less pretentious Bay Ridge on the
other, the steamer made its way, and ere long the
varied and nondescript architecture of the famous
resort came in view. The pier was reached in due
time, and the impatient passengers were soon a part
of the great host who swarmed everywhere. The
first feeling that possessed Madge was that of utter
bewilderment. Had she come from a distant planet
she could hardly have been in a world with which
she was less familiar. There were swings to right
of her, swings to left of her ; flying horses with
calliope attachment, making noise enough to suit a
Bedlamite ; toboggans where the heavy-laden cars
made a rush and roar like a train passing over a trestle-
work bridge, but neither rush nor roar could drown
the screams and laughter of the tobogganers, bump-

ing and thumping on their way; boats which hung on chains and iron rods, with motion enough to terrify the most hardened traveler, within which very uncomfortable-looking people tried to imagine that they really enjoyed it; shows in tents and shows in booths, where from the platform men with throats of boiler iron and lungs of extra leather were inviting the passing throngs to witness the marvelous exhibitions which were "just about to begin;" shooting galleries, where every few minutes might be heard the ting of a bell, indicating that some fortunate youth had succeeded in hitting one of those elusive marks at which so many aim in vain. All these, and countless other things as well, mingled with the beating of drums, the blowing of horns, the cries of venders of everything imaginable, startled Madge so that finally she looked from one thing to the other with a helplessness that was simply pitiful.

"Let us go down to the beach," said John, when he saw that Madge was a little weary; "we can get chairs there, and you will have a chance to rest."

"But, John, where did all these people come from?" gasped Madge, with the look of wonder filling her eyes and face, for the crowd had a peculiar influence upon her. It was by no means a drunken, noisy, reckless crowd, but sober, orderly, respectable, and in bearing and appearance would compare most favorably, too, with the crowds of London or Paris or Berlin. Madge was very deeply impressed, for she was quick and sensitive, and the sight of these tens of thousands moved her most strangely.

"My dear girl," replied John, "these are the

bread makers of the city in which you live. All
week they have been at work tending the ovens;
their arms have been spattered with flour, their hands
covered with dough, and they are now enjoying the
half holiday which makes life just bearable for many
of them."

"Bread makers! What do you mean?" for John's
figurative form of speech was not quite clear always,
even to his sister.

"O! I don't mean that all these people are pastry
cooks or bakers; they are the workers, the mechanics,
the clerks, the real bread winners of New York.
These are the common people of whom you read in
books, the books written mostly by men who never
saw the common people. These are the masses who
are studied by our social economists as a geologist
studies specimens—stratified and labeled in proper
order."

By this time they had come to the beach, which
was crowded with men and women and children, enjoying to the full the delicious breeze which came
in strongly from the open sea, while a goodly company, much to the amusement of the onlookers,
splashed and frolicked in the big breakers as they
rolled in from the broad Atlantic. Madge now was
quite at ease concerning the matter of recognition,
for the more she studied the people the more con-
fident she was that none of her friends were in such
a place; hence she gratefully accepted the chair
which John secured, and with simple, girlish democracy was entering into the novelty and amusement of
her surroundings, when all at once John said:

"Why, there is Dunbar! Excuse me for a moment," disappearing as he spoke, returning, however, almost immediately, bringing with him a young man of perhaps twenty-five years of age, tall, fairly good-looking, and though not in the orthodox garb of a clergyman, yet John introduced him to Madge as " the Rev. Hugh Dunbar."

CHAPTER VI.

A Reverend Radical.

"WELL! I certainly did not expect to see you down here," John said to Mr. Dunbar, after a few moments spent in the ordinary greetings.

"Why not?" responded Mr. Dunbar, regarding John with a pleasant smile.

"I thought that clergymen were not in sympathy with the pomps and vanities of such places as these," returned John.

"But 'pomps and vanities,' as you call them, are not necessarily associated with ' such places as these,'" Mr. Dunbar replied. "People who have spent all their week in the hot city are to be commended for coming here and getting a breath of the sea. O, how delicious it is!" as just then a cool wave swept through the air, tempering the hot sun and causing almost everyone to turn gratefully to the open sea, from whence the life and vigor came so richly.

"I had an impression," John went on, accompanying the words with a look and smile which Mr. Dunbar seemed to perfectly understand, "that you 'brethren of the cloth' were usually invisible on Saturdays, so as to be incomprehensible on Sundays."

"I see you are the same Disney. Your sister here may not be aware that from the magnificent altitudes of my senior year I beheld in the valley of the freshman this youth of much verdancy and small promise, whose helplessness and innocence touched me very deeply," was Dunbar's response, meanwhile turning his large, expressive eyes, full of genuine mirth, upon Madge, his earnest, almost sad-looking face lighted up with a rich smile.

"All of which translated into the vernacular means that Mr. Dunbar was in his last year when I entered college and that we became good friends," replied John.

The spot chosen by John for a few minutes' halting place was quite a little distance from the crowd, and as the tide was now receding, carrying with it the heavy fringe of spectators, our friends were comparatively alone. At John's suggestion Mr. Dunbar and himself sat down upon the sand, of which at Coney Island there is enough and to spare. The young men soon drifted into easy and familiar conversation, though Madge was not altogether pleased at Mr. Dunbar's quiet acceptance of himself as a member of the Disney party. Her coolness, however, in nowise affected Mr. Dunbar, except that now and then he looked at her with a quick, keen, curious glance; for though his eyes, as a rule, were kindly, at times they gleamed sharply and searched deeply.

"Then you have a parish?" John said in response to a remark of Mr. Dunbar.

"Yes, if you can call it so," answered Dunbar.

"In the city?" questioned Madge, who felt as if she ought, in courtesy to her brother, at any rate, to show some interest in his friend.

"Yes, in the city, but that is not very definite even to myself, for I have quite recently taken service in an East Side mission."

An East Side clergyman suggested very little to Madge beyond a superior kind of tract distributer or superintendent of some charitable institution, and as she thought of Mr. Dunbar associated with such work she wondered at John's very evident regard for him. It may have been the breeze, which was now blowing stronger and cooler every moment, but a distinct chill came upon her face, and there was something in the curl of her lips which, to say the least, was suggestive. Again Mr. Dunbar flashed upon her one of his keen, searching looks, a look of which she was conscious, though at the same moment she seemed to be absorbed in watching a vessel far out at sea.

"Then you have entered upon your work?" put in John, who knew nothing of the soul collisions which were taking place so near him, and whose only interest for the time centered in Dunbar.

"I am experimenting before reaching definite conclusions."

"You don't mean by 'experimenting' hospital and dispensary work of the same type necessary to young doctors, preparatory to a church with a big steeple and a Vanity Fair congregation?" laughed John. "Such practice is doubtless necessary, but it is hard on those who have to endure it."

"There is some truth, unfortunately, in your idea, but other things than those you suggest have influenced me;" this very quietly, but earnestly.

"Let us get back to first principles," said John, "and ask, if I may, what are you doing down here? for I assured my sister before leaving home that we would not meet a solitary friend or even remote acquaintance the whole afternoon, and yet here in the midst of the throng we find you."

"Before answering your question may I venture to hope that this accidental meeting will not interfere with Miss Disney's enjoyment," Mr. Dunbar courteously but gravely replied, for he was fully aware of certain unpleasant movements in Madge's mind.

"You will pardon me, Mr. Dunbar, if I take exception to your use of the word 'enjoyment' so far as it relates to me. Seeing you are a clergyman, perhaps it is only proper for me to confess that it was simply a spirit of adventure which brought me here. My brother was anxious to have me come, nor am I sorry that I did so; still my enjoyments are not altogether of this order." Here Madge produced what John called her "shot-tower effect," so that when her words reached Mr. Dunbar they were hard and glittering like tiny bullets. Once more the searching eyes of Mr. Dunbar looked out from under their heavy brows, and once more Madge watched with intense interest a trail of smoke as of some incoming ocean steamer.

"Your question, Disney, is easily answered. I came down here to see my brothers and sisters and enjoy part of the day with them."

"Then you still remain an apostle of the Brotherhood?" John said. "I thought those were mostly

4

college notions, and that when men got through they left them as a legacy to the incoming class."

"Not always."

"Of course there are exceptions."

"Yes, and many exceptions."

"But do not some men take these things up as fads and fancies?"

"Undoubtedly, but they soon become much more unless the men who take them up are fads and fancies themselves."

"You evidently have taken them up in dead earnest."

"No, they have taken me up in dead earnest."

"I do not quite understand."

"The fault is mine, but"—and with this he turned to Miss Disney, whose eyes were still upon the sea— but who had heard every word of the conversation, "it is not fair of me to monopolize the afternoon with matters which are largely personal."

"But these things are not personal," persisted John; "they have a deep interest for me, and the problems in which I find myself are both serious and difficult."

"That I am glad to hear. It is only the man who does not think, and who is selfishly content with things as they are, who is not troubled. How any man can face the conditions of this age and this country without feeling the burden and the mystery can hardly be reconciled with a sound mind, certainly not with a clear conscience."

This time Mr. Dunbar did not look at Madge, though she certainly was a very attractive picture, for the clear sky seemed to reflect itself in her eyes, the breeze had brought a tinge of color into her fresh young face, and if Mr. Dunbar had looked at her no one would have blamed him. But he looked along the beach down to the Iron Pier, then turned the other way only to see multitudes of those whom he called his " brothers and sisters."

"He is positively worse than Edward Vaughen," Madge said to herself, " and he, goodness knows, is bad enough."

"No wonder John has all sorts of notions," she went on with her unspoken thoughts; " what with Edward Vaughen and this Mr. Dunbar, they have filled my brother's head with the most absurd fancies."

"John," she said, after a few minutes, when there was a lull in the conversation, " is it not time that we were going ? "

It was a simple and natural question, but there was that in the tone which made it abrupt, if, indeed, not ungracious. This time just the faintest gleam of amusement stole upon Mr. Dunbar's face, for he understood the question as a polite dismissal. Madge saw the shadow of the smile, and it provoked her, for she knew then that her intent was discovered. She tried to cover up her failure with an invitation for Mr. Dunbar to return with them, and when he declined she was quite solicitous that he call upon Dr. Disney and give them opportunity of hearing further of his work.

Nothing could exceed the ease and graceful dignity of Mr. Dunbar's leave-taking, but somehow it seemed to Madge as though a spirit of mischief lurked in his eyes and as if he had come off the better in their silent contest.

"Your friend, whatever his notions may be, has the manners of a gentleman," she said to John, after Mr. Dunbar had gone.

"That is not to be wondered at," was the reply, more curtly, too, than was John's wont with Madge.

"You don't mean to insinuate that because he was favored with your graceful and dignified example for a year he must therefore be a gentleman all the rest of his life," she playfully responded; for though she could not see any disturbance in her brother's mind she felt it, and it annoyed and, if anything, made her more provoked with Mr. Dunbar as the cause of it.

"No, but if you put it the other way, you will reach a more correct view of the case."

"What do you mean? Mr. Dunbar is nothing but an East Side clergyman, probably one of those unfortunates for whom Dr. Bland pleads so earnestly on Mission Sunday."

"You poor, misguided creature," John said, pityingly. "Dunbar is rich enough to endow Dr. Bland and a dozen others beside. He is also of one of the best families we have, while he himself is as true a man as lives."

It must be conceded that though John was Madge's "own and only brother" he took evident satisfaction in making this reply, and even all the more when he saw its effect upon her.

Poor Madge! She now understood the lurking

mischief in Mr. Dunbar's eyes and the ghost of a smile with which he had taken his dismissal.

"Why, I thought he was a socialist," she hastily replied, anxious to find something by way of extenuation.

"Yes, but not the sort of socialist that you mean, nor the sort that a great many mean. I don't understand why he has taken up the work he is now in; but one thing certain, he is thoroughly in earnest."

The afternoon was now well advanced, and Madge suggested that it was time to return home, when John said:

"Father has a special engagement for this evening, and when I spoke of our coming down here he proposed that we remain at Manhattan Beach for dinner. This side trip of ours was not, however, on his program, and perhaps we had better say nothing about it."

They went over to Manhattan Beach by rail, making the run in a few minutes, and there found a crowd proportionately as great as the one which they had just left. Though not yet the fashionable hour for dining, the tables on the long, wide piazzas of the "Manhattan" were crowded, and the waiters were rushing here and there in response to the calls on every side. The benches on the plank walk facing the sea were all occupied, while hundreds of people were promenading up and down, enjoying the magnificent view and at the same time the refreshing breeze which came in from the ocean. The music from the "Pavilion" was too strong and clear to be confined within wooden walls, hence the strains of

Gilmore's famous band filled the great square with melody. Ladies in the daintiest of summer costumes gave color and vividness to the scene and rivaled in richness and variety the immense beds of flowers fronting the hotel in the glory of early July. On every hand there was evidence of wealth, and it may be questioned if in the days of imperial Rome a scene of more real splendor could be found. For here were jewels costly and gleaming, laces and silks finer and more exquisite than ever adorned Roman matron, rich attire and golden ornaments in lavish display, not barbaric as in the days of Nero, but deli- cate and elegant, of richest quality and finest work- manship.

Madge was even more amazed than in the early afternoon, for she had accepted without question the statement that "there was positively no one in New York," while here were crowds of people of evident wealth, reveling, too, in the enjoyment of that wealth as she had never even dreamed of.

She suggested something of this to John, who said :

"Down yonder," pointing to that part of the island where they had met Mr. Dunbar, "are the bread makers, while here are the bread eaters."

"But bread makers are usually bread eaters," laughed Madge, who was anxious to avoid a return to the serious discussion of the early afternoon.

"Not always," said John ; "they have the honor of mixing the flour, of making the batches, of shap- ing the loaves, and of tending the ovens, but the bread is not for them. Of course, if a loaf is over-baked or the crust browned beyond the point which is attractive or palatable, the baker may have it for his own use; but, Madge, it is true the bread makers are yonder and the bread eaters are here."

"If that is so, let us belong to the bread eaters, for I am very hungry. Only think how long it has been since lunch time, and one cannot well live on ocean breezes and band music."

To this remark John gave an approving smile, and soon they were in the dining room of the "Oriental," where surely there is "bread" in all possible varieties and forms.

CHAPTER VII.

Making Stones into Bread.

FOR the very same reason with which Mark Brompton urged his invitation Mrs. Vaughen steadily declined it, which shows that the man and the woman rarely, if ever, have the same point of view. We may discuss the question of sex equality as we please, but when everything is said it still remains the same sublime mystery. One is tempted sometimes to wonder in what this equality consists. Those diamonds so gracefully, though not unconsciously, worn by the Marchioness of Tabasco at the state ball in honor of Prince Sapolio are carbon; that wagonload of coal of which Tim O'Healy is in charge is also carbon. Does it then follow that the Marchioness of Tabasco is on terms of equality with Tim O'Healy?

Now here were Mark Brompton and Mrs. Vaughen, though of the same kith and kin, as far apart in their conclusions as their finite natures would allow. To the mind of Mr. Brompton there was no reason whatever why his sister should not come to New York at this particular time ; to the mind of Mrs. Vaughen there was a most urgent reason why she should remain at Eastwich. Mrs. Vaughen had an understanding of more things than were dreamt of in the philosophy of her worldly-wise brother. She was perfectly certain that Mrs. Brompton, had she been at home, would not have united in this invitation, and when she returned would resent such a visit as an intrusion.

Mrs. Vaughen sincerely pitied Mark. Though he was older by several years, she remembered distinctly his early ambitions and his determination to be rich and successful. She knew also that there was no romance in his marriage; that no fine, tender feeling actuated him in the founding of his home; and that from beginning to end the whole transaction was almost as definitely commercial as anything which took place in his office. She was further aware that he got just what he bargained for, nothing more or nothing less, Augusta Glenville understanding perfectly the nature of the arrangement.

Miss Glenville was no lovelorn damsel or yearning heroine, no boarding-school maiden with a heart crowded with dreams. In her way she was just as practical and matter-of-fact as Mr. Brompton was in his, and while there was the orthodox wedding, not even omitting the customary rice, neither one pretended to anything of sentiment. If the officiating clergyman had said, " Wilt thou, Half Million, take this Half Million, to have and to hold from this day forward ? " there would probably have been some indignation in the bridal party, yet in reality that was the inner meaning of the ceremony.

But Mark Brompton long since had made the discovery—a sad, pitiable discovery by whomsoever made—that man shall not live by bread alone. The loaf may be made of the finest flour, of the daintiest shape, baked most carefully, yet there is a hunger which it cannot meet.

He, foolish man, had imagined that the heart was a sort of safe ; a receptacle for bonds and title deeds; with a combination known only to himself, which he could open and close at will. Years ago he had found, but much to his surprise, that it was not a cunning mechanism of steel springs and wrought iron, for it throbbed and ached with a pain all its own. But he kept on making money, and apparently was dead to all feeling ; still there were times when there was a sense of utter loneliness, when the world was barren, and his life one of bitter disappointment. " ' A little below par,' to use the terms of the ' Street,' " Dr. Disney would say, in that bland, gracious way of his; for sometimes Mr. Brompton wondered if physical conditions were not the cause of his depression, and would therefore send for Dr. Disney, in whose skill he had much confidence.

" You require toning up, my good friend. There is nothing, however, to cause alarm. The pulse is regular, though not as full as it might be. I think, however, we can take care of that without much difficulty."

And so Mr. Brompton would remain at home for a few days, but the time was very heavy on his hands; for Mrs. Brompton had no appreciation of his moods or feelings, and her attempts at sympathy were by no means grateful.

At such times Mark Brompton went back over his life, with just the same hardness and honesty as he did everything, but the retrospect was not pleasant. He heard voices from men who had come to him pleading for some little kindness which he had failed to grant. He saw men with pale, despairing faces leave his office, his stern refusal meaning for them utter ruin. He could feel now that he had been hard, merciless, exacting, demanding inexorably his pound of flesh.

But do we not read of a famous but nameless individual who during a time of sickness expressed a strong desire to be a monk, but who when his health was restored was anything but a monk? Whatever tenderness came to Mark Brompton during these times was known only to himself, nor was he any less rigorous once he was back in his office.

"The trouble with your Uncle Mark," said Mrs. Vaughen to Edward, just a few days before he left Eastwich, and she was giving him some motherly counsel, "is that he has made stones into bread."

"In what way?" asked Edward; for while he was poetic and imaginative, still there were phases of his nature eminently practical.

"In this way," answered Mrs. Vaughen, "he has taken his youth, his ideals, his generous impulses, and by the sheer force of his will made them the servants of his ambitions."

"But had he not a right to his ambitions?" questioned Edward, drawing his chair closer to his mother's; for the conversation was taking place under the veranda of their little Eastwich home, and the evening shadows were deepening rapidly.

"Surely," was the quick response, "provided such

ambitions are not miserably selfish. As an active, useful man your Uncle Mark is honestly entitled to the honest man's loaf, but he, unlike your father," looking softly in the direction of the little cemetery, which could be seen in the distance, and which she had visited that afternoon, "is not content with his lawful portion."

"Then you think that Uncle Mark has more loaves than rightfully belong to him?" Edward plausibly suggested, for he knew that Mr. Brompton's honesty was unquestioned.

"Legally and according to the standards of business he has a right to all he now possesses, but morally no man is justified in using his superior strength and skill so as to enrich himself at the expense of others."

They were both silent for a few minutes, Mrs. Vaughen's eyes turning again to the distant churchyard, where they remained, as though searching among the shadows for the one who had made life so rich to her, Edward's eyes reaching into the heavens, following the movements of the clouds, upon which the moonbeams were now beginning to fall. These two quiet figures represented memory and hope. The one was, therefore, busy with the past, the other busy with the future.

"You will meet the same temptation as your Uncle Mark, and you will hear the same mysterious voice, 'Command that these stones be made bread,'" resumed Mrs. Vaughen.

"But success does not always mean yielding to temptation," Edward urged, not so much in defense of his Uncle Mark as in support of his own ambitions.

"No, but when one is in the wilderness which we call life, and when certain stones, which it is dishonest even to touch, are lying all around us, to take these stones up in our hands and turn them into bread is the temptation which assails almost everyone, nor are there many who successfully resist it. Remember, my darling boy," this with great tenderness, but with equal solemnity, "the wilderness in Judea is the same as the one in New York, and the temptation of the one is the temptation of the other."

Within a few days they parted, she to maintain her loving watch over the quiet grave, he to enter upon that terrible battle in which so many are slain.

.   .   .   .

To the very minute the train rolled into the Grand Central Depot, and Edward Vaughen was soon on the platform. There is nothing remarkable to the average New Yorker in the big station on Forty-second Street, but what is there or what could there be remarkable to a New Yorker? He might leave his home in the morning, passing some vacant lots on the corner, and on returning in the evening find the lots occupied by a huge apartment house, tenanted from top to bottom by families all settled and everything to rights, yet he would hardly think it a matter of sufficient importance to mention at the dinner table! He invariably reads the paper while riding over the Brooklyn Bridge, and it is only when some country friend is with him that he even looks at that marvel of engineering skill, with its threads and lacework of iron ropes and gigantic cables; as wondrous, yet as beautiful a structure as this world has ever seen. No concern of his that buildings lift themselves so high from the ground that elevators are run express; for in this busy town men cannot spare the time for an elevator to stop at each floor on the way up! But this was Edward Vaughen's first visit to New York, and before he was half way down the platform of the depot he was fairly bewildered. He followed, however, the stream of passengers, a stream which, like the river Danube, has three mouths, for some turned to the right, in the direction of the waiting rooms, some to the left, where they could reach the "Elevated," and some went straight ahead toward the street. The peculiar cry of the depot hackman, a cry which for penetrating quality is like that of the Venetian gondolier when about to make a sharp turning, attracted our young friend, and ere long he was being driven to his uncle's home on Fifth Avenue.

Mr. Brompton received him with as much cordiality as Edward had reason to expect, and for several days he enjoyed himself visiting about the city, and seeing such things as would naturally be of interest to him.

"I have spoken to Keen & Sharp, and they can make room for you in their office," said Mr. Brompton one morning, as he and Edward were in the breakfast room.

"And who are Keen & Sharp?" said Edward, smiling gratefully at his uncle.

"Friends of mine, with whom I have had business relations for some years. They do here what is known as a general brokerage business, but have interests in other things, and I think an opening with them will be to your advantage."

"It is exceedingly kind of you, Uncle Mark."

"O, I have simply made an investment in you," interrupted Mr. Brompton. "Sometimes I put a little money in wheat, sometimes in cotton, sometimes in a railroad; and sometimes I lose, and then again I don't. Just how my investment in you will turn out remains to be seen."

"When am I expected to begin work?" Edward asked.

"I told Mr. Keen you were in the city, and could begin any time."

"Then I will start in next Monday," said Edward.

"Very well. I will drop a line to Keen & Sharp to that effect."

CHAPTER VIII.

The Dream and the Reality.

TO take a young man fresh from college, and within a few weeks after graduation have him at work, was Mark Brompton's way of doing things. To him a business life meant promptness; a disregard of either convenience or personal desire, and an obedience to which everything must give way without excuse or hesitation.

"Mr. Jones," he would say to his confidential clerk, "I have a 'cable' from our correspondents in London which requires immediate attention. You will therefore take the *Britannic*, which sails to-day at one o'clock, and as you are familiar with this matter you can arrange it according to instructions," speaking as indifferently as if he had asked Mr. Jones to do some little errand in Brooklyn or Jersey City.

The fact that Mr. Jones had a daughter who was to be married within the week, and that the invitations for the wedding were already out, would not weigh even as dust in the balances of his command. So in less than three hours Mr. Jones would be on the big steamer heading for Liverpool.

"Mr. Smith, I wish you to represent 'the house' at the creditors' meeting of Bang & Crash in Chicago the day after to-morrow. You will take the train this afternoon, as I have wired some gentlemen to meet you to-morrow evening, so as to have an understanding of affairs." Then he would take up some other matter from his desk, this one being settled.

Poor Mr. Smith! And he had a christening party in his home this very evening! The baby was christened, and the party came off; meantime he was half way to Buffalo.

"Mr. Brown, there are some interests of ours in Nevada connected with that road which the T., C. & O. expect to lease. As you have this matter in your department be good enough to give it immediate personal attention. You had better start at once, and arrange to remain there till everything is settled."

And Mr. Brown had just become engaged to Miss Grey and was looking forward to a summer of outings and pleasures of the rarest kind. But he went to Nevada.

Was Mark Brompton, then, a hard master? Not at all. With him business took precedence, and everything else had to fall behind in such order and place as it was able to secure in the procession. "Seek ye first the kingdom of success, and let all other things be added unto you," was his understanding of a certain familiar Scripture.

It is most assuredly true that if Edward Vaughen had not been the nephew of Mark Brompton, his first day in the office of Keen & Sharp would also have been his last. The simple fact is, he was in no way fitted for such a place. He wrote an execrable hand. He knew nothing of figures—that is, the kind of

5

figures which are used in trade. Business forms were
all unfamiliar to him. In plain truth, any one of the
office boys had a better equipment for his work than
Edward had. Before he had been an hour in the
office he felt all out of sorts, and wondered how he
would get through the day. Just what to do with
himself was a question. True, Mr. Keen had introduced him to Mr. Singleton, the head of a department, placing him under his care, but Mr. Singleton seemed to be too busy to give him much attention,
for there were two days' mail piled up on his desk.
Then the click of the three or four typewriters; the
monotonous burr of the "ticker" grinding out its
yards of tape; the constant coming and going of
people, so that the doors of the outer office hardly
remained closed for a full minute at a time; boys
rushing in with telegrams, many of which required
immediate reply; the general air of restlessness which
pervaded the whole place—all these things, with the
many others of which these were only a part, so
affected Edward that he became confused and even
irritated, and his gratitude to Mr. Brompton for
opening his way into this eminent firm was not so
great as it had been. Ah! the reality of business
life was a far different thing from his college dreams.
Within a few hours most of the romance had gone.
In the office of Keen & Sharp there was no place
for poetry or visions. Already he was folding up
his coat of many colors, and the hard, grim, terrible earnestness of the strife upon which he was
entering forced itself upon his unwilling soul.

"Mr. Vaughen, if you have not made other arrangements," said Mr. Singleton, when lunch time had come, " I will be very glad if you will lunch to-day with me."

" You are very kind," Edward responded, grateful for this mark of attention.

" Then we will go to the 'Equitable,'" Mr. Singleton said.

" Very well," replied Edward, without, however, the faintest idea of what Mr. Singleton meant, other than that he referred to some lunching place.

To the " Equitable " they went, and such a jostling, pushing, busy crowd Edward had never imagined possible. It was men, men, nothing but men— young men in all the joy and glory of their strength; men whose youth was disappearing, whose hair was tinging, whose faces were fading, and who were beginning to show the marks of business care; men of mature years, some of whom were evidently prosperous, while others looked worn and haggard. It was a crowd made up of men of all moods and passions, of all hopes and ambitions.

" Ah ! Singleton, wasn't that a surprise to-day?" a tall, eager-faced gentleman observed, just as our friends were seating themselves at a small table in the basement restaurant.

Mr. Singleton merely nodded and took up the bill of fare.

" By the way, Singleton, can you tell me if—?" dropping the balance of the question into Mr. Single-ton's ear so that no one could hear it but himself.

Mr. Singleton quietly listened, going on with his study of the menu.

"Hallo, Singleton! Another of your plans likely to go through. Big plums for somebody," and with a knowing smile the third man went by.

"You know, Angelo, what I want," Mr. Singleton said to the waiter, "fix up something, and serve enough for two," an order which Angelo understood, for Mr. Singleton was one of his most regular guests.

But the friends and acquaintances of Mr. Singleton would not desert him in those usually weary moments which lie between the disappearance of the waiter with the order, and his reappearance with the heavy-laden tray.

"That deal brought Old Slick a million."

"Tight squeeze Drowsley got in that Sahara irrigation affair."

"Blinks & Winks have gone to the bow-bows."

"Sad about Snooks, just after he got that presidency."

And so they came and went, talking about life and death, fortune and bankruptcy, success and failure, as if they were matters of the least moment and had only a passing importance.

It is true that Snooks had dropped unconscious in his office, and was taken home to die, just when the dream of years had been attained.

It is also true that Blinks & Winks, after having made an heroic fight, were crushed and broken in the struggle.

And it was true that Drowsley was caught in an enterprise which almost ruined him.

These are the chances which men have to take.

The game of life, as it is played in New York, is full of risks. Fortunes are made and unmade by the scratch of a pen or the flash of a wire. Nowhere in the whole world is the battle of the wilderness fought with such eagerness, such intensity, such courage, such audacity. Every quality in the man, whether bad or good, is brought into play. The spring of the panther, the swoop of the hawk, the patience of the ox, the strength of the lion, are here made manifest. On this battle ground, almost every day, stones are made into bread and men are changed into stones.

After lunch Mr. Singleton and Edward returned to the office, but many times during the afternoon Edward found himself anxiously wondering concerning the things which he had seen and heard.

That night he wrote a long letter to his mother, giving her a minute and vivid description of the day, but not a word did he breathe of his anxieties or disappointments. Indeed, his letter was written in a humorous strain, and very few would have imagined anything of the heart pain and loneliness which were behind it.

Mrs. Vaughen, however, was not of that number, for when she read his letter, though her lips now and then parted into a smile, yet it was a smile with a quiver in it.

CHAPTER IX.

Angels of Flesh and Blood.

OVER on the East Side of the city, well down-town, between Second and Third Avenues, lived the Sauviers, the family consisting of Mrs. Sauvier, her daughter Oberta, and her son Fred. Mrs. Sauvier had been very seriously ill; indeed, for some time her life had been despaired of, and coming up out of much weakness and suffering her recovery was anything but rapid.

"Still you are a little better to-day," Oberta said, encouragingly, as she sat by her mother's bedside and gently smoothed the forehead which yet throbbed with the obstinate fever.

"Yes, dear, I am better," but the voice was hollow and uncertain, and the eyes drooped in sheer weariness.

Nothing more was said for a few moments, Oberta's hand moving lovingly over her mother's brow, now and then the tender fingers lightly lifting the gray hair in a cooling, grateful way.

"I wish I could have held out just a little longer," Mrs. Sauvier said, with a pathetic quaver in her voice.

"You held out too long—longer than you ever will again," answered Oberta, bending down to her mother's pale, worn face, and kissing her most tenderly.

The home in which the Sauviers lived was very different from that of Mark Brompton or Dr. Disney. At one time the neighborhood was fairly fashionable, and their house had been occupied by people of considerable pretensions, but that was before the uptown movement had become so general. As wealthier families moved out poorer families moved in. Houses were altered over into tenements. Certain forms of business made steady inroads upon the quiet and dignity which were once so essential. The street was noisy—in the summer particularly so. In the gray dawn of the morning milk wagons would clatter over the rough pavements, to be followed by trucks and carts on their way to the markets. Then would come brewers' drays, which, driven with a speed that was almost reckless, and being heavy laden, made a noise as of severe thunder. As the day wore on the lighter vehicles of the grocery store and the meat market clattered continuously. Pedlars, too, with stentorian voices and lungs as those of an organ bellows, bawled out their wares. From the avenue on either side the " Elevated " trains were rushing up and down, the noise, however, being fully equaled by the unceasing din of the surface cars, with their jangling bells, and the heavy traffic of all kinds ever on these great thoroughfares. In the winter the noises are deadened somewhat by the closed windows, together with the softer condition of the streets, but in the summer the roar and confusion in such a neighborhood were almost unbearable.

Poor Mrs. Sauvier! Her girlhood home was in the suburbs of Boston, not far from Milton Hill, where from her chamber windows she could look out upon the harbor, with the sun smiting the waves as they rolled in from the measureless sea, and the lights flashing out in the darkness. The house stood in the midst of ample grounds, and, while not pretentious, indicated both comfort and refinement.

And now she is fighting with fever in New York, in the midst of noises and confusion impossible to describe and almost impossible to endure.

How did all this come about? But what need to ask, for do we not see this same thing almost every time we look fairly around us? In every great city there are multitudes of men and women who have met with reverses and misfortunes and are hiding their poverty as best they can.

Many years ago Mrs. Sauvier with her little children came to New York. Though not entirely dependent on her needle, it was her main support. Through the long, weary hours, whether in summer or winter, she worked unceasingly. She made no complaints over her dull, cheerless life, but kept on working while strength held out. She guarded her secret, whatever it was, for she had learned the value of silence. She held herself apart from her neighbors, but not proudly, gaining in the end their quiet respect. With a fidelity which never wavered she gave herself without reserve to the one task of saving her children from the penalty which her position had imposed upon them. A sad, bitter fate seemed inevitable, but if heroic devotion could avert that fate it would cheerfully be given. She could not do much for the world at large, but she determined that in her children there would be nothing of defilement, and that she would efface everything of mark or stain which their surroundings might involve. It cost her sleepless nights, bitter tears, pain, weariness, but so far she had succeeded, and if this sickness had ended as at one time was feared, not even Elijah, in his chariot of mysterious splendor, would have been more worthy of a welcome to the eternal heavens.

"Sister Nora called yesterday afternoon," Oberta said a few minutes later, "but as you were resting at the time she would not allow you to be disturbed, but hoped to call again, perhaps to-day."

"She is connected in some way with Mr. Dunbar's mission?" Mrs. Sauvier asked.

"I am not certain, but presume so."

"How kind they have been to me!"

"Not only to you, mamma, but to all of us. Mr. Dunbar has been more than kind, and as for Sister Nora I never can forget her."

Oberta had good reason to speak so gratefully, for when she was utterly worn out with sleepless nights and anxious days, fighting for her mother's life with rare courage, these brave souls, hearing in some way of her distress, came to her help, just as angels came to One who, fighting the battle of the wilderness, was faint and in sore temptation.

The angels that we see in pictures are usually very ethereal-looking beings, with wings mysteriously adjusted, and draperies that gracefully lose themselves in the encircling clouds. We cannot, of course, but admire the seraphic creatures, still their exact use has never been made quite clear to us. For in this

world tired people need rest, hungry people need
bread, tempted people need help; hence, while the
picture angel may serve a useful purpose as a fresco
decoration, or make the chief figure in a stained-glass
window, yet as a practical, matter-of-fact, everyday
sort of being the average angel is not a brilliant
success.

In a poem an angel is almost a necessity, for a poet
without any number of cherubs and seraphs is very
badly off; indeed, they are a positive necessity, for
"sings" and "wings" rhyme with "things," and
poems are usually things, nothing more. But most
people have little time for poetry. We prefer angels
with hands, who are able to minister to our needs,
who can help us in our poverty, and render us some
definite, practical service.

It was to this class Sister Nora and Mr. Dunbar
belonged. Instead of a trumpet she carried a side-
bag, with her pocketbook inside. Instead of a halo
he wore a sensible, broad-brimmed hat. Instead of
floating mysteriously in the sky they walked through
the crowded streets. Probably no artist would have
taken either of them for the foreground of some oratorio in paint, yet for practical purposes they were
worth far more than a whole gallery of mediæval
visitants.

In that part of the wilderness to which Sister Nora
and Hugh Dunbar had devoted themselves, while the
fight for bread was no more intense or bitter than in
the region where Edward Vaughen was at work, still
the struggle was on a different plane. Here men
were not battling for mastery, but against positive

hunger. It was not brain against brain, but hand against hand. The question was not one of competition, but of starvation.

And there are storms here just as in other places, and the same temptation which assailed Mark Brompton, to which he yielded so weakly, comes in all its terrible forms. Hence men at times forget that they are men ; women forget that they are women. In this part of Gotham the sins may be coarser, more outwardly brutal, than in Wall Street or Fifth Avenue ; the sins, however, are the same.

A ring at the street door called Oberta to the "tube," when, hearing the voice of Sister Nora, she hastened to give her cordial welcome.

Not very tall, nor remarkably beautiful ; nothing at all wonderful in bearing or appearance ; no novelist's heroine, with queenly air, exquisitely formed features, having the star-like eyes, the shell-like ears, the ruby lips, with which the romancers have made us all familiar. Sister Nora was only a woman, but she was a real woman, a noble, brave, true woman ; not one of those artificial femininities whose lives are spent in milliners' shops and dressmakers' rooms, and whose highest ambitions are attained in achieving honors at the horse show or a charity ball.

"I am glad indeed to see you continue to improve," she said to Mrs. Sauvier, going over to the bed and giving her strong, firm hand to the sick woman.

"Yes, we think mamma is doing nicely," answered Oberta, sitting down on the bed near the foot, Sister Nora taking a chair not far from Mrs. Sauvier.

They talked for some minutes, going from one topic to another, Sister Nora being careful, however, that the conversation was light and pleasant, for it was important to relieve Mrs. Sauvier of any undue strain.

"Before I leave," Sister Nora said, "I wish to ask a favor."

"Anything you ask will be a favor to us," gratefully responded Oberta, looking at her mother, to which Mrs. Sauvier assented by a quiet motion of her head.

"I have spoken of you to some dear friends of mine," Sister Nora went on, "and one of them, the daughter of a physician, would like some time to call with me."

A cloud, not very large nor deep, yet a cloud withal, gathered for an instant on Oberta's face, though she tried bravely to hide it.

"O, you proud, sensitive creature!" Sister Nora said, smilingly. "You think my friend is coming here on a charity errand. Well, you are mistaken."

"Poor people, you know, are proud people," Oberta managed to say, by way of reply, but she felt that Sister Nora was meeting with a poor return for her great kindness.

"Yes, and it is better so, for, in my opinion, poverty has often good cause for pride." Sister Nora had both opinions and convictions, as her friends could truthfully testify, for she was wont to speak her mind at times with considerable freedom.

"By the way," she said, rising from her chair,

"my friend's name is Disney, Madge Disney, daughter of our family physician, Dr. Disney."

"Disney!" almost screamed Mrs. Sauvier, raising her head from the pillows and looking earnestly at Sister Nora.

"Yes, Disney," answered Sister Nora, amazed at the effect of the name upon Mrs. Sauvier.

"And his daughter is coming to see me!" Mrs. Sauvier almost gasped, her eyes now filled with what seemed a look of horror.

"Yes, such is her wish, but not unless you wish it," was the reply.

"O, the ways of God, the ways of God!" Mrs. Sauvier hoarsely whispered, falling back faint and exhausted.

CHAPTER X.

An Evening at Dr. Disney's.

MISS DISNEY had a keen but uncomfortable memory of that meeting with Hugh Dunbar, and every time she thought of it, which was quite frequently, her discomfort only increased. Of course she had not been rude, not even in the most remote way, for such a thing was impossible to one whose social adjustments were so perfect and whose motions and phrases were balanced in the highest form of art. Still there was the distinct impression of a failure on her part to meet the full requirements of the case.

Very likely some of those introspective beings who enjoy mental analyses, and who are never quite so happy as when they are reducing motives and reasons in their crucibles, could discover certain unworthy elements in these feelings of Miss Disney. Perhaps they might even go so far as to insinuate that her annoyance was not because of her treatment of Mr. Dunbar, but the result of a stupid blunder for which she alone was to blame.

Well, what of it? Most of the people now in the world are human—very human—a fact which cannot well be controverted, and yet a fact which many serious moralists are apt to ignore. It should ever be borne in mind that, originally, men (and women too, strange as it may seem) were made a little lower than the angels, and so far as can be observed the order of creation yet obtains.

The only way to have even a fair proportion of enjoyment in this world is to take things for just what they seem to be, and not be too much concerned about what they really are. No sensible, industrious, well-bred bee troubles itself with the roots of the flower upon which it luxuriates with such satisfaction to itself and profit to the community. Why should it? Honey is not found in roots, but in blossoms.

The man who would preserve his illusions must not go behind the scenes. It is a great mistake to question things too closely.

You think that Mrs. Dent's smile is hollow and insincere?

You think that Mrs. Trefousi is only acting a part, and that her sweet, winning ways have no reality whatever?

You think that Miss Jouvin is only pert and silly, and not witty and romantic as some claim she is?

Admitting that in each case your supposition is correct, what have you gained? And then, if your supposition is not correct, only think how much injustice you have done, besides the personal loss to yourself! Queer old parable that is of the "Beam and the Mote." Queer old world this is, anyhow.

Of course Madge Disney felt mortified. Why shouldn't she? Here was a young man to whom she had barely condescended; whose treatment at her hands was anything but gracious; who was practically dismissed by her—though, of course, in a very polite way—and now she discovers that socially he actually has the advantage, while in other respects his position is much superior to the one she occupies! Human nature, with all its ductility and tensility, could not endure this strain without yielding somewhere.

And in order that nothing should be lacking to complete the measure of her annoyance, she now remembers that he was positively good-looking; that his eyes were not only bright, but expressive; that his voice was pleasant and mellow, and that there was something singularly attractive about his smile. She even remembered that his exceedingly unconventional tweed suit was well made, and fitted him perfectly, and that as he stood there on the beach, talking with John—his eyes full of earnestness, his face lit up with the eagerness of discussion—he presented an appearance by no means displeasing to the feminine eye.

Would her memory have been so tenacious of these details if she had not learned from her brother of Mr. Dunbar's position and wealth? Probably not; this, however, proves nothing except that Madge was human, and consequently subject to infirmities and limitations.

In a few days John Disney called upon Mr. Dunbar to urge him to come over and spend an evening in the Disney household.

"Do some mission work with us," John said. "My mother is away—called out of town by the serious illness of her father; my father has two or three special cases which keep him busy, so that my sister and I are left very much to ourselves. O, it is pitiful, in a whole city full, friends we have none! You see I remember Hood."

"Yes," answered Dunbar, "but you always had a remarkable memory for poetry, and what you failed to remember your own fancy supplied. By the way, where is that sad-faced youth with the voice into which he used to squeeze tears, and who put us through a course of agonies with his 'Bridge of Sighs?'"

"You mean Muggs?"

"Muggs was our name for him—and an appropriate name too."

"And yet I always liked Muggs; he was a sincere, well-meaning fellow."

"Yes," Dunbar answered, "but he had no future that I could see. He could recite a little and banjo a little, but the man who expects to make his way in life must have a more effective weapon than a banjo, noble and soulful instrument as it is."

"'Shake not thy gory locks at me,'" laughed John; "'Rude am I in my speech, and little blessed with the soft phrase of peace,' but there are some sins which cannot in honesty be brought to my door."

"That being the case," was the smiling response, "you may expect me on the evening you name."

Madge Disney was one of those exceedingly fortunate, but (though the admission must be made with profound sorrow) not very numerous, young ladies who look well however costumed. Still, a white gown of some soft material, simply made, but exquisitely fitting, in no wise lessened her attractive-

6

ness. She was fairly tall, of superb figure; hair just
dark enough to escape the auburn tint, but which
had a trick of catching and holding the sunlight;
eyes that were open and clear, yet rich with mysterious life, and, while her features taken separately
may not have attained Grecian harmony, the general
expression was undoubtedly one to be desired; for
Madge Disney was just about as winsome and attractive as any one woman has a right to be. As
she came forward in the soft light of the summer
evening to greet Hugh Dunbar she formed the chief
figure in a very pleasing picture, and he thought—
well, suppose we do not concern ourselves just now
with what Hugh Dunbar thought. Thought is a
very elusive thing. It cannot be poured out like
molten iron into molds prepared to receive it.
Language is to thought as the beach is to the ocean—
a place where we may stand at times and gaze out
upon the formless and the infinite. The man who
can say all he thinks has either a marvelous vocabu-
lary or such limitations of thinking as commend him
to our pity.

"O, it is very simple," Mr. Dunbar said, in reply
to John's question as to how he had entered upon
his present work. "I have always been, just as you
are now, interested in the social problem, and I was
anxious to reach definite conclusions."

"What are social problems?" asked Madge. "The
more I hear of what people call socialism the less
I understand it."

"Your perplexity, Miss Disney, is very natural.
In point of fact there is no such thing as socialism;

neither are there distinctively social problems," Mr. Dunbar answered.

"And yet," interrupted John—for it was evident Mr. Dunbar had not completed his answer—"everyone is talking more or less about 'socialism,' 'the emancipation of the working classes,' the 'crimes of monopoly,' and things of that sort."

"Very true," said Mr. Dunbar, "but there is probably no general matter concerning which there is so much said and so little understood. The social economist, as he calls himself, has his theory; the labor agitator has one entirely different, while the philanthropist has yet another one."

"But am I to understand that you deny the very existence of socialism and social problems?" questioned John.

"As such, yes—and yes most decidedly!"

"I am afraid, Mr. Dunbar, that your very kindly efforts to enlighten me have taken us away from my brother's question—as to your reasons for the work in which you are now engaged," Madge suggested.

"No," pleasantly remarked Mr. Dunbar, "your brother's question is still in the foreground."

John, who in his way was partial to an argument, evidently had another question about ready, but Madge was too quick for him.

"Now, John, please allow Mr. Dunbar to answer your first question before you propose another," she said, hastily, for she was anxious to know why Hugh Dunbar had put aside the life which was properly his and entered upon another so entirely different.

"I said, a moment since," Mr. Dunbar remarked,

evading most adroitly a question which was almost
personal, and making the conversation more general,
"that there was no such thing as socialism, and that
the term 'social problems' was quite misunderstood.
We have just the same old problems which the world
has ever had—the problems of poverty, of suffering,
of distress, of drunkenness, of ruin, of waste—and
these we must face and solve."

"Still, the question of my brother remains, and, as
you have said, in the foreground," Madge said, with
a quiet smile, clearly discerning Mr. Dunbar's purpose to lead the conversation away from himself.

"Well, there was nothing remarkable about it,"
he replied, seeing no way to avoid an explanation.
"First I joined a mission band who went out from
the seminary. Then I connected myself with one
of the East Side churches, took a class in the Sunday
school, visited in the homes of my scholars, through
them had access to other homes—so I gradually came
to know something of the people."

"And what sort of people did you find?" asked
Madge, very much as she would have asked Stanley
concerning the people he met in Central Africa.

"The same kind of people I have known all my
life," was the reply. "Not so well housed or as well
clad, but the same people. In some cases the frame
enhances the picture, but, Miss Disney, when one is
looking at a Murillo or a Rubens the frame is not of
much consequence. There is no difference in the
book of life on the East Side or the West Side except in the binding. The story is the same."

"When it became known that you had a basket of

loaves and fishes your ministry doubtless became very popular," John good-humoredly remarked.

"I have kept the basket out of sight thus far," was the quiet reply.

"How could you? You were driven over to your Sunday school; you brought your friends at times to see what was going on. Besides, were there not ' outward and visible signs of an inward and spiritual grace?' Madge, my only and well-beloved but somewhat unregenerate sister, it is for your benefit that I am quoting from the Catechism."

"My dear friend, I do not go there as you suggest. Where you found me the other day, there I live."

This was said without the least affectation or attempt at the heroic.

"Live there!" Madge and John exclaimed, in the same breath.

"Why, of course. How else could I do the people any good? This whole scheme of charity service—throwing things at the poor, like shells from a mortar—is of no use whatever. There must be direct personal contact between the rich and the poor—another service does more harm than good."

"This is hard on many of our charities and institutions," said Dr. Disney, who had been called out immediately after dinner, and came into the room while Dunbar was speaking.

"I do not mean to be hard on them," Mr. Dunbar answered, "only on the method of administration. The remedy for the present state of things is not in soup kitchens or bread tickets. Often it seems to ine as if we tossed help to the poor as we do bones to a dog. We must adopt a very different course if we would really effect anything. But now, Miss Disney, may we not have a little music?"

There were two or three reasons why Madge was willing to accede to this very natural request: she had a nice hand; she sat gracefully; she looked well at the piano, and she played with a fair measure of skill.

There were about the same number of reasons why Mr. Dunbar rather abruptly asked for this favor: the conversation was more personal than he enjoyed; the Disney atmosphere was not seriously sympathetic; he could endure average music with a patience acquired through much suffering, and he would have a chance to study Madge more closely.

So they went over to the piano, Dr. Disney and John remaining within easy speaking distance of each other.

"Singular sort of man," said Dr. Disney to John, under cover of one of Madge's double-handed crashes.

"Very," answered John.

"Married?"

"No."

"Particular friend of yours?"

"Yes."

Madge was now rippling along the upper register, with little bits of music dripping from her fingers— like a fountain playing in the courtyard of an Italian villa. Then came another double-hander, and with it:

"He seems interested in Madge."

"Hadn't noticed it."

"Get him to come over again."

"Yes, sir."

More ripples at the piano, involving silence every
where else, but soon another crash.

"I like his appearance."

"I like him."

"Good family?"

"Very."

"I hope we may see more of him."

"So do I."

CHAPTER XI.

A Sunday on the East Side.

THOUGH Hugh Dunbar had spoken to the Disneys in a quiet, simple way concerning the opening of his work on the East Side, yet there were times when he was tempted to give up in utter despair. Everything seemed hopeless. The conditions were all discouraging. His first visit to the church with which he had resolved to connect himself was a bitter experience. The structure, though architecturally distinguished from the other buildings on the street, was anything but imposing or impressive. An iron fence, sadly in need of paint and broken in several places, straggled along the front of the edifice, enclosing a narrow strip of ground intended presumably as a grass plot, but the grass, through years of neglect, had become discouraged, hence only grew in rank, sprawling tufts, and at such distances as hardly to be on speaking terms. The spaces intervening were either bare or ornamented with scraps of dirty paper and the usual litter that accumulates, no one knows how. Over the entrance was supposedly a stained-glass window, but so covered with a rusty netting of heavy wire as to hide it almost completely. Under this window, a little to one side, was a board of Gothic pretensions, which board was intended to set forth the name of the church and the times when services were held, but the years had so bleached it as to make it practically useless. The church doors were not altogether guiltless of paint, still not enough remained to establish the original color.

On entering the vestibule Dunbar saw that the walls were dingy, the matting ragged, and everything just as cheerless as could well be imagined. He went down a short stairway of five or six steps leading to a basement, called by courtesy a Sunday school room. An ungainly, space-absorbing furnace stood in one corner, from which three or four rusty, dusty, hot-air pipes, reached out, traveling the entire length of the room. Some half dozen stiff, awkward gas lights hung from the ceiling, but the ceiling being low, and the lights not protected, the results were seen in broad sooty patches. A picture of a distressed young female, out somewhere in mid-ocean, holding a very woe-begone face to the sky, yet supposed to be singing a Sunday school hymn, filled a space on one of the walls. A big linen map, detached half way across from the bottom roller, and curling up quite extensively, with heavy lines and angles, indicating the tours of the first apostles, occupied a space on the opposite wall. Here and there were some mottoes of the old time "sampler" order, to which the Sunday school children were supposed to look for help and inspiration in their moments of weariness. The whole place was damp, grewsome, chilly, and Dunbar thought that the Board of Health should not permit children to be cooped up in such a place. Then he went up stairs, where he saw stiff, uncomfortable pews; dusty, faded carpets; cracked, discolored walls; a wheezy old organ, from which the soul of music had long since departed; a pulpit with draperies worn and ragged, and everything else to correspond.

Hugh Dunbar did some serious thinking as he went through this East Side church. He contrasted it with the churches on Madison and Fifth Avenues. He thought of the rich decorations, the soft carpets, the inviting pews, the blending of color, the lavish outlay to make the place attractive. Then he thought of the splendid organ, the carefully chosen choir, the imposing service, the fashionable congregation. "These people over here," he said to himself, "are our brothers and sisters, sharers in the common lot, children of the same Father; and yet we have deserted them. Anything more selfish or cowardly is hardly possible."

But while Mr. Dunbar met with many serious discouragements, he was more than compensated in making the acquaintance of the Rev. Frank Sterling, the senior clergyman in charge of the Mission. Mr. Sterling's seniority, however, was not so much a matter of years, for he had barely turned thirty, as of experience; he having been associated with Mr. Hartley in the Mission for some time, and now, owing to Mr. Hartley's removal to a Western city, was in full charge. Hugh Dunbar could not possibly have fallen into better hands, for Sterling was a genial, hearty, manly fellow, with enough of the Old Adam remaining to keep his feet on the ground and have human blood in his veins. He was shrewd, but not cynical; keen, but not bitter; religious, but not obnoxiously pious.

"The children of this generation," he said to Dunbar, as they stood on the street corner one evening, "are wiser than the children of light. Look in there and contrast that with the church we have just left."

Dunbar looked in and saw embossed ceilings, attractive though gaudy decorations, glittering brass work, and any quantity of light and color and warmth.

"Look across the street," he said at another time, pointing to where scores and hundreds of young people were crowding into a cheap theater. "Some of the wise men of Gotham should try to solve that problem."

Hugh made some very proper remark about overcoming evil with good, whereupon Sterling said:

"Of course those of us who have boxes at the Carnegie and the Metropolitan; who attend any number of fêtes in the season; who regard yachts and horses and country houses as among the necessaries of life; who will spend on bonbons what would support a family—we will think that those people," pointing again to the crowds who were still thronging in, "are very foolish and extravagant; but, Dunbar, do you know that that poor, cheap, miserable show, with its claptrap and tinsel, is about all the relaxation multitudes have. How so many of them live as they do goodness only knows!"

They walked out quite frequently, and within easy gunshot of the church Dunbar found almost

every form of amusement that could be devised—
music halls, dance halls, cheap shows, and drinking
places without number.

"I was a good deal of a prig when I first came
over here," said Sterling one evening, after a walk a
little longer than usual, during which they had seen
something of the seamy side of their parish, " a
proper, prudish, pious prig; but when I tried to
put myself in the place of some of these people I
found they were doing better than I would. No
man knows himself until he has been tried. You
have no desire to steal, but what if you were hungry?
You have no wish to drink, but suppose your life
was utterly dreary and hopeless? You cherish
honor and virtue, but how if you found dishonor and
vice much more profitable, and without them would
starve?"

Dunbar's first Sunday in his new parish was almost as discouraging as his first visit to the Mission.
As he made his way he could not but notice the
swarms of people who crowded the streets. Children
of all ages and conditions were playing in their usual
noisy way. Women with babies in their arms were
standing around doorways or sitting on the steps.
Younger women leaned out of the open windows,
many of them with frowsy heads, and generally unkempt in their appearance. Elderly women carried
baskets and bundles, as if they were coming from
the grocery store or meat market. Men lounged
around carelessly, most of them smoking short clay
pipes, and holding such generous conversation as
could be heard clear across the street. The younger

men had donned their Sunday raiment, and as a
further mark of Sabbath observance had exchanged
the customary pipe for a pretentious cigar.

Nominally the saloons at the corner and down the
avenue were closed, but Mr. Dunbar saw numbers of
men going in and coming out, no one seeming to
mind them. In fact, none of the stores was closed,
and people were making their purchases just as on
other days. Hugh Dunbar was shocked at what he
saw, and later when he came to know Mr. Sterling
better he spoke of the reckless disregard of the Sabbath.

"And why not?" was the startling reply of Mr.
Sterling. "Many of these people were at work till
midnight, and had no other time to do their market-
ing."

Hugh ventured on a remonstrance, but Sterling
was prompt in his answer: "Dunbar, there is a
whole pile of rubbish to be cleared away before we
can build a wall of Sabbath observance in this city.
The Saturday half holiday must apply to mills and
factories as well as banks and government offices.
Workmen must be paid off earlier. Stores must
close earlier. To talk, as many of us do, about the
Fourth Commandment and the American Sabbath is
utter folly. The old Jewish plan of beginning the
day before needs to be revived."

When Mr. Dunbar went to the Mission on that
first Sunday morning a confused, mystified expression came into his face as, in glancing quickly over
the congregation, he saw Sister Nora. Try as he
would he could not quite reconcile her with either the

place or the congregation. She sat under the gallery, on the side, in such relations to the window as to be in the shade, her face also partially hidden, and yet the impression deepened upon Dunbar that he had met her before, but where he could not recall. He tried faithfully to follow the order of service; still his mind, and his eyes too, reverted unconsciously to the quiet figure in the pew under the gallery. One moment he was certain, the next he was uncertain. One time a name almost leaped to his lips, only to be dismissed as wildly improbable.

Mnemonics is a great science; so is metaphysics; so is everything that relates to the movement of mind and spirit; but when one is anxious to connect a face with a name or a name with a face it is surprising how little help science affords. At the close of the service Mr. Sterling said :

" I am anxious for you to meet Sister Nora," and in a few moments Mr. Dunbar was introduced to the very person who had so deeply interested him. As the one looked at the other instantly there was a flash of recognition, though neither spoke, just gravely bowing. Mr. Sterling being called aside, Sister Nora quietly said :

" Mr. Dunbar, as you are here on the same errand as I am let me be ' Sister Nora,' which for the time being is sufficient for all purposes."

" Then Mr. Sterling does not know ? "

" He knows my name, and that I have come from the other side of the city, but not much more. At least I think not."

" The same is true in my case," Mr. Dunbar said.

" Then we understand each other ? "

" I hope so."

It is not to be expected that this chapter fully explains itself; still, like the stern lights of a ship, it may throw some gleams upon waters over which we have already sailed.

CHAPTER XII.

Why Elinor Became "Sister Nora."

ELINOR ARLINGTON, known to us as "Sister Nora," was the daughter and only child of a wealthy New York merchant, who died just before our story opens, leaving her a large fortune. Her life had not been a happy one. Mr. Arlington, a man of the Mark Brompton type, had given himself unreservedly to business; hence the entire burden of social duties and obligations fell upon his wife. In the beginning Mrs. Arlington was a sweet, gentle, though somewhat romantic woman; given a little to certain fancies and ambitions, but as life took on its more real phases the visions of girlhood gradually disappeared. She was rich, and according to the popular notion should have been happy, but she was not happy—far from it. She was the mistress of a large and elegant house, but there is a vast difference between a house and a home, and hers was only a house. She had that which is supposed to meet the full desire of a woman's hope—a rich and varied wardrobe, but she had an empty, desolate heart.

For some time after Elinor was born Mrs. Arlington seemed much as in the more simple and joyous days, but her husband was ambitious, social demands were inexorable; so her little daughter was given to the care of servants, and the old, monotonous life was resumed. Not possessing any particular strength

of character, and not being fitted specially for leadership, her position in the procession was not a very
conspicuous one, still she had to keep marching
with the others.

If one has any choice of position in the social
parade, the best place, most assuredly, is up close to
the band, for leadership, though attended with some
embarrassment, has the compensation of prominence.
The next best place is at the rear, as it affords opportunity of dropping out in a quiet, unobtrusive
way. The most difficult and tiresome station in the
procession is that of the main body; for it does nothing except march under orders.

Mrs. Arlington was in the main body, and just
marched with the others. She went to the opera;
she went to the horse show; she went to a prescribed
number of entertainments; she went to the usual
functions. For several seasons she kept her place in
the ranks, then she slackened; her uniform wasn't
quite so jaunty, nor worn with such effect; her step
dragged a little at times, though she smiled and pretended it was a stumble, and her face, despite its
"pipe clay," began to show the strain. At length
she dropped, dropped right down; so the ambulance
was sent for, and she was carried out of the ranks.

"Utter exhaustion," said Dr. Disney, as he laid
his practiced fingers on her wrist, feeling, in that
tender, delicate way of his, for the pulse which he
knew was both feeble and irregular. "Tired out,"
he murmured, sympathetically, after he had found
the pulse, for it was even weaker and more intermit-
tent than he had feared.

7

"Mrs. Arlington must have a complete rest," he said in the library to Mr. Arlington, when he had completed his examination. "She has been overdoing of late. Too much care; too much responsibility; too many burdens for one so sensitive and highly organized."

"Too much care!" repeated Philip Arlington, after Dr. Disney had gone, and he was thinking over what the doctor had said. "She had no care whatever, at least none that I knew of."

"Too much responsibility!" he went on. "What possible responsibility did she have?"

"Too many burdens!" he continued. "But what woman had a lighter or easier life?"

He had taken her from a little parsonage, back among the Connecticut hills, where for years her father had ministered to a well-meaning but rather austere people. In this quiet country home her life, though limited in many ways, was as free from taint as the snow, which lay a heavenly white, gleaming in the winter's sun. No flower of the early summer was more deliciously sweet or innocent as she stood beside him on that June morning in her father's little church, and repeated the solemn words which fell so impressively from her father's lips.

They had known each other from childhood. Phil Arlington had been her sturdy little champion when they both attended the district school. He fought her battles every time it was necessary, and a good many times when it was not necessary. He pulled her sled with his as they went to the top of the hill where the "coast" started, and woe betide the boy who "interfered" or attempted to "run her down." Once Bill Jukes, who was steering the "double runner" upon which she was a passenger, managed to tip over the whole load in a way which was too awkward to be accidental, but though Phil said nothing just then, yet next morning when Bill Jukes appeared in school his nose was demoralized, his upper lip was badly cut, and his face had various signals of distress. The fact that Phil could not hold either pen or pencil in his right hand for two or three days was never fully explained, but somehow there was an impression all through the school that the condition of Phil's hand accounted for Bill Jukes's nose.

After Phil went to Dan Hubbard's grocery store as a sort of clerk it was noticed that Jennie Randall had a great many errands in that grocery store, and never complained no matter how often her mother sent her to make purchases.

It was a sad day for both of them when Phil went to New York to enter upon business, but he went with her picture in his heart, her kiss upon his lips, and her father's promise to give her to him when he had a home ready.

All these things went through Mr. Arlington's mind, as with sad, anxious face he sat in his library, pondering the words of Dr. Disney:

" Too much care, too much responsibility, too many burdens."

"And what care had she?" he kept asking himself. He forgot that she had self-care, self-interests, the most distressing of care, for a life which has no interests but its own is self-absorbed, and having no centrifugal force to swing it out upon an orbit of usefulness, is soon drawn within the narrowest of circles, and becomes a poor, helpless thing.

And the same was true of her burdens and responsibilities. They were all her own. There was nothing vicarious in them. She was not bearing or suffering for others. Her life had no great motive in it, which, like the fly wheel of an engine, holds and balances the power.

The machine, therefore, went all to pieces, and though Dr. Disney knew that the case was a very serious one, yet it was even more serious than he imagined.

Perhaps if Philip Arlington had been content with his fair proportion of " bread," all this would not have happened. While he was laboring for more than he ever could consume, his wife was dying of soul hunger. He had vowed most solemnly "to love and to cherish," and while in one way he had done both, in another way he had done neither.

Mrs. Arlington would have been content with coarse, cheap "bread" if with it she could have had the joy and companionship of the one whose presence made all of life for her.

"Phil," she said one day, as he sat beside her couch, for she was now unable to leave her room, "I wish you would send for Elinor."

"I have sent for her," he answered. "She will be here to-morrow, though I meant it as a pleasant surprise for you."

"Thank you," she gratefully responded. "I am

sorry to call her home just now, but I feel very
lonely at times. You see you are away so much;"
and there was a catch in her voice which suggested
the possibilities of a sob.

On the morrow Elinor came. She had been away
a great deal during the past few years, for Mr. Arlington preferred that both her preparatory and college work should be done at some distance from the
city, Elinor not being specially vigorous or robust.

Mother and daughter soon began to understand
each other, the inner life of the one being quickened by illness, and that of the other by sympathy;
and like flowers turning to the light, so they turned
toward each other. Consequently out of a relation
which in the beginning was almost formal there
came up a holy affection which blossomed in exquisite beauty, filling the whole house with its sweet
and delicious fragrance.

"My life, Elinor, has been a sad mistake," Mrs.
Arlington said one morning, as Elinor sat beside her
mother's bed, having just closed a book from which
she had been reading. " I have lived only for myself," she went on, "and it has been poor, pitiful living."

Early that morning, long before Elinor was awake,
Mrs. Arlington's memories had gone back to the
little parsonage in the Connecticut hills. She had
heard the birds sing in the rich, sweet notes of her
girlhood, notes that lifted themselves into the bending sky, and went on to join the chorus of the angels. She had heard the hum of the bees, as they
came and went from the honeysuckle at the door of

the manse, taking something of its wondrous sweetness, but leaving enough to fill the air with that
dainty perfume.

She had heard her father's voice as in the little
garden his song broke out:

"Awake, my soul, and with the sun
Thy daily stage of duty run."

She had heard her mother calling her as was her
wont, "Jennie!" "Jennie!" a tender, loving emphasis upon each word.

The dear little parsonage is now occupied by
strangers. Her father sleeps not far from the church
in which he had ministered for so many years. Beside his grave is that of her mother, while she is
here, alone in this mighty city, looking sadly back
upon days which never can return.

"Elinor," she said, at another time when they
were alone and were having one of their serious
heart-to-heart talks, "I have heard the cry of the
children and the moan of the poor, but I was so
taken up with my own concerns that I gave them
no heed. O, I am ashamed to die, for I have done
nothing for anyone but myself!"

"Disturbed sleep. Feverish conditions. Restless
nights," said Dr. Disney, even more tenderly and
sympathetically, for he was now fully aware of the
extreme gravity of Mrs. Arlington's illness.

"Nora," she said one day, for that was her pet
name for Elinor, "I am not going to exact a promise
from you, but if you have opportunity, will you do
something for me after—after I am gone?" looking
wistfully into the tearful face of her daughter.

Elinor could not speak, but Mrs. Arlington felt the silent promise which was made.

"Then do something for those to whom life is so hard, and for whom so little is being done. Perhaps in some way you can atone for my selfishness and sin," turning her poor, worn face to the window, and looking out with weary, anxious eyes upon the sky, from which the light was now fading.

After a few moments she spoke again:

"You can do what you think best. Perhaps you might put a bed in some hospital, or a room in a home for old people, or something else may seem even better, but whatever you do, remember me, dear, won't you?"

Then came the terrible days, when Philip Arlington would joyously have given his whole fortune if he could only have gone back and started life with her once more. And how different the new life would be! But it was too late. The bread for which she had hungered so long was not now within reach, and she starved to death!

At first Mr. Arlington hardly realized the full force of the blow, but gradually there came upon him a feeling of utter desolation. For a time he tried to absorb himself even more fully in business, hoping in this way to deaden something of his pain, but when he returned in the evening the house seemed so lonely and deserted, more like a house inhabited by ghosts and shadows than by living, human creatures.

Elinor did the best she could to comfort the stricken man, but his grief was too deep and his

sorrow too heavy for even such sympathy as hers.
And then came the bitter remembrance that he had
neglected his wife, that in his eager, determined pur-
suit of wealth he had left her alone, and that had it
not been for his selfishness she might still be with
him. At such times conscience was implacable.
Sternly it directed his horror-stricken eyes to scenes
and events back in the distant years. Poor Philip
Arlington! The world said that he was a rich man,
but at heart he was poor and desolate.

One morning the rising bell rang out as loudly as
it ever did, but Philip Arlington did not hear it.
He would never hear it again!

Dr. Disney said it was *angina pectoris*, and so
filled out the certificate; but had he given the common translation—breast pang—only allowing the
pang to be of the spirit and not of the flesh, his
return to the registrar would have been the exact
truth. While yet in the very prime of life—with
what should have been his best years still before
him; with strength and time and opportunity all
spent upon pursuits that were purely selfish; with no
memorial of life or character save that which could
be written on a balance sheet—Philip Arlington
passed out from the world of men, leaving everything
behind him, and going as poor as when he was born
into the unseen and unknown.

We understand now why it is that "Sister Nora"
is present at the East Side church to give greetings
and welcome to Hugh Dunbar on that Sunday
morning spoken of in the preceding chapter.

CHAPTER XIII.

Hugh Dunbar Has a Revelation.

HUGH DUNBAR was exceedingly fortunate in being the grandson of his grandfather. Any-one can have a father. The right to have a father is generally conceded, nor is there anything remarkable in having almost any kind of a father. But when a man has had a grandfather, an actual, definite, tangible grandfather, a grandfather of material substance and earthly possessions, such a man may well be envied. For most surely it is written in the laws of the Gothamites that without a grandfather none can enter the heaven of the elect, but must ever remain outside blue-blood paradise, an alien and a wanderer.

Hugh Dunbar, therefore, had good cause for devout thanksgiving. Moreover, his grandfather was no ordinary mortal, for when certain parts of Gotham were under the control of the festive goat; when sundry other parts gave pasturage to saintly looking sheep; when City Hall Park was so far up-town as to be considered in the distant suburbs, the aforesaid grandfather invested his entire savings in Goatville and Sheeptown. Canny old Scot! And not so very old, either, for before his head was whitened with the frosts of years (he was as bald as a door knob, but "frosts of years" sounds well) he had the assurance of great wealth. Originally his family consisted of two sons and one daughter, but the sons, like good little boys in Sunday school books, refused to remain in this wicked world. The daughter tarried long enough to get married and present Hugh to the admiring gaze of his grandfather, but not even the possibilities of a residence in Sheeptown could detain her upon this sublunary sphere.

A lonesome life Hugh had during his boyhood. His father, after a term of decorous mourning, married again, this time a Southern lady, and went South, where he remained till he died, a comparatively short period. Fortunately for Hugh, his mother's cousin, Mrs. Brooke, a sweet, motherly woman, was able to assume some care over him, so that he was not entirely alone. Having no parents, no brothers or sisters, forming no companionships with those of his own age, he was thrown almost entirely upon his own resources; hence when but a lad he was grave and sober as a man of mature years. His grandfather, being quite content with Goatville and Sheeptown, had no desire to leave a world in which he was so deeply interested for one in which he had no interest whatever; therefore he remained with Hugh just as long as it was possible.

In due time Hugh went to college, this being his grandfather's special desire. At college he was not enough of a grind to call for special notice from the faculty, nor was he enough of a sport to arouse enthusiasm among the athletes. He was a good, fair student, and that was all. During his senior year he became acquainted with John Disney, whose matter-of-fact philosophy and genial cynicism quickened him occasionally to the extent of a smile. When he announced his intention of becoming a clergyman no one was surprised, though it was generally assumed that one so wealthy as he was would become the popular pastor of some chapel-at-ease rather than enter upon the duty of a regular parish.

But our lives are influenced by the veriest trifles. Just as a pebble on a mountain height may divide a stream, causing a divergence which results in rivers flowing into opposite oceans, so some insignificant thing will affect all of human destiny.

Mrs. Brooke, on her daughter Olive's birthday, gave a quiet dinner to a few friends (Mrs. Brooke now lived with Hugh in the Dunbar mansion, for the grandfather had been dead some time), and in the course of the evening there was a pleasant but animated discussion on the general theme of the relations between the poor and the rich. In this discussion Hugh Dunbar was much interested, speaking as well as listening.

" I don't quite see where rich people, as we call them, have any special duties to poor people, or any particular responsibilities in the case," young Mr Brentwood said, in a loud, assertive sort of way, at the same moment helping himself to a peach, which peach, at that particular season, cost more than the whole dinner of some of his father's workmen, for his father had a large interest in two or three of the big iron mills at Pittsburg.

" They are paid their wages—many of them well paid—and they should look out for themselves," was his next remark, as he went on peeling the peach.

"So long as the machine does its work it has a right to the oil for its bearings or the belting for its pulleys, is then your theory?" put in Fergus Finlay, a member of the same class in college with Hugh but who now dabbled a little in electrical engineering, which explains his figure of speech.

"Yes, practically so," Brentwood replied.

"Then how about repairs? How about the time when the machine is worn out, when instead of being a producer it is nothing but old iron?"

"Why not have recourse to the smelting pot?" suggested Tom Scranton, a bright, wide-awake young fellow, who already was something of an expert in mining matters, and who was supposed, with good reason too, to be considerably interested in some of Mark Brompton's schemes.

The talk soon drifted into other channels, and the little wordy boats, after the manner of the paper playthings of our childhood, sailed about, bobbing and colliding very delightfully, though sometimes very nonsensically. But what would you? This gray old world of ours would be a dull place without the light hearts and the merry voices of young people. These ancient towers in all the mystery of the departed centuries need the fresh, green ivy to relieve them of their gauntness, while in the ivy young birds chatter and chirrup and even swoop and circle over the very churchyard.

In this company was a Mr. Bramwell, a distant relative of Hugh Dunbar, who, after the more formal guests had gone, remained, going up to Hugh's den for a long, confidential chat.

"You noticed," Bramwell said, once they were fairly under way, "how easily Finlay disposed of Brentwood in the talk down stairs?"

Hugh nodded.

"And yet from his standpoint Brentwood is perfectly right."

Again Hugh nodded, but this time the nod was not so much in assent as in token of attention.

"I see you don't fully subscribe to this, and yet on the principle that 'business is business' Brentwood could take no other position."

"You think, then, that when a man has paid his workmen their wages they have no further claim on him?" Hugh asked this question with a good deal of surprise, for he knew something of Bramwell and the opinions which he held.

"It altogether depends upon what you call a 'claim' and the reasons with which it may be urged."

"A claim is something to which one has an undoubted right, and the grounds for that claim are common justice."

"Then Brentwood was right, for when you pay Smithers or Hobbes or anyone else 'a fair day's wages for a fair day's work' you have done all that 'right' is entitled to and all that 'common justice' can honestly demand."

"Then why all this strife, this terrible suffering, this fearful burden of poverty and wrong?"

"For the simple reason that there are higher obligations than those of mere business, and it is the failure on our part to realize these obligations which causes the trouble."

"What do you mean?"

"Just this : business knows nothing of the law of kindness. It is an eye for an eye and a tooth for a tooth—so much for so much. The man is put in the scale and weighed against weights of iron. So much skill, so much strength, so much labor, so much wages. When his eye dims, his strength weakens, his skill declines, then the beam goes against him. Now that is business pure and simple. It matters nothing that for thirty years that man has given the best of his life to the firm in which he has been employed. Out he must go. The firm must have younger men, fresher blood, greater skill. This, my dear Dunbar, is what the world calls business, and most of the great enterprises of to-day are conducted on this principle."

"Then what becomes of the man who has been unable to provide against this day of misfortune?"

"Ah! now you are coming to Finlay's putting of it : when the machine needs repairs, or perhaps is too far gone for repairs. What a pity that we cannot work out Scranton's idea, and when people are worn and useless put them in the smelt pot and have them made over again!"

"There is something wrong, but just what I don't know," said Hugh, in a baffled, helpless way, for he could not quite understand Mr. Bramwell's statement of the case.

"Wrong!" exclaimed Mr. Bramwell, and speaking with much feeling, "wrong is too paltry a word; say 'sin,' 'shame,' 'crime.'"

Then neither of them spoke for a few minutes,

each busy with his own thoughts, and yet each waiting for the other to resume the conversation.

"If, instead of discussing this theme as a matter of
business, we take it up as a question of divine obligation and common humanity, we shall then reach the
plane where it properly belongs," Mr. Bramwell said,
breaking the silence before it had become embarrassing.

"Then your remedy is—"

"No! my remedy is not," interrupted Mr. Bramwell. "I have no remedy. No man has a remedy.
This whole matter must be worked out upon lines
and principles altogether different from those now in
operation. But I want you to do as I have done—
see these things for yourself. Go over among the
poor of the East Side. You are a property owner in
the lower parts of this city. See some of your own
tenants. It may be that you indirectly are responsible for some of this misery."

Bramwell had no wish to hurt Mr. Dunbar; quite
the opposite; but he had a way of telling the truth
in the plainest of terms, a way, though, which cost
him many of his best friends, and a way which often-
times is very foolish.

Hugh, however, was too much in earnest to be
offended easily; still he offered such a defense as came
to him.

"Yes, I know all about the saloon, and agree with
what you have said; your remarks concerning the
waste and foolishness of our working people I also
accept, but when all is said it yet remains that there
are hundreds, thousands even, who cannot get bread

enough to keep them alive, who cannot find employment by which to earn bread, and who are positively
starving."

"But haven't we bureaus of charity and many other
such organizations for the relief of these very people?"
answered Dunbar, and with considerable warmth, for
the thought of men and women suffering actual hunger in his own city touched him deeply.

"My dear Hugh, the real poor hide their poverty
as one would a family skeleton. Charity officers
never find them out. Perfunctory visitations are
utterly valueless in their case. The terribly poor are
those who will die of hunger, and rather than tell
their poverty will carry their secret to the grave."

"Then, God helping me, I will share my life with
them," Dunbar exclaimed. "I may not be able to
build a cathedral or found a library, but I can do
something for my poor brothers and sisters."

They talked on for some time longer, and when
the conversation ended Hugh Dunbar had his plans
well in hand.

Thus it came to pass that on that eventful Sunday
morning he was in the East Side church to receive
the greetings of Sister Nora.

CHAPTER XIV.

A Tortoise and His Shell.

IN his home Dr. Disney was the same gracious, courteous gentleman as everywhere else, a fact which must be borne in mind when his case goes to the jury. This circumstance in itself will entitle him to much consideration, particularly if the jury is worthy and conscientious. For this is by no means a common rule with men, nor with women either, sad as it is to make the confession. Most of us at home are very different persons from what we are in society. In society we smile and bow; we make pretty speeches; we are gracious even to those we cordially detest; we are nothing if we are not polite; but in the quiet of our homes we are ——. Blessings on the man who invented pauses! How much one can say at times and yet not speak a word!

But at home Dr. Disney was, if anything, even more gracious than when engaged in professional service, for with the charming suavity of his general bearing there was a refined humor which made him a delightful presence.

"Madge," he said, some days after the evening of Hugh Dunbar's visit, as they were at breakfast, "John's friend seems to be a bright, pleasant sort of a fellow; a little odd in his notions, perhaps, but then young clergymen are all the more popular on that account."

8

There was no particular reason why Madge should flush just a little and for a moment or two seem embarrassed. Poor Madge had not quite recovered from the Coney Island incident and her treatment of a certain East Side clergyman.

"You mean Dunbar?" asked John, dividing his attention between the question and a huge strawberry which he was balancing on his fork preparatory to a more perfect study of its inward parts.

"Yes, I mean Dunbar," answered the doctor, a mild twinkle in his eye, for he had noticed the accession of color to Madge's face.

"His notions are peculiar, but then"—deftly dropping a slice of lemon into her cup of iced tea, and speaking in her usual easy way, Madge went on—"he will probably outgrow most of them. When he is as old as Dr. Bland he may be just as sensible."

There was no need for Madge to drop any of the sliced lemon into her voice, but she did nevertheless. Still that is a way we have. When we do a person one wrong we are wont to follow it up with another.

Dr. Disney said nothing in reply; John found his strawberry all that he had hoped; Madge, therefore, was in possession of the field.

"John," she said, a moment later, "I met the 'unearned increment' yesterday afternoon."

"The what?" asked John, glancing quickly at his sister, meantime harpooning another strawberry of goodly proportions and contemplating it with much satisfaction.

"The 'unearned increment,' the monopoly man, the champion of the downtrodden."

"You are beyond me, Madge," responded John; "it may be the hot weather, or intellectual feebleness, or a mind unaccustomed to your dizzy heights, but so far I cannot quite grasp your meaning."

"Have you already forgotten the 'evasion of responsibility,' the 'trampled sacred rights,' the—"

"O, you mean Vaughen!" laughed John. "You remember him?" turning to Dr. Disney—"a college friend of mine, who spent part of the vacation last year with us at Newport. Ah, Madge! and is this how you repay that earnest and devoted youth for his efforts to reach your misguided and untutored mind?"

"I was on Broadway yesterday afternoon, at Linsey & Woolsey's, doing some shopping, and on coming out of the store, at the very door almost, there was the 'unearned increment.'"

"He saw you?"

"Certainly he saw me, and we chatted for quite a few minutes."

"Well! I wonder what he is doing in New York at this time? I understood that he would remain in Eastwich at least through the vacation."

"Yes, that was his intention, for he spoke of it yesterday, but it seems his uncle wrote for him to come on at once, as he had found a business opening for him," Madge replied, with just the faintest tinge of satisfaction in the consciousness of knowing something which John might fairly be expected to know, but for some reason didn't.

"I wasn't aware that he had an uncle in the city," John rather sadly admitted. "Vaughen never said anything about his people. He rarely even spoke of his mother, and, of course, I didn't ask him."

"You dear innocent! Only think of your being all those years with the 'unearned increment' without knowing that he not only had relatives in New York, but that his mother's brother was Mark Brompton."

"Mark Brompton! Our Mark Brompton?" Dr. Disney said, quite interestedly.

"Yes, our Mark Brompton, and the 'unearned increment' is the nephew of the stately Mrs. Brompton, and cousin of her almost equally stately daughters," Madge returned, complacently sipping her iced tea, now that she had contributed so largely to the general information.

"What is the business opening you referred to? Did Vaughen say what it was?" John asked.

"He said he was with Keen & Sharp, brokers or bankers, or something else I don't remember, away downtown."

"With Keen & Sharp?" Dr. Disney repeated, and with an anxious tone.

"Yes; do you know them?" asked Madge, who could not quite understand the anxiety in her father's voice.

"Slightly," said Dr. Disney, but, evidently desirous that the conversation should take another turn, said:

"John, your friend Vaughen seems to have got the start of you in this matter of 'earning your bread,' as you sometimes say."

"Very true, sir, but I think there was more of an

immediate necessity in his case than mine. Though
I never asked him concerning personal matters, still
I knew he was anxious to get started as soon as pos-
sible."

"Yet there is a decided necessity in your case,"
answered the doctor, who was more disturbed than
he cared to say over John's hesitation to enter the
medical profession. "If one means to do anything
with himself, he must begin early. The man who has
not started on the ladder when he is twenty-five or
six years of age stands a poor chance of doing much
climbing."

"Something depends on the ladder," said John.

"No, the ladder is much the same, whatever the
building may be."

"But suppose one has no wish to climb. Besides,
there are far more on ladders now than will ever
reach the top. Better for a man to be on the ground,
where the walking is good, than on a ladder just
high enough to get an ugly fall, but not able to reach
the top."

"The question is, shall a man's life be a ladder
upon which he may ascend, or mere flooring for other
men to walk over?" interposed Madge, nor without
intent, as she had a vivid remembrance of her conversation with John when this very matter was discussed.

"And yet the flooring of this house is fully as important as its roof. A house without floors would be
more picturesque than useful," John said, also re-
membering the conversation which Madge undoubtedly had in her mind.

" Yes, but coarse, common timbers will answer for the flooring. Flooring can be carpeted, rugged, matted; it can be covered up in a dozen ways, whereas the roof occupies the place of honor 'twixt earth and sky, able to throw back the sun, keep out the rain, bear up under the snow, and, therefore, is far more valuable and useful," was the quick reply of Madge, for she was fully the equal of her keen, ready-witted brother.

"Roof vs. Flooring," and John laughed as he spoke; "Miss Disney counsel for the plaintiff."

" But in this instance don't adopt the usual course, which is, when you have no case, abuse the plaintiff's attorney."

" Frightened already. A poor lawyer you would make. Considering your high lineage," turning to his father and bowing with an air of profound deference, "and also the high character of your associations," gently patting his own breast, "I looked for better things from you."

" Nevertheless," said Dr. Disney, falling into the humor of the situation, "as the judge in this case, which I need hardly say is one of the most important ever brought before this court, I must give judgment for the plaintiff."

"Your honor will be good enough to note an appeal," came from John with such forensic voice and attitude as to break down all court solemnities and fill the breakfast room with hearty laughter.

" A telegram, sir," said the neat waitress, a maiden of African descent, who came in with the familiar yellow envelope. The doctor opened it and read:

"My dear father died very suddenly this morning. Will expect you all to-morrow.
                              "CAROLINE DISNEY."

"O, my poor mamma," burst out Madge, the tears rushing to her eyes.

"And from her letter received yesterday morning we thought he was getting better," Dr. Disney said, as he looked at the telegram which he still held in his hand.

Mrs. Disney's father, not a bad sort of a man, by any means, lived much as a tortoise lives—a slow, heavy, ponderous life, with very little of the man himself, almost everything going to shell. In his case it was not the inward man which was renewed day by day, but the outward man, for the inward man kept on shrinking and shriveling, so that when he came to die there was hardly enough for a proper funeral. But the seventy odd years which he had spent upon his shell had not been in vain, for there were railroad bonds, bank stock, first mortgages, several pieces of city property, together with substantial interests in two or three manufacturing concerns.

Mr. Nathan Haddon was not fitted by genius and daring to enter upon such enterprises as Mark Brompton; neither had he the skill nor ability of Philip Arlington; hence his "scales" were not the result of business energy or commercial life. But he could live as the tortoise—close to the earth and turning everything into shell. Hence he wore last year's coat and last year's hat, a rule which was enforced upon every member of his household. His

lasted him more than one year, or even two, nor
could he see any reason why it should not be the
same with his entire family. His table and general
living arrangements came under this same order;
hence the scales steadily grew, so that by the time he
was fifty years of age his shell was well developed
and his rank among the tortoises was understood.
That one son went to the dogs completely; that a
daughter ran away from home and made a most ill-
starred marriage; that his poor wife gave up in utter
despair; that his neighbors considered him only a
miserly skinflint—in no way affected his course; he
just went on, adding yearly to the substance and
weight of his shell.

After his death the several scales of his shell were
divided, Madge and John receiving their due proportion, but for some reason Mrs. Disney's interest in
the scales which fell to her was restricted to their income. The tortoise probably had its own reasons for
this. Dr. Disney was remembered only in an incidental way, which in a "last will and testament" is
usually most aggravating. Of course there were
the usual disappointments, heartburnings, jealousies,
bickerings, for no matter how large the tortoise shell
may be, or how carefully proportioned its scales,
some get too much, some get too little, while some
get nothing at all. Those of this last class seldom
indulge in expensive mourning. If the tortoises
have any place of meeting in "the great beyond,"
and if they have any knowledge of the squabblings
over their shells, what interesting and varied subjects
of conversation they must have !

Under these new conditions the Disney family could not spend the usual summer season at Newport, for Newport is no place for garments of woe. Besides, Mrs. Disney, though she was fully aware of the narrowness and sordidness of her father's life, mourned for him most sincerely, for his going left her the last one of the family. His will also gave her some unpleasantness, not because of any failure to provide for her, but it recalled certain suspicions which her father had entertained regarding her husband.

It was decided, therefore, to break away from all associations and spend the vacation at Martha's Vineyard or Nantucket, places which would at least have the charm of novelty, and where they would escape the formal, heartless condolence with which society afflicts the afflicted.

CHAPTER XV.

The Steamer and the Barge.

DR. DISNEY'S horses, which were treated with marked consideration by the entire household, most assuredly resented the insult which was put upon them in having to take the family carriage to the Fall River steamer. Every attempt at an honorable compromise had been made—the trunks and general baggage sent by express, the servants taken to the pier in a hack, as far as possible all sign of vacation travel was removed, but all in vain, and the terrible strain upon their injured feelings evidenced itself in almost every movement.

As for the coachman, words cannot describe his sense of deep, unpardonable wrong. Up to this hour he had gloried in his high office, sharing most generously in the dignity of the fortunate man whom he favored with his service. He was therefore shocked beyond measure at the suggestion of going down on the North River pier and taking his place in a line with common hacks and express wagons. Nothing but the tearful remonstrance of a pretty housemaid, who lived on the same street just two doors below, prevented him from laying down his whip and quitting the household of which he was such a distinguished member.

The horses behaved fairly well on Madison Avenue, even though they were going downtown—for there

are certain sections of the city below a given line
which are still habitable to families of the Disney
class. With the exception, therefore, of a high-bred
contempt, which in justice to themselves they could
not but manifest, the horses were passively decorous.
But when they were taken from Madison Avenue,
compelled to go down Broadway as far as Canal
Street, they became furious, and once or twice were
on the point of bolting. And yet what they felt was
not as a dewdrop to the sea in comparison with the
shame of the august Michael when a cable car hire-
ling had the audacity to stamp his bell right behind
him; nor was the base gripman content with even
this, but actually called out, " Hey ! Get out of the
way ! " Could Michael's feelings have just then em-
bodied themselves that gripman would soon have
ceased to cumber the earth with his vile presence.
But, with a superb self-mastery, Michael held on his
way without so much as turning his head or seeming
to hear the repeated shouts from behind. At length
it suited his convenience to drive a little nearer to the
sidewalk, which enabled the cable car to pass; but
the magnificent contempt with which he met the
threatening looks of the irate gripman was coachman
art in its noblest altitude.

Warren Street at length was reached, but the ap-
proach to the pier was a huddled, crowded mass of
all kinds of vehicles—hacks, wagons, trucks, drays—
some on their way from the ferries, others trying to
reach the ferries, each one in the way of some other
one, so that the street was hopelessly blocked. But
whatever Michael may have felt he allowed no sign

to escape him, maintaining his calm to the end.
Everything, however, comes to the man who waits—
hence in due season the carriage drew up within a
few feet of the gangway of the *Pilgrim*, the steamer
which was to sail that evening.

A very winsome and attractive picture Madge
made as she sat on the upper deck with John, watching the hat-raising, handkerchief-waving, tear-shed-
ding crowd on the pier, as the big ship moved out
from the wharf on its nightly beat through the
familiar waters. New Yorkers are always interested
in the coming and going of the Sound steamers. No
other such fleet is anywhere in the world. And
though of immense size, how easily and gracefully
these steamers make their way! The swing around
the Battery, where that wonderful curve is made—
and that too amid puffing tugs and crowded ferry-
boats; the passage under the Brooklyn Bridge, with
the trains running overhead, and multitudes of people on their way home from one city to the other;
the sail up the East River, with the metropolis of the
nation on either side—the towers and steeples, and
buildings over twenty stories high, standing out in
the light—these, though familiar to the average
Gothamite, never lose their freshness and charm.

It was a warm afternoon, warm even for New
York, and the breeze blowing along the ship's decks
was cool and refreshing. Madge and John were
seated on the side facing New York, both of them
deeply interested in watching the people who crowded
the piers—many of the children waving their hats or
handkerchiefs as the big steamer went by.

Madge was very quiet, and at times a sad, pained expression passed over her sensitive face. She was thinking of the people on the piers—thinking of them very earnestly. She remembered some of the things which Hugh Dunbar had said; for he had called several times, and each time had spoken of these same people. Her sense of obligation was beginning to deepen. It began to dawn upon her that there were claims which she had steadily ignored. This going away seemed selfish—like people fleeing from a stricken city, leaving the sick to care for themselves or die alone. Here was she going out upon a several weeks' vacation, and yet had made no provision whatever for those who were left behind.

"Madge," said John, speaking in a low tone, for the deck where they sat was crowded, and he detested loud talking, anyway, "I think if my lot had been cast with that crowd over there," pointing to the piers, "I would have been a rank anarchist."

"Not an anarchist, John?" answered Madge, whose ideas of an anarchist involved dynamite, arson, murder, and almost everything that was horrible.

"Yes, an anarchist. Just look on that pier. Take these opera glasses. See those scores and hundreds of women and children! Can you see the faces of the children? See the poor little babies fairly gasping in their mothers' arms. Now, this breath of air is about the only comfort that most of these people have all through the burning heat. I have been over here with Dunbar. Some of the tenements are hotter than an oven. The days are fearful—the nights are intolerable. No wonder so many of the little ones sicken and die."

Madge held the opera glasses to her eyes all the time John was speaking, but there were moments when she did not see much, for a tear would come now and then. Somehow these things had never impressed her as they did to-day. Formerly she had either listened to the ship's band or promenaded along the deck, never giving a thought to the people on the piers except to be amused somewhat. Now she was deeply moved by what she saw, for there was a tragic side to it which she could not but feel.

"I tell you, Madge," John went on, "though some of our set think Dunbar a mere enthusiast, I feel like going in for just that sort of thing."

This, however, was more than Madge was quite prepared for. She had got as far as a feeling of sympathy—a proper womanly sentiment—but she was not willing to embody that sympathy in actual, definite service; another proof that Madge was human, for most of us have any quantity of sympathy. We have sentiment in prodigious quantities; at times our emotions are almost boundless, but they are mostly of the priest and Levite order, nor do they materially help the poor fellow who is in trouble by the roadside.

By this time the *Pilgrim* was nearing the islands which the city uses for its criminal and insane poor. Upon these islands the Department of Correction has erected several handsome buildings, some of them of impressive architecture, while the spacious grounds, most carefully kept, add greatly to the effect.

"Look on this picture and then on that," said John,

glancing first to one side of the river and then to the other. "See that honest man over there, trying as best he can to get a breath of air. He comes down to the river in the evening after working all day in the hot shop, hoping for a chance to cool off on some pier or wharf, and is thankful if the police do not drive him away. Then see that miserable drunkard over there on that beautiful island, living in a home a thousand times healthier and sweeter than the man who is trying to be honest and sober."

"But what would you do with these weak and unfortunate classes?" was Madge's very natural question.

"One thing I would not do," John quickly answered, "I would not house them on the most beautiful islands we have—islands which have a money value higher than any other property on this continent. It is both a shame and an outrage to have these islands used as they are now. They ought to be opened for parks, for pleasure grounds, for public resorts, for breathing places, to which the people should have free access."

"But could that be done?"

"Certainly, and it should be done soon. These islands belong to the people, and ought not to be desecrated as they are now."

"But surely charity is not a desecration?"

"This is not charity; this is simply putting a premium upon drunkenness, dishonesty, brutality, and the common vices of all great cities."

"In what way?"

"In this way: a man is guilty of any one of the

crimes named. He is sent over here, well fed, well housed, with sea water all around him—in short, spending the summer at a seaside resort, while the wife whom he has brutally beaten or the children whose bread he has stolen are sweltering in some stifling tenement. Hundreds of our common, low drunkards are having a glorious summer at the expense of honest, industrious people."

The breeze was now freshening, for the *Pilgrim* was rapidly reaching the Sound, with its broad sweep of waters, broken on the Long Island side with all manner of little harbors and bays; while on the New York side there were numberless inlets for yachts and small craft of all kinds.

"How beautiful it is!" said Madge. "See how the hills over there stand out; and the trees, how fresh and green they are!"

Just then some children on the forward end of the promenade deck were observed waving handkerchiefs, and generally giving vent to their excitement. Many of the older passengers shared the enthusiasm of the youngsters, so that the scene was quite hilarious. On looking for the cause of these demonstrations, a great barge was seen in tow of a good-sized tug, the barge crowded with women and children mostly, on their way home from a day's excursion. The pilot on the *Pilgrim* saluted the excursionists with sundry blowings of the fog horn, to which the tug responded in its very shrill but appreciative way. As the two strangely dissimilar craft swept past each other the barge sent out a volume of cheers and shouts, which the passengers of the *Pilgrim* returned with interest, John joining in with one or two notes of his favorite college yell—a yell which, when properly given, frightens even a fog horn, and makes an Indian war whoop only a lover's whisper.

"That is one of the noblest charities in New York," said a passenger to his friend, as they stood watching the barge, which already was considerably astern.

"Who has charge of these excursions?" said the other, moving over to the ship's side, but not so far as to prevent Madge and John from hearing the conversation.

"Some church usually."

"Doesn't the city do something?"

"O, dear, no! The city can get up a junket for some alderman or other distinguished foreigner; politicians arrange such things for their workers and friends, but these," pointing to the barge, which was yet in easy sight, "are mostly the work of some church."

"Of course the rich people pay the bills?"

"Not at all. Our rich people go to Europe in the spring, to Newport in the early summer, to Saratoga later in the season, and to the mountains in the fall. Of course there are exceptions, for some people have at least a measure of conscience, but as a whole the rich people of New York do nothing for the summer of the poor."

"But the newspapers are interested, and they enlist outside help?"

"Yes, the newspapers are interested, and only for them poor people would have an awful time in New York. But take the list of subscribers to the Fresh-

9

Air Fund, the Free-Ice Fund, the People's Excursion Fund, any of the Funds brought into prominence by the newspapers, and what will you find? Large subscriptions from rich men and women? No, indeed—the money is given mostly by poor people, the rich do almost nothing."

"I wonder why?"

"Simply because they don't know of the terrible conditions under which so many live. How could they? I didn't know about these things myself until recently. You know that my business as a contractor brings me into touch with all sorts of people, and the hard, terrible struggle which many have to get even enough to eat is simply awful."

By this time the barge had disappeared, and the *Pilgrim* was moving through the waters like a huge swan. The sun, released from the smoke and dust of the great city was purpling the Connecticut hills, while the sky—a vast, measureless dome, emptied of cloud and mist—arched over hill and sea in wondrous beauty. The night promised to be one of rare splendor, when no storm would disturb the waters or fog hide the glory of the stars.

"Well! this is indeed a pleasure," broke from Hugh Dunbar, "and all the more because it was so unexpected."

"A pleasure which we fully appreciate," John answered, heartily. Madge said nothing, but there was something in her greeting which Mr. Dunbar seemed to interpret satisfactorily, for he brought over a steamer camp chair and sat down quite contentedly.

"On my way to this part of the boat," Mr. Dunbar said, "I saw Dr. and Mrs. Disney at their state-room door, and the doctor desired me, if I saw you, to be the bearer of a most important communication."

"Which is that it is time for dinner," said John.

"Another proof of your wonderful wisdom, my esteemed friend. Your college training has not been all in vain."

"'The knell invites,'" John replied, rising as he spoke. "Come, my venerable sister. Dunbar, as a distinguished member of the clergy, please take your place in the procession."

CHAPTER XVI.

A Social Science Congress.

BEING experienced travelers, and knowing just how certain creature comforts can be most easily obtained, our friends soon gathered in the dining room, where a table had been reserved for them. How many have wearily stood on the stairway, leading down to this same dining room, waiting for the distinguished son of Ham to call out the number which would give them a place! The poet surely did not have these stairs in his thought when he wrote that time was short and life was fleeting. A more sad or solemn company could not be found anywhere than that on these stairs, especially during the rush of the summer travel. Every step is the scene of an unwritten tragedy; plaints, far more dolorous than Job ever dreamed of, are in the very nails and brass mountings. The most wearisome moments that human endurance is capable of have been realized on these stairs, and the feelings with which we have seen people, like this Disney party, go calmly down without waiting to be called have made us almost long for another revolution.

"And now," said John, during one of those enforced pauses which are such a marked feature of public dining rooms, "tell us something of this place to which we are all hastening, for I understand that you also are going to Martha's Vineyard."

John looked at Dunbar as he spoke, who was seated very comfortably at Mrs. Disney's immediate right, and just opposite Madge.

"Well, the place itself came into being at the time of primeval man, and remains about as when created; nor has there been much change in the man."

"Then we are returning to primitive conditions," said John. "Some Boston man has declared that the original Eden was at the North Pole. That I never believed, just because so many expeditions have been fitted out and sent to find it."

"If you have imagination sufficient to make scrub oaks into apple trees and Gay Head Indians into Adam and Eve, you may have all of the ' primitive conditions ' you desire. But I regret to say that the man of trolleys and electric lights has descended upon Martha's Vineyard bringing his wires with him."

"That I regret to hear," said Madge.

"Still, let me assure you, Miss Disney, that you can find miles, sections, regions, where the only traces of modern civilization are stakes, which must have been driven by Abraham as tent posts when he was a stranger and pilgrim on the earth."

"I have heard something of this," Dr. Disney remarked, "but I understood that these stakes were used by the Norsemen to stay their fishing nets, which was half a millennium before we discovered Columbus."

"A few hundred years, more or less, are a small matter in the presence of these mysterious stakes. Some day when you are in the woods listening to the song of the birds, hearing in the distance the mur-

mur of the sea, with the sweet winds tempered by
the trees blowing gently upon you, wondering if,
after all, this is not the original paradise, all at once
you will see one of these stakes, and in wondering
'how it ever came to be there you will have much
food for reflection."

The waiter having emerged from retirement with
a tray of ample proportions, upon which platters
and dishes were carefully arranged, conversation was
suspended for the time being. The process of thinking, however, went on.

John's thoughts :

"Dunbar talks well ; talks much better than he
preaches. Wonder why clergymen are so dull in
the pulpit. What stupid things sermons are!"

Mrs. Disney's thoughts :

" A pleasant, well-spoken young man, but rather
light and frivolous for a clergyman. I wonder why
clergymen cannot be as serious in their conversation
as when they are in the pulpit."

Dr. Disney's thoughts :

"Bright fellow. He may have all sorts of notions,
but he is shrewd withal. I wonder why clergymen,
as a rule, have so little common sense."

Madge's thoughts—

Some thoughts there are which, like the burning
bush in the desert, are not to be approached without
reverence. At this particular time Madge was doing
some very serious thinking, nor was it concerning
clergymen or sermons ; it related to Dunbar himself. We will not, therefore, intrude.

"What a glorious night!" said John, as he and

Madge took, on the promenade deck, "an after-dinner spin," to use an ocean steamer phrase.

There was nothing of cloud or fog. The sky was wondrously clear, such as it is sometimes in June, when no haze or shadow rests upon the deep, infinite blue, and the heavens reach back to distances which are eternal. The stars were coming out, though timidly, for the moon was just attaining its zenith; and in that full, rich light the brightest stars almost lose themselves. As the night wore on, the moon, catching the glories of a hidden sun, cast them upon the sea in great sheets of silver, while the shores and distant hills served as polished reflectors, adding to the beauty and splendor of the scene.

After the promenade had disposed of itself, and our friends were seated in about the same place as in the early evening, Madge asked Mr. Dunbar how long he intended to remain at Martha's Vineyard.

"I hardly know," he answered; "a few days, possibly a week."

"That is a short vacation."

"But this is not a vacation."

"If I may ask, what is it then?"

"I am going to attend a Social Science Congress."

"What is a Social Science Congress?"

"I don't know."

"Does anyone know?"

"I think not."

"Has it an object?"

"It has."

"What is it?"

"I don't know,"

"Does anyone know?"

"I think not."

"It must be something of excessive and absorbing interest," John remarked. "The amount of your information concerning a Social Science Congress is only equaled by your facility in communicating it."

"Some men are born to wisdom, some men achieve wisdom, while some men have wisdom thrust upon them. In order that you may enter at least one of these classes, I am going to insist upon you attending this Social Science Congress," Dunbar replied.

"In that case I will look up the 'forms of prayer to be used at sea,' for the unfortunate creatures who compose such gatherings are usually very much 'at sea,'" John piously remarked.

Mrs. Disney complained of the roundabout way involved in this journey, for it was not until the forenoon of the next day that they reached their destination. Even Dr. Disney was less patient than usual, and two or three times, when the party had to change from boat to train, then from train to boat, he said very plainly that better arrangements were easily possible. John, however, reminded him that railroads and boat companies were not intended to promote the public comfort, but were institutions whose sole purpose was to make money.

"My honored father, the secret of all this consolidation business, this buying up of rivals and competitors, is simply dividends—Dividends with a big D—more Dividends—larger Dividends."

"But there is less expense in management."

"Still the fares are not reduced."

"There is less waste in the number of trains and boats which are run."

"Consequently less accommodation to the public."

"The system generally is better."

"The service generally is worse."

"My son, you are becoming a rank socialist."

"My father, you are becoming a rank capitalist."

"Oak Bluffs Landing!" called out a voice, in which the fog-horn cadence blended with the sharp strains of the piccolo, hence it was heard from one end of the boat to the other.

Then the usual scramble—the gathering up of bags, bundles, banjoes, bird cages, babies; the usual rush for the gangway, the people crowding upon one another in the most foolish way; the usual waiting company on the wharf, who stand in lines, compelling the passengers to run a sort of Indian gauntlet; the usual trouble of settling down into rooms not much larger than a good-sized trunk, and the usual lamentations over the supreme folly of leaving home with its comforts and conveniences. But the Gothamite who fails to join the great company of the vacationists, cost what it may in personal discomfort, is such a rarity that a good, healthy specimen, as a "freak," would be a startling attraction.

The Social Science Congress was a great success. Some score or so, mostly dear old men who were too feeble for outdoor amusement, attended regularly, falling asleep with commendable promptness almost as soon as the sessions opened. A few severe, rather repellent-looking females were also very con-

stant in their attendance, coming in with that stern,
defiant air which reminds one of Alexander gazing
angrily around for more worlds to dispose of.

One distinguished brother presented a paper on
" Matter: a Spirit Evolution," going back in his re-
searches ten thousand billion years.

John Disney could not quite see the bearing of
this paper, nor how it related to the questions of to-
day; but in making this remark to Hugh Dunbar
he was unfortunate in raising his voice just above a
whisper, whereupon one of the repellent-looking females gave him a look, of which, speaking to Madge,
and quoting a line of a hymn, he said, " Deep horror
then my vitals froze."

Another equally distinguished brother read an
elaborate treatise on " The Drainage and Sewerage
of the Antediluvians," in which he proved that
Noah's flood was a scientific necessity, flushing the
earth's arterial system, which for centuries had been
neglected.

The chairman declared that this was a most
timely paper, and would mark a new era in the development of the world.

"Timely it certainly was," John said, " nearly
ninety minutes."

This time a female not quite so sternly defiant as the
one who had favored him with a glare turned around,
but there was such a sad look in John's eye and
such a weary, hopeless expression on his face that
the defiant female gave him a glance which was almost sympathetic.

" Capital and Labor in the Days of the Great

Rameses" gave a little man in spectacles the opportunity of his life. "Simply thrilling," John declared when he got home; "wouldn't have missed it for anything."

"Tenement Life in Arabia Petræa" was carefully discussed by a tall, benevolent-looking old gentleman, who illustrated his paper with maps and charts of all conditions and colors.

"Dunbar," said John, when the family had gathered on the piazza of the cottage which Dr. Disney had taken for the season—a cottage which stood on a little bluff in full view of Vineyard Sound—and the Social Science Congress was being discussed, "for now some years I have been your friend. I have allowed you to carry my bag, to pay my bills—in short, to make yourself generally useful. Every honorable demand of friendship I have met, even to borrowing of your superfluous lucre—loans which remain steadfast to this day. But rather than again endure such agonies as those of this afternoon I would willingly give you up to the enemies of your country, that you might die an heroic death."

"You excite my curiosity," said Dr. Disney; "tell us of the Congress."

"I am profoundly thankful that enough of me is left to excite anything," John replied, looking out dreamily upon the sea, where the evening shadows were now gathering.

"Such humility in your case is so novel that I fear for the reaction," the doctor gravely but slyly remarked.

"My only hope of ever getting back to myself is

on the principle that action and reaction are equal," said John, still watching the shadows reaching out of the sky like dusky arms, gathering the tired earth within their embrace.

" To get away from oneself, far, far away, is a decided improvement in some cases," suggested Madge.

" Autobiography, my dear sister, is always interesting. Pray go on."

Madge was about to reply, when Mr. Dunbar said :

" So far as any discussion of present-day themes, the Congress was an utter failure."

" What did you expect ? " asked Dr. Disney.

" Some suggestions bearing upon life in our great cities—plans for tenements; hints along social lines generally."

" Then you are dissatisfied with things as they now are ? "

" Most assuredly."

" Upon what do you base your conclusions ? "

The doctor was becoming interested. Madge had been all along. John was yet sea gazing, but listening intently. Mrs. Disney gathered up an occasional word, as a bird does a crumb, flying off with it to her nest.

" Partly upon general admission ; then upon some little reading ; but mostly upon personal investigation," Mr. Dunbar answered.

" Having diagnosed the case, can you locate the trouble ? "

" To some extent, yes."

"In what part of the body politic do you find it?"

"In the region of the heart."

"Then it is dangerous?"

"I think so—very dangerous."

"Have you thought of the remedy?"

"An entire readjustment of things."

"Is that possible?" asked John.

"Yes, easily so."

"You have no reference to communities or brotherhoods?" was John's next question.

"None whatever. Such things are the veriest dreams without the least shadow of foundation."

"Then this readjustment does not relate to a general distribution of property?" questioned the doctor.

"Not at all. There are lines running through society which no scheme of Utopian communism can affect. All movements of that kind are not only senseless, but dangerous, and should be dealt with unsparingly."

Upon hearing this, Mrs. Disney, who so far had taken no part in the conversation, said:

"Then you are not a socialist, Mr. Dunbar?"

"If I only knew just what a socialist is I should be the proud possessor of the secret of this century," Mr. Dunbar answered. "Perhaps we are all socialists without being aware of it."

"But if I understand you," Dr. Disney rather abruptly remarked, "certain charges are made by the poor of New York against the rich, which charges you accept as true."

"That is a fair statement of the case."

"Would you kindly put these charges in some definite form?" There was the faintest suggestion of acerbity in Dr. Disney's voice.

"Indifference, intolerance, neglect," Mr. Dunbar answered, calmly, but with evident conviction.

"You mean, then, that New York does nothing for its working people. I am connected with some of the hospitals ; I am a director in a half dozen institutions, and have reason to know that our city is most generous." This was said with considerable emphasis.

"But, Dr. Disney, this is not a question of charity or hospital service. There are scores of thousands in our city to whom charity as such would be degrading, and who, fortunately, have no need of hospital care, but who have claims, nevertheless, which are completely ignored."

"Kindly be more explicit," the doctor said.

"Then what are we doing for the tradesmen, the mechanics, the great masses of our sturdy working people, who have really made the city? What are we doing for the industrious, hard-working women, who in their way are just as useful as the men? What are we doing for the children and young people, so as to fit them for the duties of the after years? There are half a million of people in New York to whom the proper kind of help should be given, but who receive no help whatever, not even from those whom they enrich by their toil."

"We give them parks," answered John.

"Not even parks, for what with driveways, bridle paths, police regulations, a profusion of notices to 'keep off the grass,' most of our parks are not of much value to the common people."

"Museums and picture galleries," put in John, not, however, by way of opposition, for at heart his sympathies were with Dunbar.

"But how many of them, and under what conditions? We are far richer than Paris, but in this regard Paris is away beyond us. Proportionately we are as rich as London, but so far as these things are concerned London is infinitely in advance."

"Reading rooms, free libraries, halls for wholesome recreation," suggested John, who had now turned from watching the shadows on the sea to note the perplexed look on the doctor's face.

"One or two citizens have generously made provision in the ways you name," Mr. Dunbar said, addressing himself to John, "but these are only a drop in the bucket."

"Schools," was John's further response.

"Not school accommodation for much more than a good half of the children, while many of our school buildings are most miserable affairs."

"Churches," was John's final word.

"No, not even churches. The poor people have to build their own churches. In London the poorest man in the city is welcome in St. Paul's or Westminster Abbey. I have attended services in St. Paul's specially arranged for workingmen, and have seen thousands of them there. In Paris the commonest street laborer is free to attend the Madeleine or Notre Dame. In Rome the peasant worships with the prince in St. Peter's; but it is not so in

New York. We have set the people off by themselves. Religion has lost its democracy. One of
these days—I hope before it is too late—we will
find out our terrible mistake."

A certain lightening in the sky indicated that the
moon would soon come up out of the sea, whereupon Mr. Dunbar suggested a favorable place to witness the moon rise. Neither Mrs. Disney nor the
doctor cared just then to leave the piazza, which
they found very comfortable; John pleaded social
science exhaustion; Madge and Mr. Dunbar had,
therefore, the moon-gazing all to themselves. Such,
however, is the resourcefulness of human nature
that our young friends bore up under their disappointment with a resignation that was simply beautiful.

BOOK II.—PRIDE

10

CHAPTER XVII.

The Brompton Household.

M RS. MARK BROMPTON possessed in no ordinary measure the quality of stateliness. In feature she was not beautiful, in disposition she was not charitable, in character she was not intellectual; but in everything she was stately, and what more can be reasonably expected of any one person? The old and familiar legend of a certain nobleman who generously distributed his wealth before setting out on a long journey recalls the fact that to each servant was given just one pound, and for that pound he would be held responsible. Now, Mrs. Brompton's pound was a high consciousness of her own merits—a consciousness which never deserted her, and from which she derived much personal satisfaction. Hence in her way she had a goodly proportion of inward peace, for she was on the best of terms with herself. To sit down complacently and smile in the face of a frowning world is only possible to those who are in cordial relations with themselves. No man can be really happy unless he can take himself by the hand, give that hand a good, hearty grasp, invite himself to an easy chair, make himself perfectly at home, and prove to himself that he himself is one of the best fellows in the world. No woman can be at all happy unless she can look gratefully into her own eyes, smile sweetly at her own lips, talk freely

to her own self, and prove to herself that she herself
is one of the nicest women anywhere to be found.
This Mrs. Brompton could do, and do it with an ease,
an assurance, a full-rounded completeness, which left
nothing to be desired.

We have said that she was not intellectual, but
she was well gowned ; that she was not beautiful, but
she was rich ; that she was not charitable, but she
was stately ; and when a woman is stately, rich, and
well gowned anything else is not of much consequence.

Her daughters, Ethel and Janet, in many particulars had followed her noble example, accepting this
world as intended specially for them, which they
were to use merely as a means of simple enjoyment.
Such a sublime acceptance of "the earth, the sea, and
all that in them is" invariably promotes agreeable
sensations in the minds of the acceptors, while at the
same time it obviates unpleasant discussion concerning the imaginary rights of others.

Mrs. Brompton and her daughters quietly assumed
that this world was made for them, that everything
in it was meant to promote their pleasure, and that
every other person in the world had no higher duty
in life than to serve them, when such service was
necessary.

The Brompton household was not, therefore, agi-
tated over such problems as troubled the mind of
Sister Nora or Hugh Dunbar. Why should it?
Mark Brompton was one of the largest taxpayers in
the city. The man who pays his taxes meets the full
demands of the law. Out of those taxes schools and

poorhouses are maintained. Why, then, be annoyed with piteous appeals or stories of grief-stricken homes? Such things were simply preposterous, containing demands which were senseless and absurd. Mrs. Brompton had no patience with Hugh Dunbar. The people of whom he talked were idle, shiftless, lazy, wasteful; they spent their earnings in drink; anything that was done for them only encouraged dissipation, and Mr. Dunbar was doing harm instead of good. These things and many others she said on her return from Europe, where, with her daughters, she had spent part of the season in the Riviera, not content, either, with a hotel, but renting one of the finest villas, and then afterward with the American colony in Paris living in the most elegant way.

Twice, however, it has been remarked of her that she was not a charitable woman.

"Mark," she said, a few days after her return from Europe, early in October, "as your nephew intends remaining in New York, would it not be well for him to make some arrangements as to a permanent home?"

Mrs. Brompton invariably spoke of Edward Vaughen as "Mr. Brompton's nephew," which showed on her part a fine capacity for distinction between blood and legal relationship. It is not given to every woman to have this nice sense of discrimination.

"Yes?" answered Mr. Brompton, though he contrived by means of the rising inflection to suggest a question.

"It was all right when you were alone to have him with you, but, of course, it is different now."

"Yes," Mr. Brompton again answered, but this time there was no rising inflection, which would indicate that he agreed with Mrs. Brompton that "it is different now."

"You see the girls will be going out considerably during the season. If your nephew were here, he might expect to go with them, and that, of course, is out of the question."

"Of course," said Mr. Brompton, but whether he had reference to the girls going out or Edward expecting to go with them remains a question.

"Then we must do some entertaining this fall and winter, and it would be unpleasant for him not to have some part in it. Besides, it would be embarrassing for Percy and the girls to be introducing a cousin, when he is only a clerk in Keen & Sharp's."

"That is true," assented Mr. Brompton, an assent which may have meant only one or all of Mrs. Brompton's propositions.

"Then Percy has his own set; your nephew would hardly enjoy them, and they certainly would not enjoy him."

"Probably not," was Mr. Brompton's reply, which, like a double-handled pitcher, could be taken either way.

"When we are dining *en famille* it will be pleasant to have him drop in now and then."

"Very pleasant indeed," but Mr. Brompton did not say if he meant their dining *en famille* or Edward dropping in occasionally.

"Uncle Mark," said Edward, that same evening, as he was with Mr. Brompton in the library, "now

that Mrs. Brompton and my cousins have returned,
I cannot allow myself to trespass any longer on
your kindness."

"Suit your own convenience, my boy," Mr. Brompton answered, with more kindness than he was wont
to show. Then, too, he was honestly glad that Edward had spoken of this matter, and so soon after the
conversation of the morning.

"You are exceedingly kind to put it in that way,
Uncle Mark. I have greatly enjoyed my summer
here with you, but a home nearer the office will be
more convenient."

"Have you any place in mind?"

"Yes. Mr. Singleton, the head of my department
in Keen & Sharp's, has made inquiries, and I can be
accommodated in the same house with him."

"Pleasant house?"

"Fairly so; at least it looks so."

"Where is it?"

"On a street leading from Washington Square."

"Is it a hotel?"

"No, a family boarding place."

"Expensive?"

"O, dear, no! When I am a partner in the firm
or the president of some insurance company I may
then come uptown, where I can have a suite of apartments, but for the present I must be content with a
hall bedroom and the run of the house."

"Yes, I remember. In the winter you warm the
room by leaving the door open, getting what heat
you can from the hall. Your room is just about as
narrow as this," drawing an imaginary line down the

library, "with a single bed—wooden, of course—and painted brown; one chair, a shaky little table, a washstand, a washbowl considerably chipped on the edges, the pitcher broken at the lip, a bureau over in one corner, surmounted by a mirror neither useful nor ornamental."

"Evidently your memory has not failed you," Edward said, a pleasant smile overspreading his face. "I looked into my room for a minute, and you have reproduced it exactly."

Mr. Brompton said nothing for a moment or two. Memories were crowding in upon him of his early struggles in New York. A pained, dissatisfied look filled his eyes as he glanced swiftly around the large but unhomelike library. Then he turned to Edward, and in a voice which was almost hoarse said:

"I was happier in just such a room than at any time since."

"O, Uncle Mark," Edward was beginning, in the thoughtless sympathy with which youth is so generous, when Mr. Brompton interrupted him by saying:

"Happier, a thousand times happier. Then I had my dreams, my hopes, my ambitions, but what have I now? Come in!" for some one tapped on the library door, when a servant entered with the special delivery mail, which gave the closing quotations from the exchanges.

In an instant Mr. Brompton's face resumed its usual expression; rapidly he scanned the lines of figures; once he seemed as if he would make some remark on the reports which he was holding in his hand, but he went on with study of the lists, frowning slightly once or twice; then he stepped over and laid them on his desk.

"Did you tell Mr. Singleton when he might expect you?" was his next question.

"I thought, unless you had some objection, I might go to-morrow."

"To-morrow is Saturday. Why not remain here over Sunday?"

"Saturday being a half-holiday, I could spend part of the day in getting to rights, and so be able to begin the week in my new home."

And was that the only reason, Mr. Edward Vaughen? Had not some mysterious influence informed him that the Brompton household would prefer not to be embarrassed with his presence? If he remained over Sunday he could not but accompany the family to church, for on this first Sunday after returning from abroad Mrs. Brompton would see to it that the family occupied the conspicuous pew which had been comparatively vacant so long. If Edward was in the family he must, of course, have a place in this pew. That would give him recognition at once, more especially when it is remembered that many of Keen & Sharp's clientage were in that congregation. With such contingencies as these it was not to be expected that Mrs. Brompton could be in love and charity with all men or enjoy the privileges of the sanctuary in her usual devout way.

Had she said anything of this to Edward Vaughen? It is only men who are so clumsy and awkward as to have recourse to words. To such a woman as Mrs. Brompton words are almost superfluous. She could

smile in italics. With the twitching of a lip, the
movement of a nostril, the set of her chin, she could
deliver an oration and yet not open her mouth. A
flash of her eye contained more matter than a printer
could set up in a whole day.

Hence not a word was said to Edward Vaughen,
nor did Mrs. Brompton fail in anything of courtesy;
nevertheless before even she had spoken to her
husband Edward had concluded his arrangements
with Mr. Singleton.

"Mark," Mrs. Brompton said that night, as she
came into her husband's room for a few moments before retiring, where she found him still examining
the papers which had come during his conversation
with Edward Vaughen, "have you had an opportunity of speaking to your nephew of the matter we
talked of this morning?"

"Yes," was the reply, looking up for a moment
from the exchange lists.

"Of course you mentioned it to him?" yet while
she assumed that he had, still there was a lingering
doubt.

"No," Mark answered, not without a sense of
enjoyment.

"No?" she repeated, and this time the interroga-
tion point was very manifest. "I fully expected
that this would have been arranged before Sunday."

"So it will," Mr. Brompton said, reassuringly.
"Edward mentioned the matter to me, not, however,
before he had made his own arrangements for leaving."

"He mentioned it?" Mrs. Brompton's question

was set in a delicate tracery of doubt, like a diamond pin in a bit of rare old lace.

"Yes. He has engaged rooms downtown, and will leave here to-morrow."

How many things will work out of themselves if we only let them alone! If our patience were only equal to our impatience, how much easier life would be! But, instead of waiting for the tide to come up and float the difficulty away, we tug and pull and strain, using up strength which we can ill afford.

If Mrs. Brompton had waited for but one more day, how pleasantly Edward Vaughen's leave-taking would have arranged itself! Only think of all the pleasant things she could have said—chiding him for leaving so abruptly, urging him to come in at any time, hoping he would consider himself one of the family, even regretting that he had thought of going away at all!

Just about the time that Mr. and Mrs. Brompton were discussing Edward Vaughen two other members of the Brompton household had the same theme under consideration.

"I think Cousin Edward might have remained with us all winter," said Janet. "One more or less would not make much difference in a house so large as ours."

"Janet, I am surprised at you," Ethel said, with a fair degree of sisterly asperity.

"I see no reason why you should be."

"What would people say?"

"That we had given a home to our cousin, a young man who had recently come to the city."

"It is the cousin part of the young man that causes the trouble."

"Ethel, that is downright nonsense."

"Janet, you are positively rude."

"Supposing I am, what has that to do with the cousin part of Edward Vaughen?"

"Everything. Can we have him tagging everywhere after us? Must he be included in every invitation that comes to the house? When our friends are here is he to be presented as a member of the family? Think of introducing Mrs. Sharp to her husband's clerk or Miss Keen to her father's office-boy; for he is not much, if anything, more!"

"Nevertheless, Ethel, it does not seem the right thing to have one's own cousin go off to a common boarding house, while we have any number of empty rooms."

"It is just as I said a moment since—the cousin part is the cause of the embarrassment."

"Then let 'Mr. Edward Vaughen, a visiting friend from Eastwich,' remain here; let the cousin part, which so distresses you, remain in the office of Keen & Sharp."

"Janet, you never have any difficulty in being absurd."

"Nor you, Ethel, in being unkind."

"It is but a few moments since I said you were positively rude."

"Very likely; you have a genius for saying hateful things."

"Janet!"

"Ethel!"

They were both angry by this time, and both characteristically angry.

Ethel's anger was cold, deliberate, of the cog-pinion order, the one part fitting into the other part with terrible precision. Ethel never lost her temper, hardly ever varied her tone, and among those who were not favored with her intimate friendship was regarded as of a most patient disposition.

Janet's anger was hot, impulsive, galvanic, passionate; sometimes she would get into a towering rage. Janet lost her temper, she raised her voice, and was spoken of quite freely by certain of her friends.

These sisters quarreled frequently, though never in public, and such sisterly admonitions as each felt called to bestow upon the other were given in the sacred precincts of home.

Meantime Edward Vaughen's trunk, containing most of his worldly possessions, was in his little hall bedroom, so faithfully described by his Uncle Mark. The next day he bade farewell—a farewell which cannot truthfully be spoken of as " aggressively affectionate "—to the Brompton household.

CHAPTER XVIII.

The Firm of Linsey & Woolsey.

BUT all this time what of Mrs. Sauvier? When we saw her last she was slowly recovering from a long, serious illness—a recovery which was very much retarded by Sister Nora's unfortunate mention of Dr. Disney's name, and its strange effect upon the sick woman.

Sister Nora knew Dr. Disney very well, for he had attended her mother in that long, sad sickness, the memory of which would cast its shadow upon all of life. He had also been with her at the time of her father's death, and had been exceedingly tender and sympathetic. No physician could have been more attentive, no one more willing or thoughtful or kind, no one more faithful in the discharge of every duty or more watchful of those under his care. When finally those dread moments came, in which science and skill stand helpless, how gently he led her from the room; nor did his courteous attentions cease when his duties as a physician ended, but as a friend and adviser he was most helpful in every way.

All these things Sister Nora gratefully remembered, for she was preeminently just; and yet try as she would there was a certain feeling of distrust, even fear, associated with his name. Hence when she recalled that scene in Mrs. Sauvier's she found herself wondering as to its cause and meaning.

But whatever the secret was Mrs. Sauvier kept it to herself, not even referring to it, merely requesting that the visit of Madge Disney be postponed, for the present at any rate.

As for Oberta, the summer had gone in much the usual way, for just as soon as it was possible she resumed her place in the store of Linsey & Woolsey as saleswoman.

Oberta had hardly crossed the line of childhood when she discovered that her mother's needle was the chief source of the family supplies. She determined, therefore, at the first opportunity to relieve her mother of something of the burden which she had borne so patiently all these years. The child was brave, independent, of high spirit, and though at first Mrs. Sauvier would not listen to Oberta's suggestion, yet in the end the girl prevailed.

She began her public duties one Christmas season, when the rush of trade was so great that the ordinary service was not sufficient to meet the throngs who crowd into the big stores to do their sight-seeing and holiday shopping. For nearly two weeks she edged her way through the blocked-up aisles; she dodged in and out among the customers at every counter; she carried her little basket with its tiny parcels to the nimble-fingered wrappers and cashiers, hurrying back with all possible speed; she tried her best to respond to the calls of "Cash!" or the tapping of impatient clerks on the counters, which calls and tapping hardly ceased for a moment.

As the days wore on, her eyes became larger, the hollows in her cheeks deepened, her face lost all glow and color, her tired feet ached and burned, and sometimes she could have cried out in weariness and pain. At such times she thought of her mother working patiently at home, and of what this Christmas money would mean to her. Then a new light would flash into her drooping eyes, her weary limbs would take on fresh life, the spirit of a woman would enter the body of the child, and with renewed courage she went on.

Often she found herself wondering as to the people who came in and went out, most of whom had for her only an impatient glance or an angry word, all because she had feet instead of wings, and had to take her turn at the wrapping counter with the others. Often a whole day would pass without a pleasant word being spoken to her, except by the clerks at whose counters she served. Christmas shoppers may not intend to be brutal, but they are often thoughtless, and it is at the line where " one doesn't think " that brutality begins. Oberta shed a great many heart tears during these weary days, but she never complained at home. Once in a while questions came to her which caused her trouble. As, for instance, when she saw fathers buying all kinds of presents for their children she wondered why she had no father to buy presents for her. Or when she saw mothers who had money in abundance she wondered why at that moment her mother should be sewing the commonest garments in order to have money to buy bread. Or when she looked on such an immense variety of toys—skates, drums, rocking horses, boats, bats, balls, everything that a boy could ask for—she wondered why Fred could not have some of them.

One day a man, apparently of the superior type of workman, came in accompanied by a sad-faced woman dressed in mourning. He looked at Oberta for a moment or two, and then whispered something to the woman. She turned to Oberta, who was at the next counter, and on seeing her a soft, tender mist came over her eyes and a quiver upon her lips. Poor thing! Only a few weeks before their little girl of about the same age as Oberta, and whom Oberta strongly resembled, had been taken from them, and their home was now desolate.

Watching his opportunity, the man slipped a piece of paper into Oberta's hand, whispering at the same moment, "God bless you, little one!" Before Oberta recovered from her surprise the man and woman had gone, and when she opened the paper which had been put in her hand she found it was a two-dollar bill. That night she and Fred held a long council, and for the first time in their lives had a secret which their mother did not share. But on Christmas morning, when Mrs. Sanvier went to the little kitchen to prepare the breakfast, there on the table was a nice little shoulder shawl, done up with a pair of warm felt slippers, marked, "To our darling mamma, from Oberta and Fred." The dear woman had barely read the writing on the paper (it was Fred's writing, and not very clear) when two pairs of arms were around her neck, two bright, glad faces were looking happily into hers, and two joyous voices were wishing her a merry Christmas.

11

But Mrs. Sauvier was not the only one who was surprised that morning, for when Fred sat down to breakfast he kicked something under the table which rattled in a strange way. In an instant the queer-looking parcel was opened, revealing a pair of skates, which he proceeded to try on before he had eaten a morsel. Oberta's chair was pushed in under the table as far as it would go, and when she drew it out there was just the little hand muff which she had been secretly wishing for ever since the holiday sea-son began. So there was more hugging and more kissing, and though the breakfast was very simple, yet it was a glad Christmas for them all.

The faithful little cash girl had not escaped the notice of the "floorwalker" in whose department she had served, so it was not long before a letter came addressed, "Miss Sauvier, 329 —th Street, City," which she opened with a feeling of awe, for it was the first letter she had ever received. It proved to be a request to call at the store of Linsey & Woolsey at nine o'clock on the following morning. At the hour named she was there, and to her great joy was engaged for regular work. From cash girl she was promoted in usual order, so that now, at the time suggested by our story, she is in "cloaks and wraps," on the third floor, and is regarded by the firm as a most painstaking and reliable sales-woman.

It was fortunate for Oberta that at the beginning of her working life she found an opening in the house of Linsey & Woolsey, for this firm was not only honorable in its dealings with the general public, but maintained the same high standard with all who were in its service.

Both of the partners were humane, considerate, careful of the interest of their employees, and exercised over them the most healthful influence. They were strict men, insisting upon the rules of the establishment, and demanded a recognition of their rights as employers, but they were also just men, recognizing with the utmost impartiality the rights of others. Hence they allowed no miserable system of "fines," by which a clerk will be robbed of the wages which are supposed to be paid. Nor would they permit any peremptory dismissal for mistakes—mistakes which in nine cases out of ten are caused by the carelessness or stupidity of the customers themselves.

Under no circumstances would they tolerate the "premium" business, neither would they give a reward for working off upon unsuspecting customers goods which were either unsalable or not what they were represented to be. Their clerks were not paid for lying or promoted for conniving at fraud. Both honor and honesty had place in every department of the store. Men and women could have a conscience and yet not lose their situations. To make sales it was not necessary to lie and deceive.

Most sternly Linsey & Woolsey refused to enter into that horrible strife which meant starvation to needlewomen and seamstresses. Such garments as were put upon their counters were not made by women who worked fifteen or sixteen hours every day, and even then not earning enough to keep away actual hunger !

"Are such things possible in New York?" some one once asked Sister Nora.

"Possible!" she answered, her eyes blazing with indignation. "Possible! Go over into some of the side streets; look out of the elevated trains even; see the crowded workrooms where men and women are huddled; look at the weary, despairing faces; listen to the ceaseless hum of the sewing machines over which women are bending with aching backs, straining eyes, burning foreheads, and hopeless hearts. O, it is terrible! And if you only knew the pitiful wages which these poor creatures receive, your soul would burn with holy shame, as mine does every time I think of it."

But Linsey & Woolsey had no part in this gross abomination. No typhoid-laden, death-containing, hunger-stricken bundles came to their "receiving entrance." No woman left their store with a "bargain" in which the germs of a fatal disease were mysteriously folded, hiding the ghastly outlines of sickness and death.

The result of all this was that the store of Linsey & Woolsey was never packed and crowded as some other stores are. No lines of frantic, jostling women pushed and elbowed their way to bargain counters and mark-down sales. The people who came here were of that type who expect no more than what they pay for, and who think that the principle of honesty should obtain just as much in the buying of a piece of ribbon or a pocket handkerchief as in the management of a cathedral.

On that day when Sister Nora mentioned the name

of Dr. Disney to Mrs. Sauvier, so strange was the effect produced, and with such emphasis did Mrs. Sauvier repeat the name, that it made a very deep impression upon Oberta. Most vividly did she recall that scene, earnestly wondering what it all meant.

One day a party of three young ladies came to her department "just to look around," as one of them said, with pleasant frankness. But, like many others who go into stores " just to look around," they soon became quite interested. As they seemed to have some time to spare they went from one rack to another, looking, examining, asking questions, and finally proceeded to "try on." It fell to Oberta's lot to wait upon them, which she did in her usual careful and painstaking way.

One of these young ladies was cold, curt, abrupt, with a tincture of iron in her voice, and the suggestion of early persimmons in her general bearing.

The second of the party was rather loud-voiced, needlessly frank, generously critical, and while even more imperious than the other one, whom Oberta imagined was her sister, yet she was not so distinctly offensive, and after a time settled down to a fair measure of agreeability.

Both of them, however, were careful to give proper emphasis to the one serving and the one served, nor was there in either case the slightest recognition of any human relationship. The idea that Oberta might possibly be a woman of like nature with themselves never once occurred to them; so far, therefore, as any feeling of kinship was concerned, she meant no more to them than the padded, armless dummies upon which some of the costumes were displayed.

And why should they? Was not their carriage at the door? Were they not the daughters of Mrs. Mark Brompton?

The third one of the group, as the other two were examining something which specially attracted them, spoke pleasantly to Oberta, and, finding that she responded in the same way, entered into quite a little conversation with her. Ethel and Janet not returning for some time, the conversation went on, until in some way the name of Mr. Dunbar was mentioned.

"You know Mr. Dunbar?" said Madge Disney, for it was she, a glad light filling her face. "He is a very dear friend of ours. My brother was with him in college. My name is Disney. Dr. Disney is my father."

In the hard school in which Oberta had spent most of her life she had learned to control herself under almost every circumstance, but just as a lightning flash breaking out of the black sky in darkest night reveals in that instant a whole expanse of heaven and earth, so in a moment she saw her mother lying on the bed, she heard Sister Nora mention the name of Dr. Disney, and then the mysterious cry of her mother, "The ways of God! the ways of God!"

And now here was Madge Disney speaking with her, face to face!

"We are ready, Miss Disney, when you are," came like a steel lance from Ethel Brompton, who with her sister had returned from a general tour of inspection. To the firm this was not a very profitable tour.

The visible results were seen in several heaps of tumbled garments and fabrics. They had kept two or three customers waiting while they leisurely called for one pattern after another, making comparisons and asking all manner of questions. As for thanking the clerks for their courtesy and bidding them a pleasant good morning, such a thing was not supposable in their case.

Madge, however, would allow no one to be her superior in good manners, going even so far as to shake hands with Oberta and express her pleasure at having made her acquaintance. That handshaking episode was too much for the Bromptons; Janet was almost rude enough to laugh at this display of Jacksonian simplicity, while Ethel's thin nose took on an edge which, wedgelike, cleaved the dusty air and cut an open way to her carriage.

That evening while Oberta and her mother were enjoying their usual chat Oberta alluded to the visit at the store, gradually leading up to the mention of Miss Disney's name. Mrs. Sauvier listened eagerly, but made no reply. That night she moaned heavily in her sleep. In the morning, when she came to breakfast, her face was drawn and anxious, while deep, heavy lines were under her eyes.

CHAPTER XIX.

A Downtown Boarding House.

THE change from the Brompton Mansion on Fifth Avenue to a downtown boarding house was fully as decided as Edward Vaughen was prepared for. But youth is hopeful, buoyant, adjustable, and as a general thing fairly independent.

Though Mrs. Brompton had not said anything, Edward was certain he understood what her wishes were; hence he determined to make himself as comfortable as was possible under the circumstances. He wrote to his mother, going over the whole matter in the most frank and simple way, careful, however, not to blame anyone, but Mrs. Vaughen had no difficulty in discovering just where the trouble was. Her reply convinced Edward that he was not to blame for the wordless argument between Mrs. Brompton and himself.

"Some quiet hour, my friend," John Disney had once said to him, "when you are in a reminiscent mood, and with softly slippered feet move down the aisles of the years, as a noiseless verger in a cathedral, two things will give you much satisfaction— the comfort you have derived from following your own advice, and the regret that your friends did not follow the advice you gave them."

John went on, with just pause enough to give Edward time to think over his weighty words:

"Here is a publisher's announcement—'Every man his own lawyer,' which really means, 'Every man his own adviser.' That is right. The wise man gives advice, but takes none. It is perfectly true that 'in the multitude of counselors there is safety,' for the simple reason that they never agree; thus the man is free to follow his own judgment."

Edward, however, would have attached great weight to his mother's opinion, whichever way she had decided. Still he was all the more satisfied now that she agreed with him.

That "third floor, hall back" of his was not a bad little snuggery, after all. True, it was furnished about as Mark Brompton had described; in addition, however, it contained an easy chair, or, rather, rocker, "with arms," as he wrote to his mother, from which letter we may quote:

" . . . Yes, with arms, only think of it! One of the arms is rather shy, and so sensitive that anything like undue familiarity is resented by a collapse, which for the time is serious. The other arm, however, is more accustomed to the ways of mankind, though there is nothing tenderly affectionate in it; still it permits of a fair measure of attention without serious protest.

"The back of this chair, with a spirit which one cannot but respect, covers up the ravages of time with a fretwork of rare handicraft. I regret, though, that it eludes all efforts at investigation, so that whether it is a 'tidy' of the prehistoric period, or the remains of a Grand Vizier's towel of the time of Aladdin, cannot well be determined. One of the rockers is somewhat demonstrative. It has a way of responding with a 'click, clack' which, while it does not take away from the actual comfort of the chair, interferes with that sense of motion which is the peculiar charm of this article of furniture. But it is quite a chair, and as I sit in it smoking my evening pipe I am far from uncomfortable.

"My one window commands an extensive view of my neighbors' backyards, with fences and clothes-lines in mathematic order. For utilization of space a backyard in New York is a study. Hothouses, graperies, flowerbeds, lawns, shrubbery, beautifully laid out, within boundaries of about twenty feet square! Sometime I must tell you of my neighbors, with whom I have formed an imaginary acquaintance, and in whom my interest steadily grows.

"My landlady is not a bad sort; indeed, she is disposed to be kind, at times almost motherly, but her name distresses me—Mrs. Jemima Gubbins. The 'Jemima' I can understand, for it was given by Job to one of his daughters (Jemima Job doesn't sound nice, though we are told the girl was), but Gubbins has an origin more mysterious than the sources of the Nile.

"Mr. Gubbins so far has not been presented nor even visible, but, then, he may have a milk route or a market stand, in which case he gets not only the early worm, but the early bird. Miss Gubbins, however, is here—a blushing, gushing damsel of stalwart proportions and marked opulence of flesh. Miss Gubbins has mental limitations of a high order, but as most of her blushing and gushing is done when the grocery clerk is here in the morning taking the orders for the day, she is within the pale of forgiveness.

"I have already described Mr. Singleton, so you are fairly acquainted with him.

"One of our family is a Mr. Rodney Wright, a gentleman of theatrical propensities, who has written two or three very fair plays which would be quite successful only that he insists upon playing the star part himself. To write or not to Wright?

"Then, of course, we have our humorist, the man of antique conundrums, of jokes unrolled from Egyptian mummies, of wit cobwebbed by centuries. The humorist is great sport, but as Miss Gubbins invariably laughs at what he says, and we invariably laugh at him, all are accommodated.

"We have also an artist. He affects the Bohemian, comes down to breakfast in a velveteen jacket, wears loose, low collars à la Byron, allows his necktie to divide in streamers, with picturesque results. He is a good-looking fellow, and so far as I can judge he is a good fellow, which is of more importance.

"Then we have a newspaper man who is full of all sorts of public gossip, who has the names of nearly all the prominent people at his tongue's end, and who rattles along very pleasantly. He is about my age. I am going to like him.

"I must not forget Miss Pollok, whose course of time has run through at least forty annual editions. The light of hope, however, burns upon the altar of her maiden heart with undiminished ardor, and her eager, yearning eyes but faintly express the desire of her soul.   Her Christian name is Felicia; her occupation is that of school-teacher.   She indulges in love songs and ballads, the ballads usually of the tearful order.

"I have not time just now to write you of our family life, but as things come to me I will share them with you.   I am beginning to get hold of my work in the office, but, of course, everything is comparatively new.

"I had a letter this morning from John Disney in which he says that Mrs. Disney wishes me to take dinner with them to-morrow evening.   You would like Miss Disney; she is a bright, nice girl. . . ."

Good for you, Edward Vaughen!

Not a whimper in his letters, nor a sign of loneliness or homesickness.   Not a grumble at the hard, dull work in the office, nor a complaint at the barrenness of his life.

But did he deceive his mother?   His letters were merely an open latticework through which she saw the brave fight her boy was making.   She could not forbear a smile occasionally at his pleasantries.   Yet to her these were but tear drops through which Edward flashed arrows of light.   He often wondered at her replies, for she without advising yet advised, and without restraining yet restrained, showing on her part a tact and delicacy of which only wise mothers are capable.

Being yet in the shadow of recent bereavement, the Disneys could not give a regular dinner party, so only a few special friends were invited.   John was most desirous that Edward Vaughen be included, urging it strongly upon both Mrs. Disney and Madge.

"Just think of him in such a city as this without a soul to speak to except the people in his boarding house or the clerks in the office."

"He has the Bromptons," said Mrs. Disney. "Besides, they are his own people."

"In a sense they are his own people, but you see how quietly they have disposed of him." John spoke with some heat, for though Edward had said nothing about his eviction from the Brompton mansion, he understood it perfectly.

"But how can we take up a young man when his own relatives, who are our friends, will not do it?"

"Remember, my dear mother, that he was my close, intimate friend for four years, and a straighter, manlier fellow is not in New York. I have no patience with such silly pride as that of the Bromptons. A real top-lofty, 'come over with the Conqueror' aristocracy I can forgive, but heaven deliver us from shoddy!"

"But, John," put in Madge, "it is not the Bromptons who trouble us, only how are we going to explain—"

"Don't explain," John said, before Madge had finished her sentence; "let things explain themselves. There is no need to say anything whatever. Edward Vaughen is more than Mr. Brompton's nephew. He can get along without the background of Mrs. Brompton's tiresome, stately airs. Gracious! how that woman wearies me, and Ethel is almost as bad. You mark my words—Edward Vaughen will make his

way in New York, and unless I am very much mistaken the Bromptons will be glad to own him one
of these days."

"You and your 'unearned increment' have played
the Damon and Pythias act so long that I suppose
it must continue to the end," Madge suggested
with a pleasant smile, for in her heart she sided with
John.

"I hope so," John answered, heartily. "I know
the 'unearned increment,' as you call him. He is
as straight as a gun barrel, as true as steel, as open
as the day, and simply incapable of meanness or
trickery. Now, when a young, clean, bright fellow
such as he is comes to New York, to have people
like the Bromptons treat him as they have done is
enough to provoke a saint."

"I have heard of St. John, and even read some of
his writings," Madge quickly replied, "but to behold
him in the flesh was something for which I never
ventured to hope."

"It was your eyes which were holden, my dear
sister. You can see men as trees walking, but when
your own brother by his illustrious example reproves
your frivolous life you are not able to recognize his
saintly ways."

"Is it catching, John?"

"You need have no fears, Madge."

"Have you had it for any length of time?"

"I was born with it."

"Strange I never noticed it before."

"It is not in your line, which explains your lack
of recognition."

"When does it trouble you most?"

"When I am reaching down to the level of your comprehension."

"What are you taking for it?"

"Qualms of conscience with grains of sense—a remedy which might be of service to you."

"You poor thing, how you must have suffered! And such a powerful antidote!"

"It would have killed you, Madge."

"Yes, but you see there was no need of my taking it, John."

With this Madge turned to the writing table to finish the letter upon which she was engaged when John came in to speak of Edward Vaughen.

In the matter of argument Madge quite frequently had the advantage in her encounters with John, but in this particular instance he secured the desired invitation, which to him was the main thing.

A woman is usually content if she comes off first in a discussion; a man generally prefers to gain the point which is under discussion. A debate, therefore, which closes with both parties perfectly satisfied is eminently pleasing, and when properly conducted ministers to the good of all concerned.

Madge finished her letter; John wrote his; and it was to John's letter Edward referred in his epistle to Mrs. Vaughen.

CHAPTER XX.

The Marriage Syndicate.

THE complications which Mrs. Disney and Madge so clearly foresaw, but which John distinctly refused to see, were not long in presenting themselves. Edward Vaughen had hardly arrived at the Disney home when Mr. and Miss Keen were announced, and on glancing across the room Edward saw the senior partner of the firm with a young lady, whom he suspected was his daughter. He went on chatting with Hugh Dunbar as easily and pleasantly as before the Keens came in, for it never once occurred to him that there was anything embarrassing in the situation. A moment or two later, however, when the Bromptons came, a feeling of discomfort presented itself, for he had not seen any of the Bromptons, except his Uncle Mark, since he had gone to live downtown. Mr. Brompton greeted him heartily. Mrs. Brompton evidently did not expect to meet him, still she did fairly well. Ethel, taking her cue from her mother, was moderately kind, while Janet was openly friendly. Percy, a youth of the elaborate and gilded order, who had just returned from a yachting cruise, at first was disposed to be condescending, but behaved better as the evening wore on. Mr. Keen, knowing that Edward was Mark Brompton's nephew, was quite cordial in his greeting, while Miss Keen, having no knowledge of any rela-

tionship, accepted him just as he was introduced—
"Mr. Vaughen, a college friend of my son."

The pairing arrangement Madge worked out most
judiciously—Miss Brompton under the care of Hugh
Dunbar, Janet with her brother John, Miss Keen in
charge of Percy Brompton, appropriating Edward to
herself. The others her mother disposed of. A
visiting friend from the South, Mrs. Austin, a quick-
witted, nimble-tongued woman, with snappy black
eyes, enabled Mrs. Disney to avoid the dreaded thir-
teen and also to give a Joan to each Darby.

"To have the pleasure of inviting an honored
friend and then deny that friend an acceptance of
such invitation," said Dr. Disney, looking at Mr.
Keen, shortly after the company had sat down, "is
rather an unusual proceeding, but I trust Mrs. Keen
will forgive me. Still, professional honor should always take precedence of personal friendship."

"Mrs. Keen fully appreciates Mrs. Disney's kindness," turning to Mrs. Disney, "and also Dr. Disney's
thoughtful courtesy," was Mr. Keen's fairly graceful
acknowledgment.

"You think, then, that a man's public duty is a
stronger obligation than his private interests?" questioned John, who saw that conversation was sagging,
as is not unusual at dinner parties.

"On general principles I should say yes, though,
of course, there are exceptions," the doctor replied,
glancing around the table as though he would like
the discussion to become general.

"It seems to me, though, that many of our most
serious embarrassments come from this very matter

12

of 'exceptions.' If no exceptions were allowable, the
situation would be greatly simplified," said John,
who had waited for some other one to take up the
case.

"But how dull a thing you would make of life!"
Hugh Dunbar answered; "everything on schedule
time like a railroad, each train with a given number
of cars, stopping at a given list of stations, the whole
business simply a mechanical arrangement."

"If your illustration is to apply generally, I most
certainly accept Mr. Disney's position," Mr. Keen
remarked. "To roll down an embankment, or crush
through a bridge, or be run off by a broken rail, may
be variations in the monotony of life, but I prefer the
common, everyday roadbed."

Mr. Keen smiled as he spoke, and enjoyed something of that satisfaction which laymen generally
experience when they have a clergyman at a disadvantage.

"Yes, but it is the constant travel over the road
that causes these very troubles," Mr. Dunbar answered, without a moment's hesitation, much to the
delight of Madge, for the laugh which had not quite
died away was decidedly against him, neither could
she see just how he would escape from the dilemma;
"embankments crumble, bridges weaken, rails wear
out, all because of this ceaseless, monotonous going
and coming."

It was now Mr. Dunbar's turn to enjoy something
of the satisfaction which Mr. Keen had experienced.

"Meantime we are sidetracking the real question,"
said John, "which is, How far should the professional

control the individual? Now under the law of the 'excluded middle' a thing must either be or not be; the exceptions suggested by my illustrious father are therefore not admissible."

"Granting that this position is the correct one," said Edward Vaughen, speaking for the first time, "a doctor's first duty is to his patient?"

To this there was general assent.

"A lawyer's first duty is to his client?"

This also was agreed to.

"A clergyman's first duty is to his parish?"

This, too, was accepted without question.

"Then an employer's first duty is to his employees?" was Edward's next question, a question to which there was no immediate reply, but which lay like an unexploded shell with a slowly burning fuse attached —an ugly, dangerous thing, full of unpleasant possibilities.

"There is this difference," said Mark Brompton, after allowing the fuse to smoke itself close to the shell: "the parish employs the clergyman, the client employs the lawyer, the patient employs the physician; this 'first duty,' therefore, of which you speak is simply in each case an honest return for a fair equivalent; whereas it is just the other way with regard to employers and employed. Using these same illustrations, we can all see that the first duty of the employee is to the one who employs him."

By this time Edward's shell, which had seemed so dangerous, was seen to be only a *papier-maché* sham, and the fuse had burned itself out.

"Very true," said Hugh Dunbar, coming to the

relief of Edward Vaughen; " but just as the parish
needs the clergyman, the client the lawyer, the patient
the physician, so the master needs the man. The
question is more than wages and work; it is rather
one of mutual obligation."

Mark Brompton made no reply other than that
conveyed by an incredulous smile; but Mrs. Austin,
who had closely followed the discussion, broke in
with :

" It seems to me that we are forgetting the very
plan upon which society was founded. What about
hewers of wood, drawers of water, the one serving,
the other served? Even the patriarchs had servants
and slaves."

" I most cordially agree with you," said Mrs.
Brompton, looking across the table at Mrs. Austin.
" The woes and wrongs of the poor have become exceedingly tiresome. If our workmen are not content
with their wages, let them go somewhere else; if
they are not pleased with their employers, let them
find others. My own opinion, however, is that much
of the agitation is caused by meddlesome reformers,
who had better be minding their own business."

" Thanks to agitation of one kind and another, the
time has now come when a man must send for a
walking delegate or a committee of some brotherhood and say, ' Please, sir, may I build a mill?'
' Please, gentlemen, may I start a foundry?' ' Kindly
give me permission to put a ship on the stocks.'
Before a person may venture to repair his house or
put a new stove in his kitchen the consent of certain
organizations has to be obtained. Talk about the

'tyranny of capital!' It is not to be compared with the tyranny of labor." Mr. Keen spoke with some irritation, though this was not to be wondered at, for complications in the labor market had affected him quite seriously in some business matters.

"For my part," said Mr. Brompton, speaking in a very positive way, "I never permit dictation from outside parties in matters that concern my business. I pay my men what I please. I dismiss them at my pleasure. It is my money that they earn, and they must earn it in my way or not at all. No man need work for me unless it suits him; no man shall work for me unless it suits me. These worthless schemers who agitate strikes and cause trouble should be summarily dealt with. They are more dangerous to the community than thieves or firebugs."

"I am right glad to hear you say so," Mrs. Austin eagerly said, her snappy black eyes full of Southern fire. "What do such men know of your business or of any business? And yet they order strikes; they persuade men to give up their places; they disturb the public peace, and all the while enrich themselves at the expense of the very ones whom they pretend to help. I know you Northerners fought for 'freedom,' as you call it, but it seems now as if the hod man and the knight of the shovel had the upper hand."

Mrs. Austin was "reconstructed" only in part. Her father had been an officer in the Confederate army, and was killed at Gettysburg. The proclamation of Lincoln had emancipated their slaves, leaving their plantations deserted and useless. Though only a girl, she remembered that terrible time ; there was, therefore, more than a tinge of bitterness in her voice when she spoke of " Northerners " and " freedom."

Madge saw by a certain light in Edward Vaughen's eyes, together with an eager expression on his face, that he was about to reply, so the instant Mrs. Austin had finished she put a quiet question to him which took his attention for the time.   Janet, with equal adroitness, engaged the battalions of Hugh Dunbar's speech, holding them effectually in check.   The two dangerous ones were thus disposed of, leaving Mrs. Austin in possession of the verbal heights.

Telegraphic signals having been exchanged, Mrs. Disney made that mysterious motion which is so well understood, and in a few moments the party had exchanged the dining room for the parlors.

When Dr. Disney suggested that in view of Mrs. Keen's very delicate health the utmost carefulness was necessary, and then pleasantly proposed that she send a substitute in the person of her daughter, he was speaking one word for Mrs. Keen and two for himself.   Dr. Disney had his own reasons for hoping that in the near future John would see that Miss Keen was a very attractive young lady, whose fortune and connections were both highly desirable.

When Mr. Keen accepted Dr. Disney's kindly suggestion he also was speaking one word for Mrs. Keen and two for himself.   His hope, however, was not in John Disney, but in Percy Brompton, for he had his own reasons for desiring an alliance with the Brompton household.

We have all heard of matchmaking mothers, who

in the most adroit way get their daughters " listed "
on the matrimonial exchange, and then form a
little syndicate of cousins and aunts to manage the
market as Wall Street never dreams of. Dick
Verdant, a good, simple-hearted fellow, had hardly
been fairly introduced to Miss Pausay before he was
taken possession of by the Pausay combine, and what
with " dear, sweet girl," " so kind and devoted," " a
perfect treasure," " worth her weight in gold," followed up with urgent invitations to all sort of functions at the homes of certain members of the " combine," Dick was bewildered, nor could he recover
himself before he was being received as the accepted
suitor of Miss Pausay.

But she made him a capital wife, and he was much
better off than if he had married some Dresden shep-
herdess, with staring blue eyes and a lot of fluffy
flaxen hair.

What delicate management was required with the
rector of St. Veronica's ! The dear man was tall,
gaunt, ascetic, with his head among the stars, and
hardly a thought for the common things of earth.

But Mrs. Wiseman had a daughter, in whose gentle
bosom there throbbed more hopes than probabilities.
Miss Wiseman was famous for her skill in working
altar cloths. She had a genius for Dorcas meetings.
Her fame as a zealous leader in church activities had
gone abroad. When the right time came Mrs. Wiseman formed a little syndicate ; St. Veronica's became
the center of attraction ; the congregations increased ;
broader plans of church work were devised ; Miss
Wiseman had frequent consultations with the rector,

so to-day she is the rectoress, and Mrs. Wiseman has not lived in vain.

Lord Piccadilly had hardly come down the gang-way before he was in a network against which nothing availed. He was deluged with cards for everything in town and out of town. He had calls and callers at all times and seasons. The hospitalities that were crowded upon him—rides in the park, dinners at Tuxedo, trips to Newport, moonlight sails up the river, boxes at the opera, attentions of every imaginable description—were more than he could number. He wrote to his father, the Earl of Cheapside: "These Americans are the most hospitable people I ever met. Their kindness is really wonderful."

He was not then aware that he was in the hands of the Shrewdly syndicate, whose one purpose was to have a daughter marry into the English nobility.

Miss Shrewdly is now the Countess of Cheapside, her husband's noble father having quite recently departed this life in that full odor of sanctity which is the special privilege of the highly born.

She carried a bagful of American securities to her British home, by which the Cheapside estates and baronial halls were taken out of pawn, but she left behind her a man's broken, shadowed life, and memories from which her heart would never be free. Still, she is a countess, is addressed as "my lady," visits at Marlborough House—enough, surely, to satisfy the pride of any woman.

It was a pity that Dr. Disney and Mr. Keen should differ so widely in their plans. The one thought of his son, the other thought of his daughter, but in reality each man was thinking of himself. In his way Dr. Disney had quite an affection for John, just as Mr. Keen had for Rhea, but often these affections of ours are only envelopes in which much of down-right selfishness is inclosed.

Mrs. Shrewdly would have been indignant if any-one had charged her with selfishness, but she was selfish—cruelly, heartlessly selfish—and to gratify that selfishness she sacrificed her daughter's happiness, and was guilty of soul murder.

"Rather a pleasant young man Mr. Vaughen is," said Miss Keen to Madge Disney, as they chatted together after the party had returned to the parlors.

"Very," Madge answered, for though she had a way of speaking of him to John as the " unearned in-crement," and was disposed to regard him as somewhat visionary, still there was no denying the fact that he was a most agreeable young fellow.

"You have known him some time?" was the very natural question, and the one next in order.

"He was in college with my brother. They are classmates. He spent part of the vacation with us one year."

" Of what family is he?" came next.

Madge was fully aware that the ice here was thin and the skating dangerous.

"I really don't know," which was literally true. "I think he is an only son. His mother lives in Eastwich, a little place somewhere down East."

" He seems intimate with the Bromptons."

The ice was not quite so thin here. Madge could skate, therefore, in comparative comfort.

"Yes; he is Mr Brompton's nephew. His mother and Mr. Brompton are brother and sister."

"O!" not very loud, but significant.

Then, as things will, changes took place in the groupings, so that in due time Edward found himself talking with Miss Keen, evidently finding something of interest to talk of, for they remained together for nearly the rest of the evening.

Dr. Disney was too courteous to show any disappointment, yet he found himself wishing that John was in Edward's place, chatting so easily and pleasantly with Miss Keen. Mr. Keen was too much a man of the world to betray the least annoyance, still at heart he was angry with Mark Brompton's nephew for taking the place which he had intended for Mark Brompton's son.

As for John and Percy, all unconscious of the plans which were in the minds of the two matchmakers, they were discussing the possibilities of a yacht race, the one yacht with a hull of aluminum, the other one of celluloid.

"Who is the Mr. Vaughen we met at dinner?" said Miss Keen to her father, in the carriage on their way home.

"A clerk in my office," was the angry reply. Mr. Keen was thoroughly angry—angry with the Disneys for having invited Vaughen, but more angry with his daughter for wasting the evening as she did.

"I understood Miss Disney to say that he was Mr. Brompton's nephew," said Miss Keen, very much surprised at her father's reply.

"So he is; but he is a common clerk in my office, not much better than an office boy, and poor as a church mouse."

"O!" responded Rhea, but not in the same tone as earlier in the evening.

Nothing more was said and very soon the carriage drew up at their door.

CHAPTER XXI.

Wee Jamie.

BUT we must not forget Hugh Dunbar nor the work to which he had given himself—a work which he was finding exceedingly difficult and complicated. Though he was young, strong, eager for experiments, and still more eager for results, yet already he had discovered that neither "fashionable slumming" nor spasmodic charity was of the least avail.

The fashionable slummer he regarded as a vain, silly person, whose motives were chiefly sentimental, and who usually did far more harm than good. Spectacular charity excited his utter abhorrence, for it only mocked the awful misery which it failed to alleviate.

In his parish were multitudes of people—thousands upon thousands—whose condition was not so much that of poverty as of dense, terrible ignorance, in many cases reaching to semi-barbarism. That a large proportion of these people were aliens, of foreign language, with habits peculiar to themselves, entirely unfamiliar with American life, in no wise lessened his sense of responsibility, but rather added to it.

Many of these people—it might hardly be fair to say most of them—but very many of them had thrown aside almost everything by way of religious tradition, and despite earnest efforts refused to have anything to do with churches or church people.

When Sunday came, and the season would admit of it, many went to the beaches, to the common summer resorts, of which there are scores within an hour's ride from the city, and to places of public entertainment. Others were not able to afford these luxuries, but had to content themselves with such inexpensive enjoyments as Central Park could give. In the evening the beer gardens along the river front filled up with their usual crowd, who patronized the swings, the dance rooms, contriving in various ways to put in the time till about midnight. Sunday had no religious significance whatever. It was simply a holiday, just a day in which they were not compelled to work, though for that matter Hugh Dunbar found that hundreds of them plied the needle or ran the sewing machine on Sundays the same as on other days.

At an early age the children were taken from the day schools—many of them were never sent at all—for such money as they could earn was needed to support the home. They drifted into factories of one kind and another, of which there are hundreds in New York. They were crowded into workrooms of innumerable varieties, some so filthy, so foul, so illy ventilated, as to be little better than pesthouses.

They took whatever employment was offered, coming into contact mostly with those of their own class, only, of course, more hardened, as well as more familiar with the coarse vulgarities of life.

When the day's work was over there was nothing for them but return to the crowded tenement, which in the summer was stifling, compelling many of them to remain out of doors all night rather than suffer the awful heat of their rooms.

Not infrequently the small "flat," or even "side" of a flat, would be divided with another tenant, so that a score of families would sometimes be occupying a building not much wider and only a story or two higher than an ordinary house!

The walls were usually so thin that the common conversation of the people across the hall could be heard easily, nor was this conversation always such as one wished to hear. At night the hallways and narrow passages were dark, so that going up or down stairs was attended with considerable annoyance, if not danger.

As Hugh Dunbar went through this parish of his he wondered if such a city as New York was doing all that it might do for these people. Speaking to John Disney, he said:

"When the city puts a light on the street corner, stations a policeman with a club, arranges for the visits of a garbage man, has it done its whole duty in this matter?"

"Ask me not in sadful poetry. I am no alderman with a pocketful of franchises, listening eagerly for the voice of some street car company."

At heart John Disney was just as serious as Hugh Dunbar, but he did not show it in the same way.

"A grave problem is this of municipal government—one that must be solved, or trouble will come to us," Dunbar answered, putting aside John's pleasantry.

"A grave problem it is; we are always burying something or other. One time it is wires, another time it is gas pipes, another time it is water mains, and no sooner have we fairly buried them than we dig the poor things up again."

Dunbar looked at John half reprovingly, but John went right on :

"The graves we dig in the streets of New York are long enough, deep enough, broad enough, to bury everything and everybody four times a year. You are right, Dunbar ; municipal government is a grave problem."

"And to these thousands we have given the ballot, men who are utterly incapable of an intelligent vote," Dunbar replied, as seriously as he could, for John's humor was not without its effects.

"And also the box," added John. "These friends of yours are not satisfied with the ballot, but take the box as well, stuffing it to their hearts' desire. No wonder some wards roll up such big majorities."

Hugh Dunbar was proud of his native city. Its magnificent enterprise, its commercial supremacy, its genius for vast undertakings, the ease with which it accepted the heaviest responsibilities, the earnestness of its life, the power which it exerted all over the nation, the broad, generous way in which it responded to every appeal, together with its manifest desire to be worthy of its high rank among the great cities of the world, produced in the mind of Dunbar a feeling such as Dante felt for Florence, or the ancient Hebrews for Jerusalem.

But the first six months of earnest work in his

new parish brought him face to face with conditions
against which he dare not close his eyes, for he saw
possibilities of danger on almost every side.

It was well for him that he had the help and inspiration of Sister Nora at this time, for often he was
almost discouraged at the vastness of the work upon
which he had entered.

"Jamie Smithers is very sick," she said to him one
morning, when with Mr. Sterling and some members
of the sisterhood connected with the church they
were planning the work for the day.

They were all interested in Jamie, who was a dear,
wee chap, growing up as a flower in a wilderness of
sand. When about five years of age one day while
playing on the street he was knocked down and run
over by a brewer's wagon, just escaping with his life.
He was taken to the hospital, where one of his legs
was amputated, and, though he had the use of the
other one, it was so bent and weakened as to be
almost valueless. If Jamie had been the son of a
rich man, who could have paid lawyers' fees and secured witnesses, the brewer would probably have
been held responsible for the reckless driving of his
drayman, but at the trial it was made out somehow
that the boy had tried to run across the street almost
under the horses' feet, and that the driver could not
possibly have prevented the accident. The fact that
most of those who gave testimony had been visited
by the brewer's agent, while others of them were in
the employment of the brewer, evidently did not
affect the jury, for the case was dismissed. The
brewer, however, was not utterly heartless, for when

Jamie came home from the hospital he sent him the price of a handsome pair of crutches! Of course the boy was deprived of the enjoyments and pursuits of the other children of his class, and his pale, sad face, as he sat at the window looking out upon the street watching the boys and girls playing about in heedless glee, was most pathetic. Neither could he attend the public school, for the school was some blocks distant, and he could not walk so far.

But Jamie did not give up in despair. No sooner did his little sister Effie begin to learn her letters than he had her teach him. By degrees he took on spelling, then writing with the help of slate and pencil, then something of arithmetic, so that he not only kept up with Effie, but even went ahead of his brother Bob. His father being a carpenter, a first-class one, Jamie came naturally by a desire to work with tools, nor was it long before his chair at the window was exchanged for a seat at a bench which Mr. Smithers had put up for him. Here Jamie made all manner of things—salad sets, paper knives, napkin rings, and as he grew older he ventured on more ambitious work. At first his father only humored him in this carving pastime, thinking it would help the poor boy to get through the day. He soon found, however, that there was genuine merit in Jamie's work, so he cast about for some way to dispose of it. Not far from where the Smithers lived, just down the avenue a little way, there was a curio store whose proprietor handled all sorts of wares, particularly rare old carvings, Flemish and Swiss.

Jamie's work went in here, coming out again in a

13

few weeks with the marks of centuries upon it!
Many a dear man proudly exhibited to his admiring
family a bit of "genuine Flemish" which he had
picked up in this curio store for a mere song.

But Jamie knew nothing of this, neither did his
father. The curio man, who was shrewd enough to
keep his own counsel, was the only one in the secret.

For a time things went on pleasantly in the Smithers
household, for Silas Smithers, being a good workman, had steady employment in a shop not far from
where he lived.

But his employer (there was only one, Mr. Wood
having succeeded to the business, but keeping the old
firm name) was not content with the way things were
going, so he branched out quite extensively. He entered into some heavy building operations in Harlem
and on the West Side, but all at once business became unsettled, money could not be had to meet his
obligations, so that eventually the firm of Wood &
Stone was forced to suspend.

Silas Smithers was very sorry at the misfortune
which had overtaken Mr. Wood, for he had been a
kind, considerate employer; still there were other
shops in New York where he would find work to his
hand. But when he started out he learned that
many other of the building firms were in the same
plight as Wood & Stone. Steady work was nowhere
to be had. He tramped mile after mile, inquiring
everywhere, but to no purpose. Things began to
look serious. Shops in which two or three hundred
men were wont to work stood idle. Then Silas was
glad to get short jobs, working a few days now and

then. Mrs. Smithers made the very most out of
what he earned, but when five people are to be fed,
and the wages of the breadwinner cut down more
than half, to keep actual hunger away was almost impossible. Then it was that Jamie came to the fore.
Like a little man he worked so as to make up, in
part, the shortage in the family income. Hardly
would he have finished his breakfast before he was
at his bench, where he remained the whole day. His
work was so fine and delicate, involving the play of
long, slender fingers, that his father could not help him
very much. But he carved and rasped, he filed and
polished just as merrily as ever. Poor little fellow!
Sometimes when he went to bed he couldn't sleep,
he was so tired, and there were pains in his back
and chest which distressed him greatly. Once in a
while he would get on his mother's knee, just as he
used to do when he was younger. She would gather
him up in her arms, sing to him, croon to him, talk
to him out of her mother heart, then he would hob-
ble over to his bench and take up his work again.
He never said anything about the pains in his chest,
or the hours that he lay awake in the night. His
face, always pale, grew whiter and thinner, but he
smiled just as bravely as ever, hiding even from his
mother every sign of weakness. When he heard his
father coming up the stairs he would begin to whistle
some little air which he had learned from Effie or
Rob, just as though he would greet with boyish glad-
ness the weary, discouraged man.

Sister Nora accidentally (Sister Nora's "accidentally" might be changed to intentionally in many

cases) made the acquaintance of the Smithers family, and it was not long before her visits were times of great joy to little Jamie. She took a deep interest in his carvings, disposing of many of them at much higher prices than the curio man was willing to pay. This she explained by saying that her friends made their purchases through her, thus saving the usual charges of the dealer.

At the right time she mentioned Mr. Dunbar, with the hope that he might be permitted to come in some day and see Jamie at work.

When Mr. Dunbar came Mrs. Smithers was nervous and embarrassed, but Hugh soon made himself so much at home that the good woman got over all her fears. He talked with Jamie about the different kinds of wood upon which he was working. He went over to the bench and examined the various tools that he used. He got Jamie to explain how certain carvings were made, and, all told, spent nearly an hour, talking mostly with the boy, who was delighted with him.

"It is very kind of you, sir, to come an' see my poor boy," said Mrs. Smithers, as she held the little lamp over the stairway, so that Mr. Dunbar might have the light on his way down.

Mr. Dunbar stood for a few moments on the landing, for he saw that Mrs. Smithers had something more to say.

"I hope, sir, it is not askin' too much if sometime you might call again."

Mr. Dunbar promised to do so, also expressing the pleasure which his visit had given him.

"We ain't much on goin' to church that I know, an' still my husband an' me wants to do what is right."

With this they parted, Mrs. Smithers holding the lamp, while Mr. Dunbar cautiously made his way down the flights of stairs.

"The nicest-spoken gentleman I've ever met," she said to Silas, when he came home that evening. "An' he talked to Jamie just as if he knew all about carvin', an' he knows of a man who wants half a dozen of them Swiss frames."

"One of them minister chaps?" questioned Silas, but not unkindly.

"Yes, but he's got no minister manners like as ye hear of. He's just plain an' sensible, like common folks. He talked about you an' what you worked at, an' s'posed times was dull. He invited Effie an' Rob to go sometime to the Mission, an' shook hands with me an' Jamie when he went out."

All the time Mrs. Smithers was talking she was busy setting the table, lifting lids from sundry pots that were on the kitchen stove, and preparing generally for the evening meal.

"He's going to bring me some models which he wants copied," added Jamie, whose pale cheeks were flushed with the excitement of Mr. Dunbar's visit.

Silas Smithers said nothing, but went over to the "sink," where he washed his hard, rough hands; then splashed some water on his face, which he wiped and dried; then he combed out his dusty, matted hair before the little mirror, which hung on the side of the sink next the window. By this time Mrs. Smithers was ready to dish out the supper.

After supper he lighted his pipe, a cheap brier, with a supposedly amber tip, which Mrs. Smithers had once given him for a Christmas present. The amber tip was gone; the bowl was considerably charred all around the top, but, withal, that was his favorite pipe. The fact that "Mollie," as he called her, gave him that pipe may have had something to do with his regard for it.

The pipe was smoked half way before he said anything in reply to what he had heard about Hugh Dunbar.

"An' so you liked the minister," he said, looking at Jamie, who was finishing "one of them Swiss frames."

"You'd like him," answered Jamie. "One sure thing, he knows about carvin'."

"Ministers an' me don't see much of one another. I lets them go their way, and they mostly lets me go mine;" and Silas gave an extra tug or two at his pipe, which was threatening to go out.

"Well, you'd like this minister," Jamie said, with confidence, holding out the Swiss frame and looking it over critically.

"You think so, my son? Then I must try an' be here next time he comes."

With this Silas emptied the ashes out of his pipe, tapped it on his boot heel, and laid it down on the mantelpiece. Then he went out to see the secretary of his "union" about a special meeting which was called for the following Sunday afternoon.

CHAPTER XXII.

A Trades Union Meeting.

"YOU think nothing can be done for the Smithers people just now?" Hugh Dunbar asked Mr. Sterling one morning, as they were talking the matter over. "That boy appeals to me most strongly, but I am afraid to suggest his going away, for now that Smithers is out of work Jamie is needed at home."

"That is just where the trouble is," replied Mr. Sterling. "They cannot afford to send him anywhere, and if we should undertake to do it Silas Smithers is so proud and high-spirited that he would resent it."

"What a pity that people have such foolish notions about receiving help! When a man is down why can't he let some one give him a lift."

Mr. Dunbar had a perplexed, anxious look, for he was troubled about these Smithers people.

"You never were down, Dunbar, so you can't tell how it feels. Besides, a great deal depends on how the help is offered. Let me tell you that the real honest, deserving poor are the very last to accept charity—at least such charity as is generally attempted. You go, for instance, to the dispensaries. Inquire of the doctors and those in charge, and they will tell you that most of those who come there for treatment do it to avoid the expense of medical service, for which they are abundantly able to pay. The same is true of about everything else."

Mr. Dunbar made some remark by way of reply, quoting Dr. Disney, who had spoken of the dispensary system as one of the finest charities in New York.

" With all due deference to Dr. Disney," Mr. Sterling said, " he knows nothing about it. I do. I have gone to these dispensaries; I have talked with the doctors in charge, and my opinion is that they are about the most abused charity in New York, for the very people whom they were intended for seldom receive any service from them."

" Of course there are opportunities for abuse; still I hardly see how your remark about our other charities applies."

" Well, I tried it once,·and that once was enough for me. I went to a certain much-advertised institution just to see, as some people say, ' how it feels.' An elaborately dressed female, the daughter of an empress by her airs one would imagine, turned upon me a pair of glass eyes—not glasses or spectacles, but cold, unfeeling glass eyes—and in words which were shot from her mouth like bits of ice from a catapult she made inquiries of my general needs and condition. Then I was passed along to the tender mercies of an official, who put me through such an examination as a police captain gives to a man arrested for murder. After this I had to interview some ' visitors,' with the hope of discovering that I was a ' rounder,' or some other equally estimable member of the community. Now, red tape and detectives are very well in their way, but every poor man is not a tramp or a drunkard, and should not be treated as such. When charity is administered out of a hand that is as hard and as cold as iron it is more of a punishment to receive than to starve or go to jail."

Hugh Dunbar made no reply just then, though he did not agree quite with Mr. Sterling.

Shortly after, and having met Silas Smithers a few times, he invited him to come to the Mission and hear Mr. Sterling preach. "He is a good preacher, much better than I am, and short," he added, smiling.

"I'm much obliged to you, I'm sure," said Silas, "an' sometime Mollie an' me will go, though we hain't been much to church for a long while."

"Mr. Sterling preaches next Sunday. Why not come then?"

"Next Sunday we have a meetin' of our union."

"What time does your meeting begin?"

Hugh was anxious to get a hold on Smithers, not only for his own sake, but that in some way he might find an opportunity of doing something for Jamie.

"At two o'clock," said Silas; "but I belong to a committee which meets half an hour earlier, an' we have some special things to report on."

"Suppose, then, you come to the Mission in the morning, remain with me to lunch, then I will go to your meeting in the afternoon."

In view of Mr. Dunbar's kindness to Jamie, not only by his visits, but in disposing of a goodly number of his carvings (indeed, between Sister Nora and Mr. Dunbar the boy was kept so busy that the curio man complained), it seemed an ungracious thing of

Silas Smithers to refuse. The fact is, Silas was well aware that at the meetings of the union ministers and churches were spoken of quite freely, not always, either, in very respectful terms, and he was afraid Mr. Dunbar might feel hurt if he heard some of these things.

A compromise finally was agreed upon—Silas could not go with Mr. Dunbar on the next Sunday, but would take him to the union meeting in the afternoon.

"An' then some other Sunday Mollie an' me will go to the Mission," was his last word, as Mr. Dunbar got up to leave.

"I'm kind of afeerd he won't like it," Silas said to Mrs. Smithers, after Mr. Dunbar had gone. "You see, times just now is bad, heaps of our men is out of work, an' there is considerable feelin'. I wish he hadn't wanted to come. Still, it ain't no fault of mine."

Silas consoled himself by bringing out his old brier pipe, which he proceeded to fill in his deliberate way. Then lighting it he sat down, and began to meditate upon the possibilities of the coming Sunday afternoon.

There was not much of the clergyman in Mr. Dunbar's appearance, at least so far as dress was concerned, when he presented himself at the time appointed, to go with Silas to the union meeting.

"Just say I am a friend of yours," he said to Silas, as they went down the avenue.

Silas was greatly relieved at the change in Mr. Dunbar's costume. He had not said much about it

at home, for both Mrs. Smithers and Jamie felt
highly complimented at Mr. Dunbar's desire to attend the meeting in his company, and nothing would
have pleased them better than for the young clergyman to appear in regular church garb; but Silas knew
more about these matters that they did. Mr. Dunbar's tweed suit, with soft, broad-brimmed hat, had
therefore his unqualified approval.

It was expected that the meeting of the afternoon
would be of special interest, for, as Silas explained to
Mr. Dunbar on the way, delegates were coming from
some of the other unions with proposals and resolu-
tions.

The hall where the meeting was held, though not
large, could easily accommodate about five hundred
people, but it was comparatively empty when Silas
and Mr. Dunbar arrived. This, however, was not to
be wondered at, for Silas had a committee to attend
which met a full half hour before the regular meeting. Following the lead of Mr. Smithers, Hugh
Dunbar went up to the front seats in the hall, going
over close to the wall on the side, to the right of the
speaker's desk, as this would give him opportunity of
seeing the people as well as hearing the speeches.
Being alone, Silas now attending his committee, Mr.
Dunbar watched the men as they came in, in knots
and groups, though occasionally one came in by himself. They were mostly men in middle life, many of
them with strong, resolute faces, good, square foreheads, and frank, clear eyes looking out from under
bushy eyebrows. There was quite a sprinkling of
younger men, but they were not so serious as the

others, and by the way in which they addressed each
other the meeting was evidently a social occasion.

" How goes it, Bill ? "

" Put it there, Davy."

" How's your fightin' weight, Tim ? "

" Sam, give us your paw."

Many such expressions passed freely around, some of
which were so quaint and so accompanied with gesture as to cause a quiet smile on Dunbar's face at times.

The usual tobacco smoke imparted a fair degree of
pungency to the air of the room, but the ventilation
was tolerably good, for which Dunbar was grateful.

By the time the chairman called the meeting to
order the hall was full, and men were standing in the
side aisles as well as back by the door.

The usual routine business was got through in
regular order, when the chairman announced that
two special committees were now prepared to report.
Upon this there was a buzz of excitement, which
broke out into vigorous applause as Silas Smithers
stood up to read the first of the reports called for.
It may have been that the presence of Mr. Dunbar embarrassed the worthy Silas, or that he was
afraid of the effect of the discussion upon him, but,
be the cause what it may, he began reading in a
nervous, timorous way. As he could not be heard,
except to those who were quite near the platform,
instantly there were cries of " Louder ! " " Platform ! "
" Can't hear ! " with the result that Silas had to
get up on the platform and begin all over again.
By this time he had recovered his nerve, and so
read as to be heard all over the hall.

The report set forth the work of a committee which had been appointed to confer with the firm of Mantel & Sill as to the employment of non-union men. Mantel & Sill, the committee reported, refused absolutely to discharge the non-union men who were now at work for them.

Tom Williams reported for the second committee, and gave the results of a conference with Locke & Barr, iron founders and manufacturers of builders' hardware. This firm declared its intention of selling goods to any man who would buy them, whether or not such man complied with the conditions of the union.

The reading of these reports was greeted with cries of "Shame!" "Scabs!" "Strike!" the excitement increasing every moment.

Hugh Dunbar vividly recalled the conversation in Dr. Disney's, when Mark Brompton defined his position with such emphasis, though no more positively than Mr. Keen had done.

"By what right do we interfere with the business of these firms?" said one of the visiting delegates, who without wasting time upon preliminaries struck boldly at the very heart of the question. "Simply the right of self-preservation, which is the first law of nature. Unless we interfere, and unless we combine to interfere, we'll be crushed into ruin. All I have in the world is this pair of hands," holding them up so that everyone in the room could see them; "upon these hands my family is dependin' for support. Deprive these hands of labor, an' you deprive my children of bread. But if these hands are not backed

up by other hands, an' if there is no unity among us,
then the man who employs me has me at his mercy.
He can pay me what he pleases. He can make my
hours as long as he likes. He can discharge me
when it suits him an' for any reason, little or great.
Havin' nothin' but my hands to depend on, I am
helpless unless others unite with me. Your fight for
us and our fight for you is not against Mantel &
Sill or Locke & Barr. These firms simply represent a combination of capital, an' unless there is on
our part a combination of labor the workin'man is
not much better than the slaves before the War of the
Rebellion. In some respects not so well off, for it
was the master's interest to feed an' clothe and
shelter his slaves, but you know just as well as I do
that there are thousands of horses in New York city
who have better homes, better care, better food, than
the same number of honest working people."

At this point shouts of "True!" "Shame!" were
heard all over the hall, and Hugh Dunbar, who
knew something of uptown stables and downtown
tenements, could not but admit that the speaker was
right.

"An' we must make this fight for ourselves," the
delegate went on. "There is no one who will make
it if we don't. The newspapers won't. Capital controls newspapers. These reporters at this table are
even more at the beck and call of the capitalist than
we are. They can be dismissed on the spot, an' if
one word is put in the paper that is against capital,
the whole lot of them editors will be bundled out
instanter. It ain't no use to expect much from

newspapers. The newspaper lives by its advertisin',
an' it is not the workman who advertises. He has
nothing to advertise. But the capitalist is the ad-
vertiser, and even if he hain't got any stock in the
paper he controls it all the same."

Here one of the reporters, a young man with
long hair and a shirt collar of magnificent altitude,
pushed back his chair from the table and looked
at the speaker in superb disdain. The reporter was
a green hand evidently.

"Our young friend has stopped writin'," said the
delegate, pointing to him, which secured for the
reporter rather more attention than he desired.

"An' why has he stopped writin'? Just because
he dare not put in his paper the things which I have
said. He can get room for a whole pageful about a
boat race. An' why? Because the crews are the
sons of rich men, who are takin' a college course
in athletics. No fear of that bein' crowded out. O,
dear, no! But you look to-morrow in his paper for
a report of this meetin'. Well, you needn't. It
won't be there. Not that this young man is to
blame. Not at all. He simply dursn't put it in.
An' he couldn't put it in if he wanted to. The editor
would have it taken out, if he stopped the press to do
it. You are quite right, my young friend, in sittin'
back an' enjoyin' the meetin'. It shows you have
good sense, for what's the use of scribblin' a whole
lot of stuff an' get nothin' for it but the grand
bounce?"

It should be said right here that ever after, when
this reporter was sent to union meetings, he was

exceedingly careful to pay minute attention to the proceedings, nor was he ever known to practice the "lofty scorn" air again in public.

"But then the newspapers are no worse than the others," the speaker went on, leaving the reporter to enjoy himself as best he could. "There's the politician, for example. Will he help us in our fight? Not a bit of it. You can depend upon the politicians just about election time makin' all kinds of promises. An' how they love the workin'men! They can't sleep nights just for thinkin' of them an' how much they respect them. An' then we vote as we are wanted to, an' the politicians are never seen or heard from till next election.

"An' then there's the Church."

Here Hugh Dunbar leaned forward with renewed interest, but Silas Smithers turned away his face so that he could not even see the speaker. Silas was very uncomfortable at this stage of the proceedings.

"Does the Church help us any?" asked the delegate. "They come over here with their soup kitchens, their coal yards, an' their bread tickets, makin' a big parade of what is bein' done for the poor, an' yet in the church itself, in the broad aisles, on the best seats, are the very men who grind the faces of the poor. This mornin' most of us didn't go to church. Perhaps we ought. To stay away from church is not much to brag of. But in some of the churches there were men sittin' as pious as saints, owners of tenements, for which we have to pay such awful rents; directors in corporations, which are the first to cut down wages and the last to raise them;

men singin' about heaven and the New Jerusalem who are mean enough to do things we'd scorn to do. The preachers talk about the 'Carpenter of Nazareth,' but I tell you if he went to some of the churches in this city it's a poor welcome he'd find. S'pose this mornin' he'd gone to some of them churches uptown, an' the marks of toil on his hands, an' his clothes plain an' commonlike, would he have been taken up the broad aisle an' sat down with all them corporations an' syndicates? Not likely. There isn't a preacher in New York who dares to say the things that the 'Carpenter of Nazareth' said. The men who makes corners on wheat an' cotton, on 'most everything, don't want any such preachin' as the Carpenter preached. The Church nowadays is for rich people. The poor man is not wanted there. They say he is, but when one goes he knows enough not to go again. We must just fight our own battle. We can't count on anyone but ourselves, but if we will only stand to-gether we are bound to win."

Long-continued applause was given the speaker as he concluded, and to the amazement of Silas Smithers, who stealthily glanced around, Mr. Dunbar was applauding as vigorously as anyone in the room. "Clappin' his hands, and stampin' his feet," was how Silas described it to Mrs. Smithers when he got home, Jamie's blue eyes lighting up with wonder as he listened to his father's description of Mr. Dunbar's excitement at the meeting.

The next speaker was of more refinement than the first one, but no less honest or frank.

14

" My friend who has just sat down very properly asked the question, By what right do we interfere with the business of Mantel & Sill or Locke & Barr? and he has answered that question in a way which admits of no further discussion. May I say but a word or two concerning this matter of interference? Our armies, under General Grant, interfered with the business of the merchants in Vicksburg; not that there was any quarrel with the merchants themselves, but because a great principle was involved; hence individual rights had to be sacrificed. When Sherman undertook his march to the sea he infringed upon individual rights in the sharpest way. Every great event in history is marked by the loss of individual rights. One of the oldest and most commonly accepted laws in the world is that which gives a man rights in his own property, but there are times when even his ownership must be put aside. Wellington and Napoleon had no legal business on the fields at Waterloo, and the notices, " Trespassers prosecuted " and " Keep off the grass," so far as actual law was concerned were entitled to recognition. But there were more matters in Waterloo than the rights of the individual. Now, Mantel & Sill or Locke & Barr have individual rights, and while these rights do not conflict with others of more importance they are to be respected. But just as in war, when the rights of the individual must give way before the higher laws of necessity, so the rights of the individual employer must yield to the larger rights of the community."

Hugh Dunbar again recalled Mark Brompton's

positive statements that no man had a right to interfere in the affairs of another, and that an employer
had no interests except his own to consider. He
wondered how Mr. Brompton would meet the cool,
measured words of the delegate.

Continuing, he said:

"We say quite often that a man has a right to do
as he pleases with his own. That is not so. Even
a man's house is not his to do with as he wishes. If
he attempts to pull it down he must see that other
houses are not endangered thereby. A man can be
indicted for setting his house on fire if it adjoins
other houses. A man cannot even take his own life!
We see, then, that in every instance the rights of
the individual are subordinate to other rights. Hence
Mantel & Sill or Locke & Barr, being only members of the community in which there are interests
paramount to theirs, must abandon their claims in
favor of that principle which is the basis of all true
government—'the greatest good to the greatest number.'"

Here the speaker closed, and though the enthusiasm
was not so great as when the other delegate had
finished, yet the impression was even deeper.

The meeting then adjourned, Mr. Dunbar leaving the hall with Silas Smithers.

CHAPTER XXIII.

Mrs. Gubbins Asks Questions.

IT so happened that one of the reporters at the meeting of the union—not the callow youth to whom the delegate paid such generous attention —was the newspaper man referred to by Edward Vaughen in his letter to his mother. His name was Faber—Dixon Faber when it was written in full—and Edward was discovering him to be a first-rate fellow.

Mrs. Gubbins, who really was a well-meaning woman, tried to exercise a sort of motherly care over her boarders, and usually on Monday evening, when most of her household would be at dinner, took occasion to introduce topics which related more or less to the preceding day. In this she was seconded by Miss Pollok, for Miss Pollok disapproved most strongly of the way in which many of the boarders spent Sunday, particularly certain heathenish young men who went off in the morning on excursions of various kinds, seldom returning before night.

Miss Pollok was a devoted member of the Church of St. Elijah—attended low celebration in the morn-ing, high celebration at noon, evensong late in the afternoon, and vespers in the early evening; so that, like a certain pious sparrow and an equally pious swallow, both of which are mentioned in holy psalm, she had found in the church a house and a nest for herself.

There were those unkind enough to intimate that the incoming of a fresh, marriageable curate quickened her religious zeal; but such remarks are unworthy of any well-disposed person.

There is no doubt but that she was considerably taken up with Chasuble, a round-faced, fair-haired divine, who so robed himself, even for street wear, as to suggest the Litany on legs, and when Chasuble, using certain mediæval tones, spoke of "the holy altaws of the chauch," Miss Pollok listened in a rapt, ecstatic way. It is also true that when Chasuble allowed himself to become engaged to a brewer's widow, of voluminous person but of ample fortune, Miss Pollok experienced such a sense of grief as interfered for the time with her church-going propensities. During such time her harp hung silent on the willows, and her sweet voice was not heard in quivering melody.

She thought the artist was a heathen—a handsome heathen, she admitted to herself—one well worth reclaiming, but the artist refused point-blank to be reclaimed. Then she essayed the humorist, only to meet the same sad result. As a missionary to the heathen Miss Pollok was not a brilliant success. Her efforts might possibly have been more favorably received had she been twenty years younger and fairer to look upon.

"I was not at church yesterday," said Mr. Faber, in reply to a question of Mrs. Gubbins, "yet I heard a good sermon."

"Where were you?" asked Mr. Wright. "I have been taught to believe that the sermon and the sanctuary sustained and supplemented the Sabbath."

Mr. Wright, let it be said, was an ardent believer in the power of alliteration. He followed this order not only in the building of his plays, but in ordinary conversation.

"Terrible truths tellingly told," he said, after Faber had spoken of the address of the first delegate.

"But are they truths?" Edward Vaughen questioned.

"Well, concerning the newspapers, I thought the only way to decide was to put the delegate's charge to a test. I therefore wrote a fair account of the proceedings, half a column, perhaps more, but the city editor, though he said the 'stuff' was good, ran the blue pencil right through the very parts which I was anxious to keep. Then, as a matter of curiosity, I got the other papers which had reporters at the meeting, but not one of them gave the proceedings a full 'stick.' Only one paper alluded to the visiting delegates, then merely mentioning their names."

"You think the other charges equally true?" Vaughen further questioned.

"Not a doubt of it to my mind," Faber answered. "Perhaps our friend Singleton here, who is something of a politician, may not agree with me. Miss Pollok probably will defend the church. Still, I think the delegate was right."

Mrs. Gubbins, having met the demands of her conscience, was satisfied with the results of her inquiries, but seeing that the discussion was likely to reach beyond the limits of the usual dinner hour, proposed that the company adjourn to the parlor, where the conversation would not be interrupted. But an easy, informal dinner-table talk, with its "Yes, I will, thank you;" "The olives, did you say?" "May I trouble you?" "Thanks, you are very kind," and all the other trifles which redeem the meal from being a mere feeding time and prevent the table from becoming a trough, cannot be carried to the parlor without losing almost everything of interest.

Especially was this true of Mrs. Gubbins's parlor, for it was a long, narrow, dark, and rather depressing room, somewhat sparsely settled with furniture of the horse-hair persuasion.

There was, of course, the inevitable piano, but it was closed, for this was one of the seasons referred to, when Miss Pollok's harp was on the willows, she being the only member of the household who had the courage to attack this treacherous and elusive instrument. The carpet had that strained, weary look which one sometimes sees in people, as though it had been so beaten and trampled on as to have lost almost everything of cheerfulness and color.

A mysterious but pretentious set of steel engravings, relating in some vague way to the "voyage of life," occupied prominent places on the walls. There were also some oil paintings, portraits—one of Mr. Gubbins at the time when he endowed Mrs. Gubbins with all his worldly goods; one of Mrs. Gubbins in the robes of festal glory in which she received this endowment; and one of Miss Gubbins when she was a cherub of about five years' growth. The cherub had wide white pantalettes coming down almost to her shoes; a light but ample dress, belted with a broad blue sash tied in a huge bowknot, with streamers nearly to the floor; fat, puffy cheeks, between which a nose lay somewhere, and a smile which must have cost the artist hours of inspired labor.

A "clock set" in black marble had the place of honor on the mantelpiece, but the clock preserved a rigid silence concerning all its movements, while the other pieces of the "set," being of the Egyptian urn order, added to the general solemnity.

"As gloomy as a church," was the comment of the artist, but not said in the presence of Mrs. Gubbins, for the artist was a gentleman.

"Silent and stately, chaste and charming," was the comment of Mr. Wright, but said in the presence of Mrs. Gubbins, for Mr. Wright was fond of an audience.

"Third floor, hall back, chairs for two, bed for one, tobacco for three," said Edward Vaughen to Singleton and Faber, as they came up from the dining room.

To Vaughen's room they went, Singleton taking the rocker, Faber the other chair, Edward sitting crosswise on the bed, with his back against the wall.

"That must have been quite a meeting yesterday afternoon," Edward said. "I wish I might sometime attend such a gathering."

"Then come with me," answered Faber. "You look almost intelligent enough to pass for a reporter. With a little coaching you might manage to sit at a table, scribble on some rough paper, and seem to be taking in the whole business."

After a few quick puffs, so as to get a good "fire on," he said:

"There was a chap there yesterday who greatly interested me. He came in with one of the men who read a report; but he was no mechanic, for his hands were white and smooth. Besides, he didn't have the 'shop' air."

"One of the enemy," Mr. Singleton suggested. "A spy in the camp."

"No. He was evidently in sympathy with the men. I sat where I could see him, and I confess to a curiosity as to who he is."

"Young man?" questioned Edward, with a certain eagerness.

"Yes, somewhere between twenty-five and thirty."

"Large gray eyes?"

"I should say! Bright and quick as lightning."

"Good-looking?"

"As good-looking as a man has any business to be."

"Did you notice him when the delegate was speaking about the Church?"

"Yes."

"Particularly?"

"Yes."

"How did he take it?"

"His eyes fairly burned. Once or twice he acted as if he wanted to say something. His face was very pale."

"That young man was Hugh Dunbar," Edward said, in a tone which admitted of no doubt.

"And who, may I ask, is Hugh Dunbar?" said

Mr. Singleton, reaching for the tobacco jar, which stood on the bureau, and proceeding to refill his pipe.

"I can tell you," answered Faber, "though I never saw him before yesterday. He is a rich young clergyman, who, instead of settling down in some elegant parish, has gone to the East Side, and is doing all kinds of work in a Mission over there."

"Then you know something of him, after all. I was afraid he was not being known," Edward said.

"That is where you are mistaken, nor understand Dunbar's way," Faber replied. "True, he has not sent his picture to our office, which explains my not recognizing him yesterday. Neither does he deluge us with typewritten 'pickings' from his sermons, as some prominent divines are in the habit of doing. But we are keeping track of him, for he is going to make a stir one of these days."

"Queer line, though, for that sort of man to take," Mr. Singleton said.

"Just the right line," answered Faber.

"How do you make that out?" Singleton asked.

"Easily. Here is the Church, which is supposed to stand for the enlightenment of the people, claiming, too, to have a special mission from heaven, and yet, instead of making common cause with the people, it has abandoned them, it has curried favor with the rich, and when the delegate said that there was far more pride than piety in the Church he was saying the truth."

"Why, Faber, for a newspaper man you are almost pious," Singleton said, good-humoredly.

"O, that's the way we get it from you Wall Street

saints when we reporters talk about churches or
religion," Faber answered, with a smile. " Still,
when we see a gritty, plucky chap, like this Dunbar,
trying, man fashion, to do some honest work, it is
something to be proud of."

This time it was Faber who reached for the tobacco
jar, which Edward usually kept well stocked up.

" Then you agree with the general charges of the
delegate?" Mr. Singleton asked.

" As a broad statement of the facts, leaving a mar-
gin, however, for exceptions, yes," Faber answered,
without a moment's hesitation.

"Kindly explain," asked Edward Vaughen. "Remember I am a stranger, and not familiar as you are
with the conditions of the city."

" I will," responded Faber, tilting his chair back
against the wall, at the same time working his head
out from under the short, straight gas pipe, with
which he was in some danger of colliding. " Speaking in a general way, the churches in this city have
less interest in the masses of the common people than
they have in the pagans of Central Africa. I am
familiar with New York, for my work on the *Trombone*, with which I have been connected for a
number of years, has sent me to every part of the
city. There is a lot of talk at public meetings now
and then about the ' masses,' but most of that talk is
either rant or cant. To put it plainly, the Church
has deserted the common people. It has no use for
them. They are not wanted. The fact is, and we
all know it, the lines between the rich and the poor
are drawn more sharply in the churches than any-

where else. A man can go to the theater and not
feel his poverty as he will in a church."

"Because he can go to the peanut gallery," interposed Mr. Singleton. "The other man can go to
the boxes."

"Exactly," replied Faber. "The theater is a
financial matter from beginning to end; the Church
is not. The Church is supposed to stand for brotherhood, for equality, for great principles of benevolence
and love. Hence it should be the last place on earth
to mark differences or set one class against another."

"Evidently you have studied the situation," Mr.
Singleton said, looking at Faber with more interest
than at any time during the evening.

"I have, experimentally as well as theoretically.
But," looking at his watch, "you must excuse me.
I have an assignment at an uptown affair and must
be off."

"Bright fellow," said Singleton, after Faber had
gone.

"Good fellow, too," added Edward.

As Mr. Singleton had now got up, and was preparing to go to his room, Edward pulled down the
window so as to get rid of the tobacco smoke. Then,
on Mr. Singleton leaving, he put on an overcoat,
closed the door, and started out for a walk in the cool
night air.

CHAPTER XXIV.

Broadway by Gaslight.

EDWARD VAUGHEN was yet so much of a stranger in New York that when he went out for a stroll in the evening he generally contented himself with a turn or two around the square close to his boarding place, after which he would go back to his room, where he read or wrote until it was bedtime. He tried to be neither lonely nor homesick, but often he was both. Sometimes he was half angry with himself for leaving the Bromptons so abruptly, for he was genuinely fond of his Uncle Mark.

The conversation with Faber and Singleton had so excited him that his customary short walk was not quite satisfactory. He therefore went as far as Broadway, where he stood for a few moments undecided as to what he should do next. A cable car going uptown, with a few seats to spare, looked inviting, and in an instant he had boarded the car, which, starting with the usual but always unexpected jerk, deposited him with some abruptness in a seat near the front door, but not before he had sprawled over the long legs of a young man, knocked an elderly lady's bonnet almost off her head, and excited a general smile among the other passengers. The young man with the long legs did not smile; neither did the elderly lady with the bonnet; but there are some

people who have no sense of humor; though, for
that matter, Edward did not smile, at least not just
then. But when the long-legged young man, who
evidently was going somewhere on Fourteenth
Street, got up before the car had turned the curve,
and played the game of "pillar to post" in a most
reckless way, Edward smiled with a visibility that
was almost cruel. He tried, though, not to smile
when the elderly lady with the bonnet, as she rose
to go out, and the car stopping with characteristic abruptness, was carried as by some mysterious
force into the unwilling arms of the conductor, the
poor bonnet faring this time even worse than before.
Edward had already discovered that while, in itself,
to get on or off a New York cable car may not be a
remarkable achievement, yet to do either without
loss of dignity or grace of attitude is an accomplishment which attains the standard of the highest art.

It was yet early in the evening, possibly not much
after nine. Crowds of people were moving about;
lights streamed from the shop windows, for this particular part of Broadway has all sorts of things to
sell, and it sells them by gaslight as well as day-
light. There were displays of fruit, the richest and
most tempting to be seen in the city. There were
also some wonderful displays of flowers; people
gathering around the windows, admiring not only
the flowers, but the artistic way in which they were
arranged. Watching his opportunity, Edward got off
the car, and walked along for a few blocks enjoying
the novelty and excitement of the scene, when suddenly he came upon a group of young men, some

half dozen or so, standing on the steps of the main entrance to a hotel. They were all dressed in the extreme of fashion, but talked loudly and under much excitement.

"Come on, Brompton," one of them said, taking another one by the arm, as though he would lead him to some place to which the other did not care to go.

"What's the use?" replied the one addressed as Brompton, speaking thickly. "You fellows have cleaned me out. Haven't a stiver. This isn't my night. Some other night. Must excuse me."

The voice, though so thick and guttural as to be almost indistinct, Edward recognized as that of his Cousin Percy.

"O, come on! What's that got to do with it? A quiet little game, with a chance for you to even things up is what you want," was the reply of the one who first spoke, still holding on to Percy, and making an attempt to lead him down the hotel steps.

"Not to-night. I know when I've had enough. Some other night, when 'twill be my night, I'll have it out, but I'm going home."

Percy's answer was not firm, merely stubborn, which angered the other.

"Mamma's boy! going home to his mammy," he sneered, letting Percy's arm go, that he might accompany his mocking words with contemptuous gesture.

Edward was now standing near the door of the hotel, where he could see and hear everything, though in the shadow, for he did not wish Percy to see him. He was anxious to help Percy, but hardly

knew just how to do it. He saw that his cousin
was in a state of almost helpless intoxication, and if
left to himself would be exposed to both danger and
disgrace. He also saw that two or three of the
group were determined in some way to take advantage of the young man's miserable plight, lure him
most likely to some gaming den, and there fleece
him to their hearts' content. Edward noticed that
these two or three were perfectly sober, while the
others were nearly as helplessly drunk as Percy was.
He was determined, therefore, not to let his cousin
fall into their hands any more than he was already,
for with "I. O. U.'s" and notes of hand they would
make it a costly night for his cousin. Still he
thought it best not to interfere unless driven to it.

But Percy's wine, or whatever drink it was, had
not so dulled his wits as to allow him to ignore the
sneer and scornful gesture of the one who had, as
he thought, grossly insulted him. Indeed, the opposite was the case, for in his inflamed condition he attached to the mocking words a significance which
was never intended. The speaker, therefore, had
barely finished his taunting sentence, before Percy
had struck him a stinging blow full in the face.
Coming so suddenly, as well as with passionate force,
and taking the young man by surprise, it caused him
to stagger back and almost fall down the hotel steps.

Instantly there was a great commotion. Men
rushed out from the hotel. Passers-by assembled in
scores. The sidewalk and hotel steps were jammed,
and in a few moments the crowd was so great as to
reach well-nigh across the street. But no sooner had

the blow been struck than Edward rushed forward and with the cry, "O! Cousin Percy," he took hold of young Brompton, and by sheer strength forced him within the hotel. Percy struggled and resisted to the utmost, but Edward was a tall, powerfully built fellow, and as it was not a question of moral suasion, but of physical force, Percy had to yield.

The crowd, seeing that there was no immediate prospect of renewal of hostilities, disappeared almost as rapidly as it had formed, so that with the exception of a few curious stragglers the hotel and street resumed their wonted condition. The friends of the man who was struck took hold of him, as Edward had taken hold of Percy, only instead of bringing him into the hotel they led him off in another direction.

Great excitements and great shocks will soon sober the most drunken of men. It was not long, therefore, before Percy began to realize something of what had taken place.

"The cad!" he muttered; "wasn't satisfied with winning my money, but must insult me on the street. Confound him! I'll break his neck."

After a few moments he broke out again:

"I believe that hound is a regular sharper. Just look here," turning his pockets inside out; "he hasn't left me a copper. But 'tisn't the money I care about. The miserable whelp!"

In a little while some of the young men who were with Percy on the steps of the hotel at the time of the row came into the room where he was with Edward. The incident, however, had not sobered

15

them; they were not principals, only onlookers; their
reckless hilarity, if anything, was, therefore, increased. They complimented Percy on his courage.
They agreed with him in his estimate of the one
whom he had struck. They insisted upon having up
a bottle of wine to drink Percy's health. They
made silly speeches. They sang silly songs. They
acted like a lot of young fools. Finally some of
them, having worn themselves out with

> "For he's a jolly good fellow,
> Which nobody can deny,"

had either sobered sufficiently to go home, or being
known in the hotel were given rooms for the night.
So Edward, when it was almost midnight, ordered a
carriage and took Percy to the Brompton mansion.

Some years before, Mark Brompton, seeing that
Percy was not likely to make much headway in
scholarship, and had no taste whatever for anything in scientific lines, proposed that he go into
some business. To this Mrs. Brompton made strenu-
ous objection. In a voice that was as clear as a
piccolo in Alpine air she declared that there should
be "at least one gentleman in the family."

Mr. Brompton intimated that it was possible for
one to be a gentleman and still to be in business.

"You know what I mean, Mark," said Mrs.
Brompton, still using the piccolo, though the finger-
ing was not skillful.

"I probably know what you mean better than
you know yourself," retorted Mr. Brompton, upon
whom the piccolo had an irritating effect.

"I hardly see how you could know very much

about either gentlemen or their ways," replied Mrs. Brompton, raising the last finger of her right hand on the piccolo.

When a family matter is being discussed by a bassoon and a piccolo, though the bassoon has a range of three octaves, the piccolo invariably comes out ahead.

Janet was the only one who favored the idea put forward by Mr. Brompton, but as Ethel said:

" Janet has difficulty with herself. Naturally she is inclined to be vulgar."

" You sweet saint ! What a gentle, kindly way you have ! With what tender delicacy you convey your feelings ! " and Janet flared up in her hot, impulsive way.

" But why should Percy be tied down to a desk or slave in an office when there is no need of it ?" asked Mrs. Brompton, when they were discussing the matter among themselves.

" No need of it so far as money is concerned, but other things have to be considered. Percy would be very much better off if he had something to do. For some time past, a whole year or so, he has not been doing well. His rooms and mine are on the same floor. I hear him when he comes in, and he nearly always comes in late. You know that he is rarely down to breakfast. Then, too, he never has any money. What he does with his allowance goodness knows. I don't like to say it, mamma, but I think Percy is in a bad way."

" Janet, you ought to be ashamed of yourself, talking in this way about your brother. He is no

worse than hundreds of the young men of his class.
What would you have him do? Perhaps papa
could get him into Linsey & Woolsey's as floorwalker,
where he would have a chance to associate with that
girl in the cloak department of whom Madge Disney
is so fond."

This little speech of Ethel's thoroughly angered
Janet, and when she was angry she spoke right out,
irrespective of consequences. Even her mother's
stateliness had not the least effect.

"Better for him to be a floorwalker, earning an
honest living, than to be hanging around theaters,
dangling after actresses, drinking with all sorts of
people, and spending money in the most reckless,
foolish way. Perhaps he is no worse than the other
young men of his class. But that is not saying
much. Carl Von der Plonk was so intoxicated the
other evening at the Snipkins's reception that he had
to be taken home. Young Fitz Noodle got himself
into such a scrape with that variety actress that his
people had to send him away. And we all know
what happened to Charlie Blobbs. The sooner we
do something for Percy the better for him and for
us as well."

"Now that you have shown such an intimate acquaintance with your brother's habits and private
affairs, perhaps you would kindly suggest just what
you want him to do. The least hint of yours could
not but be valuable."

"Ethel, I love Percy just as much as you do, perhaps more, if it comes to that, for you are not willing to sacrifice any of your pride so as to really help

him. Why should he waste himself as he is doing now?"

"He is not wasting himself," corrected Mrs. Brompton, again having recourse to the piccolo.

"He is wasting himself," returned Janet, heedless not only of the piccolo, but of the fifth commandment. "He plays golf; he plays tennis; he plays polo; he goes about town with a set of fast young men. At night he plays cards and billiards, and comes home at all hours, and if you don't call that wasting himself, then I don't know anything about it."

It was now Mrs. Brompton's turn to be angry. Not that she could dispute the truth of Janet's words; indeed, it was their simple truth which made her so angry.

"It seems to me, Janet, that you have been playing the spy upon Percy, which in my opinion is a mean, low, contemptible proceeding. Young men will be young men. Young sinners often make old saints. But it is just as Ethel says—you would like him to be some miserable counterjumper or pettifogging clerk. Why didn't you suggest his going over to the iron works in which your father is interested? A place might be found for him in the yard."

With this Mrs. Brompton left the room, departing in high wrath, leaving the girls to fix up matters as best they could.

"Janet, you should not annoy mamma so," Ethel said, tightening up the keys of her verbal fiddle, preparatory to a general attack on the strings.

Janet made no reply. She had no piccolo at com-

mand like her mother. She had no keen, delicate
violin such as her sister handled so skillfully. Her
weapon was only a trumpet which consumed more
breath than she could usually spare. So Ethel went
on, bowing on the highest register:

"You know that mamma will not consent to any
such arrangement as papa proposes. Besides, what
would the Von der Plonks say? or the Fitz Noodles?
If you have no pride for yourself, Janet, you should
have some for the family."

All this, as has been said, took place some time
ago. But Percy was not put at any business.

On reaching the house, Percy, after he had fum-
bled in all his pockets, gave Edward his night key,
with which he opened the door, and then, taking
Percy's arm, helped him up stairs to his room. No
one was in the hall or parlors, for it was now after
midnight. A light, however, was in the library,
showing that Mr. Brompton had not retired.

"I'm much obliged to you," Percy said, when
after a few minutes Edward rose and was preparing
to leave. "I'm ashamed of that miserable row down
there, but that fellow angered me more than I could
stand."

"Have you known him for any length of time?"
Edward asked.

"Not so very long, but it has been an expensive
acquaintance."

Edward said nothing, having a suspicion that
Percy had been losing money at cards.

"Why, it isn't more than a month since I first met
that fellow, and he has worked me for over a thou-

sand dollars," said Percy, answering the question which Edward did not ask. "But, confound it all, what can a fellow do? Here I am all alone in this big barrack of a house. Mrs. B. is always out somewhere. The Misses B. are always out somewhere. Mr. B. is everlastingly busy with papers and things in the library. The only one who takes any interest in me is Janet."

Edward went down stairs as quietly as he could, but on reaching the hall Mr. Brompton came out of the library.

"Why, Edward!" he said, "how is this?" looking at him keenly, though not unkindly.

"I met Percy downtown and came home with him," was the reply.

Whatever suspicions Mr. Brompton may have had he kept them to himself, for his next question was:

"You still like your place with Keen & Sharp?"

"More than I did at first," Edward was able to say truthfully.

"Are you in the inner-office yet?"

"No, Keen & Sharp evidently do not intend that I shall know much of their private business, for I am still on an outside desk."

"Who has charge of your department?"

"Mr. Singleton, who, by the way, lives in the house with me."

"Is he treated as a confidant?"

"I think not. Indeed, I am sure of it, for it was only the other day that he was speaking of this same thing, and complaining that the firm was managing the business very differently from what they used to."

"Then there have been changes in the work of the office?"

"Yes, a good many; particularly within the past six months."

"Or, in other words, since you went there," said Mr. Brompton, with a meaning look.

"Edward," he said, a moment later, "I don't want you to be a spy, or in any way act dishonorably to your employers. But let me tell you something which very few people know—you are in my employment when you are with Keen & Sharp, for I am a large though silent partner in the firm. Now, I am afraid there is something wrong. You can, therefore, serve me by keeping your eyes open. I have confidence in you and am willing to trust you."

So the uncle and nephew parted—the one to make his way to a downtown boarding house, the other to go back to his chair in the lonely library.

CHAPTER XXV.
Dick-Whittington's Cat.

WHEN Edward Vaughen left the house of his Uncle Mark it was his intention to walk down Fifth Avenue to Fifty-ninth Street, cross over to Third Avenue, where he could take the "Elevated" to Ninth Street, which would bring him within a few blocks of his home. But walking briskly, and thinking intently of what Mr. Brompton had said, he was at Fifty-ninth Street in what seemed only a few minutes. He determined, therefore, to go on down Fifth Avenue, for though the night was cool it was pleasant—just the night for a brisk walk. Nor was it late—that is, in the New York sense of lateness—for while the New York clocks synchronize with all others of the Eastern section, still the hours on Manhattan Island do not mean the same as in some other places.

Now, in Eastwich, until Edward went to college, "Curfew" meant for him, as for all others in the village, the solemn departure of another day. The little children were then supposed to be fast asleep, and the young people were all expected home. The grocery store put up its shutters, put out its lights, and closed its door. The houses generally were dark and still, and to be on the street after this hour would either have to be explained or open the way to unpleasant criticism. A quiet place indeed was Eastwich once nine o'clock had rung.

The broad church steps, which run the entire length of the church front, leading up to the ample porch with its Corinthian columns, where the children gathered almost as soon as school was over, were now deserted, and the church, so white and stately, lifted itself into the mysterious shadows of the night.

The pump and horse trough, which stood right opposite the forge of Andy Smith, usually one of the most active and populous parts of the village, gave no sign of life whatever. Nor would anyone, except a resident of the place, ever have imagined the gossiping, the chaffering, the disputing—equine, canine, and, of the human, masculine—on this very spot an hour or two before. Occasionally a light would be seen in the back parlor of Mrs. Paletot, which suggested a funeral or a wedding somewhere in the neighborhood, for which she had special orders. But as a rule Mrs. Paletot kept regular Eastwich hours.

The medical establishment of the village was fairly primitive; still it had certain advantages over many more pretentious concerns. It was all under one roof, for the doctor kept the drug store and the drug store kept the doctor. The doctor first wrote the prescription and then proceeded to fill it up, careful never to prescribe anything which was not in the drug store; thus much time and trouble were pleasantly avoided. A light was always set in the drug store window, the doctor slept in the room overhead, but this was usually the only light on the street.

By ten o'clock there would not be a sound anywhere in Eastwich except the crying of a sick child, the bark of some restless dog, or the step of a belated traveler, lover most likely, hastening to his home.

The contrast was therefore very marked as Edward stood on the Plaza at Fifty-ninth Street, for it was brilliantly illuminated, and the big hotels which border on the Plaza were full of life and gayety. Carriages were coming and going. Such of the hotels as kept public cafés had large companies of ladies and gentlemen enjoying after-theater suppers, and the scene reminded Edward very distinctly of the few weeks which he had spent in Paris one vacation with John Disney. No place in New York, perhaps no place in the whole world, has a greater aggregation of wealth than this Plaza and its immediate neighborhood. In the hotels themselves the dreams of the "Arabian Nights" are more than realized, for no prince or king could maintain such establishments as these. In them is everything that the most fabulous wealth can command—porticoes, with carvings in the stone worthy of a cathedral altar ; staircases and corridors in Sienna marble and bronze, in which are chiseled and traced the most exquisite designs; Pompeiian billiard rooms; First Empire drawing rooms ; Versailles bedrooms, parlors, and dining rooms, after some of the daintiest in European palaces. No Monte Cristo, in whose hands millions were but trifles, could have devised for himself anything more luxurious than these palatial abodes.

Within these superb buildings are hundreds of New York's wealthiest families, permanent residents,

who maintain their suites of apartments all the year
round, living in a way that is almost bewildering, so
rich and extravagant it is. Everything that the
brain of man can suggest; every invention which in
the least measure will promote comfort and ease;
every hint of science which might add to health
and safety; every tint of artist's brush; every cut of
sculptor's chisel; every dainty touch of decorator;
hangings of silk, of lace, of rich tapestry, are all
here, and in such profusion as to reveal the possibilities of wealth illimitable.

Whence came these colossal fortunes? This was
the question Edward Vaughen was putting to himself as he stood within stone's throw of the huge
hotels. Some of them—not all of them—may be accounted for.

.   .   .   .

" It can be bought for— "

Mr. Trawleigh hesitated at naming the amount,
though he knew it perfectly.

" Five millions," put in Mr. Keen.

" And capitalized for— "

Mr. Trawleigh again hesitated.

" Thirty millions," said Mr. Keen, in a calm, matter-of-fact tone, as if the sum named were a mere
trifle.

" Can the stock be placed at that figure ? " asked
Mr. Albright, rising from his chair and going over to
a table, upon which some maps were spread, through
which certain red lines were drawn.

" Not a doubt of it," answered Mr. Keen. " Hunt
& Steele, who are in this thing with us, have so far

arranged for about a quarter of it. Deale, Dicker &
Smart, who are also in the syndicate, report about
the same figure. Our firm has not been idle, so the
stock will sell at par right off."

"How long will it remain there?" Mr. Albright
asked, still looking at the maps, and following some
of the tracings with a lead pencil which he held in
his hand.

"Until the syndicate has disposed of its holdings,"
answered Mr. Keen, in the same cool, matter-of-fact
way.

"Brompton in this?" asked Mr. Robb, a member
of the firm of Robb & Gouge.

"No; he didn't get the chance," Mr. Keen said,
who seemed to be in charge of the proceedings.

"Any trouble with the city?" questioned Mr.
Albright, now looking up from the maps and facing
Mr. Keen.

"None whatever. Our Mr. Sharp has been doing
some missionary work with a few of the more noisy
ones. Everything is all right."

"I am afraid of it," said Mr. Wise, a careful but
reputedly wealthy banker. "Here is a proposition
to take property which is worth in actual value five
millions and put it on the market at thirty millions.
Now, to make dividends on this enormous increase
of capital we must cut down the wages of every man
on the road, and some of them hardly get enough
to keep body and soul together. Gentlemen, this is
not the kind of business I take stock in."

"Neither do I," said Mr. Albright; "there has
been altogether too much of this sort of thing."

Was the syndicate formed?
It was.

.   .   .   .

"You think it can be done?"
"I know it can be done."
"You speak confidently."
"Because it is practically done now."
"Explain."
"There is now in hand, and in easy reach, a controlling interest in the road. It hasn't met its fixed charges for some years. The stock has been going down and down. We can control things when we please."
"And then?"
"Reorganize; drop out the old stockholders; float the new certificates; officer the road ourselves; make the biggest strike this city has known for years."
Was it done?
It was.

.   .   .   .

"It is a great scheme," said Mr. Furroughs.
"A scheme with money in it, which is more important," said Mr. Granger.
"It will excite the opposition of the newspapers."
"What of that?"
"These reformers and radical preachers will denounce it."
"Let them."
"It will squeeze a good many people."
"What odds?"
"It will mean an increase in the price of bread."
"Suppose it does?"

"The poor have it hard enough now, goodness knows."

" A penny in a loaf isn't much."

"Not to you ; it is to the poor man."

" You needn't go in unless you want to. This thing is going. If you want to ride, better jump on."

Was it done ?

It was.

At whose cost ?

At the cost of the man who had to pay the extra penny on his loaf.

.   .   .   .

"Edward Vaughen, give an account of yourself! An hour after midnight and you wandering around the streets of New York ! "

It was John Disney who spoke, laying at the same moment his hand upon Edward's shoulder.

"I am looking for Whittington's cat or Aladdin's lamp," Edward answered.

" New York has not, within my time at any rate, been troubled with a scarcity of cats ; the Whittington brand, though, is rare. As for lamps, the Aladdin make is hard to get hold of."

John said this as they turned from the corner and were walking down the avenue.

"Strange, isn't it," Edward said, " people nearly always associate good fortune with luck or magic, and seldom with plodding and hard work ? "

" Not strange at all, my philosophic friend. Many of the great fortunes right round us were not attained by patient ' plodding.' Whittington's cat or Aladdin's lamp had something to do with most of them."

"Then the man who contents himself with plain, hard work doesn't stand much chance of success?"

"If that man but knew it he has found Aladdin's lamp, only instead of ghouls and goblins and all manner of strange creatures from the specter world he has spirits of life and health and peace to wait upon him. The man who has a clear eye, a clean heart, a conscience which does not need to be drugged; who can stand on his own feet and look the world in the face—he is the successful man. The trouble is, he seldom knows it. Now, here is Edward Vaughen, a friend of mine, my college classmate, fairly good-looking, with a reasonable measure of ability; strong, hearty, healthy, a promising career opening before him; but because he must for the present be content with a 'third floor, hall back' in the house of the esteemed Mrs. Gubbins, and cannot have an uptown hotel all to himself, I find him wandering discontented and distressed through the streets of New York, as unhappy as a spring poet overtaken by a blizzard, or a park policeman in a rain storm."

Edward knew John too well to attempt anything by way of protest, for that would only add fuel to the flame. John therefore went on:

"Now, some of these people," with a wave of his hand in the direction of certain pretentious houses on the avenue, "may have, for all I know, the veritable Whittington cat or the genuine Aladdin lamp. But the cat is eternally humping itself, and is a cross, spiteful, disagreeable old thing. The lamp, moreover, only calls forth little devils of pride, avarice jealousy, and all the rest of them, so that the owners of the lamp are to be pitied."

"But these are the successful people," Edward managed to edge in, taking advantage of a slight pause in John's oratoric flow.

"Successful in what?" John asked. "Success means achievement; it means the overcoming of difficulties; but tell me, I pray thee, thou man of wisdom, what mighty genius is required in finding a stray cat which turns out to be a 'Whittington,' or in tumbling over an old lamp which proves to be an 'Aladdin?'"

"What, then, is real success?" Edward asked, for John's mood was one with which he was perfectly familiar. Hence he dropped a question now and then, like a nickel in the slot, just to keep the machine going.

"Success, my respected and venerable brother, is the art of life. The newsboy who sells his papers, the peanut man who sells his peanuts, the street pedlar who sells his suspenders and shoe laces, equally with the merchant, the banker, or the senator, may attain the highest possible success. All that anyone has to do is to live up to the measure of his abilities. A brook trout doesn't require an ocean; a daisy can grow in a patch of ground as well as in a prairie. But here we are down to Madison Square! All good, nice little boys should be in bed. The anxious soul of your dear Mrs. Gubbins will be distressed."

And so they parted, John Disney taking a Madison Avenue street car, Edward Vaughen continuing his walk, for he was now within a few blocks of home.

16

CHAPTER XXVI.

The Real Dr. Disney.

DIXON FABER, in an irreverent way not uncommon with newspaper men, referred to
Mr. Singleton as "something of a politician,"
but Mr. Singleton was much more than a politician;
he was a philosopher. Anyone can be a politician.
All that a man has to do is simply to study his own
interests, and then advance them in every possible
way. But it is not everyone who can be a philosopher.
This requires patience, large-mindedness, and mental
aptitudes of no common order.

Mr. Singleton (Benjamin he was called at baptism;
Ben he was dubbed when a boy at school; but now
that he was full forty years of age, was quite bald on
the top of his head, and had charge of a department
in Keen & Sharp's, he was addressed usually as
Mister) was a genuine philosopher, and in Edward
Vaughen's "third floor, hall back" he often discoursed in the wisest way. The rocker was his
favorite seat, and when Faber wasn't present Mr.
Singleton added to his comfort by making a foot rest
of the other chair.

He had a history as well as romance, the romance
accounting for his being at Mrs. Gubbins's and unmarried. The history he kept to himself. There
was a little packet of letters, yellow, faded, in a girl's
handwriting, securely locked in a tin cash box which

he kept in one of his bureau drawers; but whatever was written in these letters only Mr. Singleton knew.

"You ask," he said one evening, turning to the bed, where Edward was sitting in his free and easy way, "why there are so many failures in business. The reason is simple. It is not the business that fails, it is the men."

"As a remark, that sounds well, but I confess I don't understand it," Edward said, pleasantly, for by this time he was on quite familiar terms with Mr. Singleton.

"Then let me illustrate. Some people, I am sadly aware, must have things made very simple so that they can understand them. Hence I proceed. There is a certain fish which, because it has pectoral fins of unusual strength and size, assumes that it can fly. At times, therefore, it leaps out of the water, just to show how superior it is to the other fishes not so endowed. But sooner or later that leap is a sad one, for the real birds of the sea are watching for it. The result is that before the poor, vain thing can fold its wings and drop back to its natural place it is caught. True, the fish becomes fowl; only, however, after a process of mastication."

"Now, if you will only illustrate your illustration or explain your explanation I shall be much obliged," said Edward, pulling up one of the pillows which had fallen down, and trying to make himself more comfortable.

"Very good. Line upon line, precept upon precept. 'There are those to whom even the alphabet has to be graduated. So I go on. The seal lives partly on land, but mostly in water. But the seal makes the mistake of its life in ever leaving the water. If it knew the first thing of grace of attitude or poetry of motion it would forever abandon all claim to feet and content itself with swimming. Now, the seal, in its silly desire to do something which it never was intended to do, had to exhibit itself on the rocks and ice as a champion walker. The consequence was that men saw what a fine coat it had; so since then it has been skinned without mercy."

"What on earth have seals and flying fish to do with my question? I should have thought that—" Edward was saying.

"Anything in nature that does two things equally well is a freak, and does both things badly," Mr. Singleton said, calmly ignoring the interruption, then proceeding with:

"What need was there of Melton & Tweed going into real estate operations? None whatever. They had a first-rate clothing business and were making a good living. But the fish would fly, and in one of its leaps landed in the Bankrupt Court."

Edward was now beginning to see the drift of Mr. Singleton's mind. He listened, therefore, all the more intently as the philosopher went on.

"The same thing happened to Herring & Salt. As ship chandlers they stood well on Water Street. But the seals had to get on the rocks. So they dabbled in Western lands and two or three other things; hence their handsome skins now adorn other but shrewder men. Mr. Edward Vaughen, do you see?"

At another time, as Mr. Singleton and Edward were having one of their after-dinner chats, Mr. Singleton asked:

" Vaughen, how many of us are in this room ? "

" Only ourselves," Edward answered, in an amused way, for Mr. Singleton had been discoursing of psychology, and, as is not unusual in such cases, had got out of sight of land.

" Correct, my friend; only just define what you mean by ' ourselves.' "

" I mean you, Mr. Singleton ; myself, Edward Vaughen."

" ' Mr. Singleton ' and ' Mr. Vaughen ' are merely visiting cards. My body, which you are doing me the favor of accommodating with this chair, is only an envelope. You have not yet made my acquaintance. I don't know anything whatever of you. The man who is sitting in this chair is a man whom you have never met ; the man who is sitting on that bed is a total stranger to me."

In an indirect way these conversations relate to Dr. Disney, though it may be noticed that his name was not mentioned, neither did either of the speakers have him in mind.

Things were not going well with Dr. Disney. Some of his plans, plans upon which he had spent much care, were not working out as he had hoped.

So far as actual money was concerned—that is, money for the general needs of life—Dr. Disney should have been one of the easiest men in New York. Mrs. Disney had a good income, for her father's investments were all interest-bearing. Madge and

John were also well provided for under their grandfather's will. His own practice was large, and one
of the best paying in the city. But Dr. Disney was
not satisfied. To use Mr. Singleton's figures, it was
another instance of the flying fish or the walking
seal. Hence he went into all sorts of schemes. He
had almost a mania for speculation. He dabbled in
nearly everything. Cotton, grain, railroads, gas,
mines, quarries, were taken up one after the other,
and though the doctor would have been terribly
shocked had he heard it, yet he was spoken of by
those who operated for him as a confirmed gambler.
Some of his ventures turned out well, upon which he
went into others which turned out badly. Then he
became reckless. He increased his holdings. To
carry all that he was doing required a good deal of
money. So he was forced to borrow, and borrow
largely. This meant accommodation notes, and as
he could not ask certain men to indorse his paper
without being willing to indorse in return, his liabili-
ties one way and another were very heavy.

He had hoped for relief when Mrs. Disney would
inherit her portion of the Haddon estate, but Mr.
Haddon for some reason so tied up everything that
the doctor could do nothing with it. Sometimes he
was in the direst straits, resorting to all manner of
expedients to keep himself afloat.

Then he was troubled about John. The silly
notions, as he thought, of Hugh Dunbar had sadly
interfered with John's life and prospects. Why
couldn't he give up this folly, settle down properly,
marry Miss Keen, instead of throwing himself away?

Even Madge disappointed him. She also had come under the Dunbar influence, whereas it had been his long-cherished wish for her to become a member of the Brompton family.

But did Dr. Disney show anything of the anxieties and disappointments which came one after the other, and, pressing the hidden spring of his secret life, passed through the mystic door to take up their abode in his heart?

Most men would have given some sign of the inward unrest, but Dr. Disney was the same calm, suave gentleman that he ever was, with every indication of a spirit at peace with all mankind.

The Disney household, with the exception of the doctor, have retired for the night. Dr. Disney, who has had a very busy day, is in his own room sitting by the fire. The chair he occupies looks comfortable, for, in addition to its own thick cushions, Madge has provided pillows, the covers of which she embroidered with her own dainty hands. The room is cheerful and bright, having not only the ruddy glow of the fire, but a lamp sending out a mellow light from under a rich shade. Soft, heavy draperies, oriental in pattern and material, hang from the windows. A massive but inviting-looking lounge, upon which an afghan of Mrs. Disney's handiwork is thrown, occupies a nook within reach of the bookcase. On the table at which the doctor is sitting are books, papers, magazines, reviews, all cut and ready to his hand.

But surely this anxious, worn-looking man, sitting so dejectedly in the big chair, with drawn forehead, compressed lips, harassed face, is not our Dr. Disney! Ah! this is the real Dr. Disney. At other times he was in stage costume; he was before the footlights; he was merely playing a part. Here we see him as he is, as he sees himself. To-night he is going back over the years. Memory, with mysterious mechanism, is moving slides before the calcium light of conscience, and the pictures are being thrown upon the outspread curtain of his soul. Sharp, vivid, intense, these pictures are, and the figures in them not only move, but speak, and their voices are awfully distinct.

He sees a young woman of some twenty years of age standing in the moonlight, but almost in the shadow of her father's house. Her face is singularly winsome; such a play of light; so much of real womanhood. Then he sees tears gather in her eyes and hears sobs break in her voice. "No! It is impossible. Nor should you have spoken as you have. Walter Disney, I never thought that you would ask me to forswear myself. You knew that I was engaged to your cousin, Fred Sauvier, and that we are soon to be married. Have you no honor, no sense of manhood?" With a proud, angry look she turned away, leaving him alone in the moonlight.

The picture dies out, but another instantly takes its place.

The scene now is in his own room, three years after the one of the moonlight. His Cousin Fred, a simple, honest, but easily influenced young man, enters, and with pale, anxious face cries out:

"Walter, I'm in great trouble! Can't you help me?"

O how he hated Fred Sauvier, and in his heart had registered a cruel vow of revenge!

"You indorsed his note for two thousand dollars. Well, what of it?"

"But you know, Walter, when Grandfather Arlow started me in business I promised him that I would not indorse notes for anyone. Now, this note is due the day after to-morrow, and it will go to protest."

"Why can't Howell meet it?"

"The people for whom he made the goods have failed. Howell will have to go under too. If I had only another week I could manage, for Bertha has some little money in New York, but I can't get hold of it in time."

"That money of Bertha's sure of being on hand next week?"

"Sure. She telegraphed the agent this morning."

"Grandfather Arlow keeps his account in the same bank as you do?"

"Yes."

"They know you at the bank?"

"It was grandfather who introduced me."

"Then why not use grandfather's name for a week? There is no need for him to know. Bertha's money will be here in a few days, and the note could then be taken up."

"But, Walter, that would be forgery!" Fred said, in a frightened voice.

"Yes, I know, but men do it. I wouldn't, though. There is some risk about it—not much, but some."

Careful, cunning Walter Disney! He pushes a

plank over to a drowning man, but suggests that there are nails in it which may tear his fingers!

His cousin goes out of the picture, and he sees himself carry to a typewriter in a public office a letter:

"DEAR SIR: A note with your indorsement for two thousand dollars will be presented at your bank for discount to-morrow. If you doubt this letter make inquiries."

Once more the slides dissolve. This time he is in a court-room. His Cousin Fred is within the prisoner's bar, for Mr. Arlow had instantly telegraphed his bankers, with the result that Fred Sauvier was arrested for forgery. Now he hears the sentence, "Fifteen years!" also a woman's heart-broken cry; then he knows that his cousin's wife has fainted in the court room.

Another slide is noiselessly moved along the holder. A stern, pitiless woman, with a face set as iron and terrible as fate, looks implacably into his.

"Walter Disney, you tempted my husband. You suggested the crime which has broken his heart, desolated our home, and ruined the lives of two infant children. You have the curse of the man you have murdered, for he is now dying of remorse and shame. You have the curse of the woman whose soul you have destroyed, for I shall hate you eternally. You have the curse of my children, for I will train them up to curse you. Walter Disney, if there is a God in the universe, and if there is justice with him, a judgment will come to you."

The picture slowly faded out, leaving him with a face as the ashes in the grate and his forehead beaded with soul tears. Then he rose to his feet, almost staggered across the room, opened a small case, took out a tiny bottle, poured into a glass a few drops of some powerful drug, which he diluted with water before drinking, and soon after was fast asleep.

CHAPTER XXVII.

Madge is Worldly Wise.

AS the nephew of Mark Brompton, but perhaps still more as the friend of John Disney,
it was inevitable that Edward Vaughen should
soon find place in the social life of New York.

At first Mrs. Brompton was not over pleased at
meeting the young man so frequently; still he was
such a nice, gentlemanly fellow, never in the least
presuming upon his relationship; so her resentment
materially declined.   Indeed, there were times when
she was almost sorry that she had been so anxious
in the matter of his downtown lodgings, once even
hinting to Mr. Brompton that his nephew might re-
enter their household, but Mr. Brompton did not
accept the suggestion.   The present arrangement
suited Mark Brompton, for it gave Mr. Keen the
impression that Edward was simply a poor country
relation who had to be provided for.   So long, therefore, as he remained in the family of Mrs. Gubbins
it was ample proof that the relationship between
uncle and nephew was one of mere blood, and nothing more.

If Edward had been awkward, gawky, unused to
the ways of society, dull, stupid, everlastingly in
people's way, possibly Mrs. Brompton might not
have been so willing to give him a place in her family.   But that is no concern of ours.   To look too

closely into a kindness is as bad as to submit a gift horse to a dental inspection.

"Well, my young friend, you seem to be going out quite a good deal these days," Mr. Singleton said one evening, as he saw Edward take out his "claw hammer" and proceed to array himself in evening dress.

Edward smiled and nodded, after which he went over to the mirror on the bureau to enter upon the soul-distressing concern of tying his necktie.

"You have heard Madame Screechoni warble?"

Edward confessed that he had heard Madame Screechoni make some extraordinary noises; the warbling he would not vouch for.

"You have seen the performance of the eminent Digitaliski?"

"Why do you say 'seen?'" Edward asked, evening the ends of his tie, so that it would not hang lopsided, as it was disposed to do.

"Because the hearing, in the case of Digitaliski, is of small moment compared with the seeing. People get up on the seats. They crowd around the instrument. The whole thing is an exhibition."

Edward was now having trouble with his cuff buttons. The cuffs were stiff as sheet iron. The buttons were of the old-fashioned order, solid and good, but not amenable to kindness.

"Then you have properly admired the work of Signor Paletto?" Mr. Singleton questioned as with an amused but sympathetic smile he watched Edward labor with the cuff buttons.

"Hang Signor Paletto! If he would only wash his face and comb his hair—"

"In that case you would remove his chief claims to distinction. Ah! now that you have those cuff buttons disposed of, you will be more kindly."

The average man when he is working his way into evening dress prefers to have his room all to himself, for there are certain gestures, not to speak of phrases and terms, which he enjoys most in solitude. But Mr. Singleton was not only a philosopher; he was the head of a department in Keen & Sharp's.

"The other evening you met the Winks, the Jinks, and the Blinks contingents. This evening you will meet the same people, only the order of the procession will be changed. Also some of the women's gowns. But that is all there is of it. When you are as old as I am you will have got through Winking and Blinking and Jinking. Still you are not a bad-looking fellow. Going to Von der Plonk's?"

Mr. Singleton on going to his room locked the door, opened the little cash box, took out reverently the packet of faded letters, and read until after midnight. In the office of Keen & Sharp he was one of their most capable managers; in the house of Mrs. Gubbins he was a genial, cynical philosopher; but in his own room he was Ben Singleton, whose sweetheart had died nearly twenty years ago, but to whose memory he was ever loyal.

Being in the same set with the Keens, Edward quite often met Miss Keen, and after a time they began to look for each other at the different functions. On entering a room, as soon almost as he had paid his respects to the hostess (the host in these matters is not usually of much consequence),

Edward would glance quickly around, and though he was wise enough not to show it, still a deeper, gladder light would flash in his eyes if he saw Miss Keen anywhere in the company. And then there would pass between them some mysterious sign of recognition, a smile of the broken sixpence order, divided about evenly.

When they had opportunity to speak with each other it was not so much what was said which made their conversation interesting, but rather an undertone of sympathetic relationship. Once in a crush at the Bromptons', when the young people were glad for a little while to sit on the stairs, Edward managed to get on the same step with Miss Keen. By accident their hands touched, but somehow that touch made Edward's blood fairly tingle. Miss Keen possibly had herself in more perfect control; still there was a look on her face which was not there before.

Knowing of the close business relations between Mr. Brompton and Mr. Keen, also that Edward Vaughen was Mark Brompton's nephew, the Gothamites generally allowed the young people a fair measure of latitude.

Still there were those who studied the situation with much interest.

"John," said Madge, after this gathering at the Von der Plonks', for which we saw Edward array himself, when they were having one of their confidential confabs, "have you observed how very devoted the 'unearned increment' is to Rhea Keen?"

"No," answered John, going over to the rack for his pipe, for this was John's snuggery.

"Well, I have," said Madge, unfastening her gloves, and making herself very much at home in what John called "Madge's chair."

"You must admit," replied John, going on with the filling of his pipe, a work with him of some deliberation, "that Edward Vaughen has good taste, for Miss Keen is a very attractive girl."

"The taste I am prepared to admit, for Rhea Keen, to my thinking, is one of the few really beautiful women in our set. The judgment, however, I am disposed to question."

"In what way?" asked John, now prepared to go into the question on its merits, for his pipe was well started, his chair was just at the right distance from the fire, and there were few things he more thoroughly enjoyed than a bright, breezy chat with his lively sister.

"Edward Vaughen has no money," Madge answered in a tone of profound conviction, emphasizing her statement of plain fact by a look of almost unnatural seriousness.

"And what has that to do with it?" John asked, with an air of genuine surprise, for Madge was usually free from mercenary motives.

"A great deal. Mr. Keen has other plans for Rhea. He is one of the most ambitious men in the city. Mark my words," this with great impressiveness, the emphasis strengthened by a fairly vigorous use of the right hand, in which Madge held her gloves, "when Mr. Keen begins to suspect anything he will put a stop to it in short order."

"But Vaughen isn't going to marry Mr. Keen,

nor Miss Keen either, for that matter, for he is only
beginning, and probably hardly earns enough to pay
his way. But why Mr. Keen should interfere does
not just occur to me."

It must be confessed that John was a little bit disappointed at the worldly wisdom of his sister.

"It will occur to you before long, for I tell you,
John Disney, that Mr. Keen will interfere, and that,
too, in the most vigorous way."

This time Madge brought down the gloves on the
palm of her left hand with considerable energy.

"And yet why should he?" persisted John after a
few moments' silence, during which time he nursed
his pipe into a state of more visible combustion.
"Edward Vaughen is a clean, honest, manly fellow.
He comes of a good family. He is a thoroughbred.
I know him through and through. Now, simply because he hasn't yet 'made his pile,' why a man like
Keen will throw him over and give his daughter to
some man without honor or character to me is not
merely incomprehensible, but—"

"That may be, John, but Mr. Keen is no worse
than other men. You remember how Mr. Blobbs
interfered between Fanny and Sidney Davenant, so
that finally everything was broken off, Fanny at
length marrying Mr. Hyde, the rich leather man,
who was old enough to be her grandfather."

"Yes, I remember it, and Fanny Blobbs was a
fool for doing it. There are times when a daughter
owes something to herself. When a woman does
what Fanny Blobbs did I am not certain that even
'fool' is strong enough to cover the case. I know

17

Sidney Davenant, and if Fanny had married him she would have been a much happier woman than she is now. I met her the other day; it was on Fifth Avenue near Madison Square. I hardly knew her, she was so pale and old-looking. But I have no sympathy to waste on her."

Nevertheless in his heart John pitied Fanny Blobbs, though he was provoked with her.

"That is all very well, John, but what else could Fanny do? Sidney Davenant had nothing to offer her, and, brought up as she had been, it would have been folly for her to think of making a home with him."

"Nothing to offer her! A healthy, wholesome, strapping fellow, with a heart full of love, a mind full of ambitions, and a future as certain as to-morrow's sun. Do these things count for nothing in the esteem of such women as Fanny Blobbs? What had old Hyde to offer her? A big warehouse full of leather, and when you have said that you have said all there is to say."

"Meantime, what of Edward Vaughen and Rhea Keen?" Madge asked, for they were more on her mind than Fanny Blobbs and her leather man.

"The best thing is to let them manage this business themselves. It may not be as serious as you think. Vaughen is disposed to be romantic. He always was. As for Miss Keen, she knows what she is doing. You need have no anxiety on her account. But I hope Vaughen won't get in beyond his depth. You don't meet fellows of his type every day."

"But, John, it seems to me you are prejudiced against Rhea Keen. Now, you stand up for Edward Vaughen, so I mean to do the same by Rhea."

"That is right, Madge, but Miss Keen can get along without any special help. She may do any amount of high thinking, but not much plain living; and if it comes to a choice as between Edward Vaughen and shekels she will take the shekels."

"John, you are mistaken."

"Madge, I don't think I am."

And so they separated, each convinced that the other was wrong.

"Rhea," said Mr. Keen that same evening, after their return from the Von der Plonks, "that clerk of mine seems disposed to be quite friendly. I noticed him fairly attentive to you."

"You refer to Mr. Vaughen?" said Rhea.

"I mean Mr. Vaughen, of course," Mr. Keen responded, with an irritation which was very palpable.

"You would not expect me to be rude to Mr. Brompton's nephew?" Rhea answered, an answer which fully justified John Disney's remark that she was perfectly able to take care of herself.

"There is a very great difference between rudeness and encouragement," Mr. Keen replied, for he felt that his daughter had discovered the weak place in his armor.

"Papa," said Rhea, "when Mr. Brompton's nephew is considerate enough to treat me as a lady expects to be treated by a gentleman am I to reward him by intentional discourtesy?"

"You are altogether too provoking," said Mr. Keen, now quite angry, for he saw that he was overmatched.

"Not provoking at all. Merely definite and practical," answered Rhea, and the conversation ended.

CHAPTER XXVIII.

The Mysterious Consultation.

A NEW curate had come to St. Elijah's; consequently Miss Pollok's heart beat high with hope, for though he was of a certain maturity of years he was unmarried. And now that the brewer's widow was no longer in the way, who knows what may happen? Miss Pollok determined, therefore, to resume some, if not all, of her former duties, and as a first step in this noble resolve she entered vigorously into the work of the chapel Sunday school. It was, of course, a mere coincidence that the new curate was in charge at the chapel. But such enthusiasm as hers could not be restrained in any formal service. Hence she attacked the piano in the parlor of Mrs. Gubbins, and with its help voiced her joy and hope in wondrous melody.

It must be confessed that the effect on the household was somewhat depressing, and Miss Pollok had the parlor all to herself. Her heroic attempts to reach the altitudinous termination of "The Maiden's Prayer" deserved recognition, and the pathos with which she gave "O Promise Me" was unmistakable. Still the parlor remained a sacred inclosure, across whose portals none would dare to step.

The artist, ever the true gentleman, occupied the room overhead. No sooner did Miss Pollok begin "Some Day, Somewhere" than he would move softly to and fro, lest he might disturb her, after which he would be seen on the stairs, stepping quietly down, then going out, not to return for some hours.

Mr. Wright, who had the room next to that of the artist, was not so fine in his grain, for he would tramp about in the most reckless way, finally pounding down stairs, and pulling the door after him with an energy entirely unnecessary.

Mr. Faber, being on the floor higher up, could not hear with the same distinctness as either Mr. Wright or the artist ; and as there is nothing more tantalizing to a fine musical taste than to get only snatches and stray measures, he would close his door, preferring to shut the music out altogether when he could not have it in its completeness.

Mr. Singleton was not musical at all—philosophers seldom are. He therefore spoke of the performance in the parlor in a way that was certainly irreverent, if not profane.

As for Edward Vaughen, when he had a spare evening now and then he devoted most of it to writing to his mother, but Miss Pollok's music was neither soothing nor inspiring. He kept on bravely, but when he wrote, " the thing is horrible," right in the midst of a description of a dress which Madge Disney had worn the night before, one that he particularly admired, and at another time put in, " will she never stop ? " when he was referring to the gathering at the Von der Plonks', he thought it wise to give up writing for that evening. Accordingly he put his papers aside, pulled on his overcoat, and went out, slowly and carefully, however, for Edward was too considerate to disturb Miss Pollok, who just then was plaintively warbling "Left Blooming Alone."

Having been uptown quite a good deal in the evenings, Edward thought that a walk through the business section would afford him the opportunity of contrasting the busy day with the silent night, and at the same time furnish a new experience.

It was about nine o'clock. With anything like rapid walking he could be at the Battery at ten. There he had a choice of a cable car or the "Elevated," returning in good season to finish his letter.

The night was fairly cold, though not rough and blustering, as it sometimes is in New York about mid winter. It was one of those still, quiet nights when the stars hang low in the heavens and sparkle wondrously in the frosty air.

With his fur cap pulled well down on his head, his ulster buttoned up to his chin, his hands in heavy gloves and swinging at his side, Edward strode along most joyously. And why not? Was he not just crossing the threshold of young manhood and entering upon the very fullness of life? With a magnificent physique worthy of a young Apollo; with blood throbbing and tingling in exuberant health; with hopes that stretched out before him as clearly as the street upon which he walked, why should he not stride along in all the vigor and daring of youth?

How quiet and almost deserted Broadway was as Edward walked along! What a sharp contrast with the earlier hours of the day! In the forenoon the crowds keep growing, until one wonders where all the people come from. How difficult it is to make our way, and how much more difficult to cross the street! The endless procession of vehicles, or, rather, the double procession—for there is a stream going up as well as one going down—causes some lively and even daring movements on the part of those who must pass from one side of the street to the other. The wonder is not that so many people come to grief, but how few; for we are a reckless folk, taking all manner of chances to save a minute's time.

And when we are in the region of City Hall, where the Brooklyn stream coming and going from the Bridge falls in with the streams coming and going from the Jersey ferries, what an amazing number of people are going either our way or the other way!

But Edward could walk now as rapidly as he pleased, for the crowds had utterly disappeared. The only signs of active life were in Newspaper Row, where lights were streaming from the windows in the tall buildings and the papers were being prepared for the morrow.

So deeply did Edward feel the contrast that he resolved to go down to the street where Keen & Sharp had their offices, so he turned off Broadway at Wall Street and walked through to the street where these offices were. How quiet everything was! He could hardly realize that these were the same streets through which he had walked only a few hours before. They seemed uncanny. It was unnatural that they should be so empty and still. Edward felt as if he were in a dream.

The high buildings lifted themselves into the silent night like the walls of some mighty fortress, with doors securely bolted and barred. He looked for the crowds of eager, anxious men, but none could be seen. He listened for the noises of the beating footsteps, but none could be heard. The arena was deserted. The gladiators had retired. The amphitheater was empty. The hope, the eagerness, the ambition, the strife, which during the day were so manifest, had departed. Nothing remained but shadows.

He soon came to the building of which Keen & Sharp occupied the first floor, intending to simply glance at it and pass on, but seeing a bright light in the inner office he went over and looked in. This he did not out of curiosity merely, for he remembered Mr. Singleton telling him that during exciting times on the "Street" the partners would remain in the office all night planning for the strife of the coming day. But to his surprise, on glancing through the window, he saw not only Mr. Keen and Mr. Sharp, but Dr. Disney. Dr. Disney evidently had just arrived, for, though his hat was on the table at which the stenographer usually sat, he had not removed his overcoat, and was standing, taking off his gloves in that graceful, deliberate way in which he did everything.

What this visit meant Edward could not possibly imagine. Of all men Dr. Disney, and at this hour! He had never heard Dr. Disney's name mentioned in the office. So far as Edward knew, it was not on the books of the firm. He could not, therefore, connect

him with any movement or speculation in which
Keen & Sharp would be likely to engage. Surely he
was not there on professional business. Edward was
completely nonplused.

The clock on old Trinity now struck ten, and as
Edward was too much of a gentleman to wait or spy,.
he went back through Wall Street out to Broadway. ·
He admitted that the circumstance was a strange one.
Seeing Mr. Keen reminded him of Rhea, though he
did not require such remembrance, and as he went uptown in a cable car it was Rhea he thought of. Still
now and then he wondered at seeing Dr. Disney in
the office at that hour.

" The situation is critical, but the chances are in
our favor," Mr. Keen said, in reply to a question of
Dr. Disney.

" I had hoped that by this time our chances would
have become certainties," answered the doctor.

"And they would," put in Mr. Sharp, " but there
was some countermining on the part of the enemy."

" You mean by this that some other parties are
after the same combination ? " questioned the doctor,
a shade of very perceptible anxiety crossing his face.

" That is just what I mean," replied Mr. Sharp.
"And the trouble is, we cannot find to what extent
the countermining has been carried on."

" Then the chances are not so distinctly in our favor
as Mr. Keen seems to imply ? " was the doctor's next
question, the anxiety deepening on his face and even
sounding in his voice.

" Mr. Keen is very hopeful ; more so, naturally,
than I am. This is a big scheme. If it goes through

all right we will make a whole pot of money. But I
have had my doubts all along."

Mr. Sharp pulled out a drawer in the desk close at
his hand, took from it a cigar, but did not light it,
contenting himself with holding it in his mouth and
chewing the end in a way that was more vigorous
than picturesque.

"Have you any suspicions as to who the party or
parties are who are in this 'countermining' business?"

The doctor had regained something of his com-
posure, and asked this question in his usual bland
way.

"We have," answered Mr. Keen, "and that is
where the situation is unpleasant. Mark Brompton
is the man who is making the trouble."

"Mark Brompton!" exclaimed Dr. Disney, rising
from his chair in great excitement. "How did he
ever get hold of it?"

"How does he get hold of everything?" Mr. Keen
said, almost savagely. "I confess that he beats me
even at my own game."

"There was nothing said in the office?" the doctor
asked.

"Not a word. We have kept the thing a dead
secret. How Brompton got wind of it is more than
we can make out." Mr. Sharp spoke with considerable emphasis, for he was plainly anxious as to the
outcome of the affair.

"You have young Vaughen in your office. He is
Brompton's nephew. He may have heard something."

Dr. Disney had the utmost confidence in Keen & Sharp doing their best to keep this thing a secret. Still some one had played the spy.

"Yes, Vaughen is with us. You know our relations to Mr. Brompton. Well, he wanted a place for this nephew, so we made an opening and ran him in. But he is not in Mark Brompton's confidence, for he boards somewhere downtown, while Mrs. Brompton gives him shoulder *à la frappé*. Besides, he is not in our confidence."

"Is there anything we can do? Mark Brompton is dangerous. If he knows we are in this thing he will ruin us;" and as the doctor spoke his voice was husky, so great was his anxiety.

"Can't you, as Brompton's physician, tell him that he is overdoing? Work some kind of a nervous gag. Advise him to take a trip to Europe. Get him to give up business for a time. Threaten him with heart failure, and all that sort of thing."

Mr. Sharp made these suggestions in a light, flippant way, so that the doctor might regard them as pleasantries. But in his heart Mr. Sharp was neither light nor flippant.

Dr. Disney made no reply. He could not make the reply which his professional honor demanded. These men held his signature for an amount which he dare not lose. Virtually he was in their power, and so Mr. Sharp's words stung him almost beyond endurance. Quick as lightning his thoughts flashed back to that time, now over twenty years ago, when he suggested an even greater crime to one who came to him for help, and he could see the horror-stricken

face of Fred Sauvier as he answered, " But, Walter,
that would be forgery ! "

And now after all these years he is asked to per-
jure himself, to break the sacred oath of his profession, and for the sake of a false, wicked pride dishonor his position as the trusted adviser of Mark
Brompton.   In what way would such advice differ
from the course of the midnight thief who holds the
saturated sponge over the mouth and nostrils of the
sleeper, drugging him into almost deathly unconsciousness, and then robbing him of his goods ?

And so it had come to this !   The very mention of
such a thing was a crime.   But his lips were sealed,
for he dare not break with Keen & Sharp.   There
was too much at stake.   But wherever he looked
around the office of Keen & Sharp he saw the pale,
anxious face of Fred Sauvier.   He could see it looking from the map which hung over one of the desks.
He could trace it in the rug before the fireplace.
And with the face he could hear, "But, Walter, that
would be forgery ! "

Nothing more of any moment was said, and just as
the Trinity Church clock was striking eleven Dr.
Disney left the office and went uptown.

BOOK III.—AMBITION

CHAPTER XXIX.

John Disney's Scheme.

ONCE upon a time, a long, long time ago, there was a man who was very much pleased with himself. He was also equally satisfied with the results of certain of his undertakings. He therefore resolved that when the right time came he would go in for a regular course of pleasure, and enjoy the good things with which he was so abundantly favored. Unfortunately, however, when the time arrived for this enjoyment the man's energies and vital forces had all been expended, so that while he retained the desire for ease and merriment he had no capacity for either. The consequence was that the man had no further reason for living, so he died with an abruptness that was startling.

Now, here was Mark Brompton, getting really nothing out of life, except the grim sense of satisfaction which comes from mastery. In a hand which was like iron he had taken the world by the throat. With a strong, resolute voice he had demanded payment even to the last farthing. And the world paid him in full, but it had ample revenge, for it took more out of him than he had taken out of it. He had made money, but he had unmade himself. He was what some people call rich, but what wiser people call poor. What he had was not his, strange as it may seem. He did not own his money; his

money owned him. He could buy pictures, any
number of them, and he did ; but he had no soul with
which to interpret them. By the simple writing of
a check he could purchase a whole library, but the
books had no message other than their bindings.
Music was not even the least distressing of sounds,
for when Ethel played or Janet sang, though the one
played superbly and the other had a rich, vibrant
voice, to him it was only unmeaning noise.

On Sunday mornings, with fair regularity, he
went to church, but he got nothing from either
service or sermon. And how could he, for he
had no interest whatever in the things for which
churches are presumed to stand? He was not a
pagan, for he hired one of the best pews in Dr.
Bland's church ; his name also appeared well up on
the list of subscribers to missions in Patagonia and
Timbuctoo. Such a thing, however, as personal responsibility never once occurred to him. Movements like the one led by Mr. Dunbar excited his
hardly disguised contempt. His home life was absolutely barren. All possibilities of love and tenderness he had put aside. The romance, the poetry, the
glad, sweet hopes which redeem life from utter sordidness, he had crushed as flowers under the ruthless
feet of his ambitions. He treated Mrs. Brompton
with respect, of course, but in no way did she touch
his heart or enter the mysterious depths of his being.

For his children he entertained much the same
feeling as a godfather is supposed to have. He admired Ethel for her beauty. He was quite interested in the idea of her marrying young Von der

Plonk. He liked Janet. Sometimes her frank, fearless tongue did not please him. He did not trouble himself very much about Percy. Percy was fond of yachting; he cared nothing for yachts. Percy liked horses, and would often go to the races ; he had no interest in horses, and held races in contempt. Percy was disposed to play the rôle of the man about town ; this he thought only a slight remove from idiocy.

Now, when you take a man who has no love in his heart, no uplifting, inspiring motives in his soul, no interests outside those of his office, it is difficult to see just what life means to such a man, or what possible good he gets out of it.

"Mr. Brompton," said John Disney one evening in Mr. Brompton's library, "I have come to ask your advice and assistance."

"Your note suggested as much," replied Mr. Brompton, but without any special encouragement in his tone. He liked John Disney, but there was a vein of romance in the young man with which he had small sympathy.

"The special matter which prompted me to solicit this interview was that I might consult you concerning my own career," John answered, with more hesitation than was usual with him.

"In what way can I serve you?" Mr. Brompton spoke just as he would in the office—direct, abrupt, curt.

"I have concluded to go into some kind of business, and I thought you might help me."

John was finding it hard work to talk to Mark Brompton. He had met him a number of times,

18

but always socially. Now that he was talking business and asking a favor the footing was very different.

"Is not this contrary to your father's wishes? My understanding was that you would enter his profession." Still not the least show of interest; the voice exactly the same as with Mr. Jones at his own desk.

"My father was disappointed at first. Of late, however, when we have talked about this he has rather favored my plan."

"What is your plan?"

"I really haven't any, other than to get into something which will give me an idea of business, and at the same time come into contact with working people."

Mr. Brompton's face hardened. An unpleasant light gleamed in his eyes. His lips curled in a way that was almost contemptuous.

"You are asking something beyond my power to grant," he said, very curtly.

"But I don't want any position of trust or responsibility; just some common kind of work in one of your mills or shops."

John spoke so earnestly and with such evident desire that Mr. Brompton looked at him sharply.

"Some of Mr. Dunbar's notions?" he tartly suggested.

"No. Mr. Dunbar has had nothing to do with this. We have not even spoken on the subject."

"What, then, put such a notion into your head? Young men with your training and advantages usu-

ally aspire to something higher than working in
foundry yards or machine shops."

"The notion has been in my head for a long time,"
John answered, frankly. "You see, up there at college we heard a great deal about what is called the
'social problem.' Professors who never saw the inside of a workshop, and who know nothing whatever
of the real life of the people, used to talk in a very
profound way of the new social conditions, and all
the rest of it. Then the men in their rooms would
take the matter up, talking what to me was nonsense. None of them, either professors or students,
had any practical knowledge of the subject. I used
to laugh at them, the professors especially, for they
should have known better. It seemed a ridiculous
thing for men who never did a day's work in their
lives, and who had no business experience whatever,
to go on discussing such a question as this. But I
made up my mind, if I ever got a chance, to go into
the matter for myself, as it would help me to decide
upon my own future. My grandfather, as you know,
left me a little money, not much, still enough for
present purposes. And now that I am free, and not
quite clear as to what line of business I may take up,
I thought this would be a good time to work out
my experiment."

Mr. Brompton listened with much interest, looking closely all the while at John. Though his face
was always stern and set, there were times when an
expression almost kindly came upon it, like sunlight
on a rugged mountain. This statement of John's
impressed him. It was not such a romantic under-

taking, after all. As he saw it, this was simply a close investigation such as any wise man of business would encourage.

After a short pause he said:

" This everlasting discussion of the ' social question,' as people call it, by men who don't know what they are talking about is a serious injury to the business of the country. In college you say the professors talked about it. As most of the college professors are well-meaning, inoffensive men in themselves, their talks would not do any harm. But newspapers get hold of these things. Then agitators take them up. The next thing the workmen themselves are talking about them. After this come strikes of one kind and another, keeping business unsettled all the time. If men knew what they were talking about it would not be so bad. One thing I like about Dr. Bland—he does not bore us every Sunday with tiresome harangues on the ' Responsibilities of Wealth ' or the ' Duties of Employers ' and such stuff. A few Sundays ago, when he was away somewhere, an apostle of the new order held forth on the ' Wrongs of the Poor,' making out that we were to blame for the present state of things. What did he know about it? Nothing whatever. He reminded me of a tonguefish floundering about in muddy water."

This little speech seemed to relieve Mr. Brompton of much of the bad feeling which he had when the conversation opened, so much so that he even smiled upon John in quite a friendly way.

But words are queer things. Sometimes they go

up like a rocket, coming down again in showers of
variegated light, while at other times they will rush
into the sky with a great noise, only to end in smoke
and sound. When properly understood words are only
poles upon which to string the wires of our thought,
not flagstaffs for the display of mental bunting.

Now, all the time Mr. Brompton was speaking
John Disney, though listening to every word, was
making applications very different from those which
the speaker intended. He thought of the sleek,
well-fed, complacent congregations who gathered
every Sunday in the church where Dr. Bland ministered with such eminent favor. Then he thought
of the hundreds of plain, common people who attended the Mission church of Hugh Dunbar. And then
he thought of the great gulf which separated the one
company from the other, a gulf wider and deeper,
than in any other city in the world.

But John did not give Mr. Brompton any inkling
of his thinkings. There are times when a close
blockade upon the mouth is scientific warfare, and
when silence rises to the dignity of statesmanship.
Mr. Brompton, looking at John from under his
shaggy eyebrows, never once suspected that behind
that quiet face of his there was going on a process of
thinking just the very opposite of that which he desired. Such, however, was the case. Mr. Brompton was now quite disposed to help John, and on the
following Monday John Disney was installed as assistant timekeeper in the Hematite Rolling Mills and
Tubal-Cain Machine Shops, a concern in which Mark
Brompton was a large stockholder.

That same Monday evening when Fred Sauvier returned to his home, and when he, with Oberta, as was their custom every evening, went over the affairs of the day, he spoke in glowing terms of his new assistant.

"Handsome and unmarried," he said, glancing mischievously at Oberta.

"How do you know?" a very natural question of Oberta's, seeing she was a woman.

"First from my eyes, for he is tall, well formed, not so fine in face as Mr. Dunbar, but more rugged and manly-looking, with a pair of eyes that can cut leather, and about as shapely a head as ever sat on a man's shoulders."

"Your description has my approval, and you say he is unmarried."

The look which Oberta returned to Fred as she said this was brimful of mirth, sharing part of it with Mrs. Sauvier, who listened with much enjoyment to the lively chat.

"I say it because he told me so himself, and I presume he knows; still these are the days of the 'new woman,' so that a man may be married and not know it."

"Speak for yourself, Fred Sauvier! Who are you to talk of the 'new woman?' Remember that I am in 'suits and wraps' in the well-known house of Linsey & Woolsey, where every day the 'new woman' appears in state. But let the 'new woman' alone. It is the new man I am interested in."

"He is a gentleman."

"Handsome, unmarried, and a gentleman! Then

why has he become your assistant at the Hematite
Rolling Mills? The plot thickens, the mystery
deepens; hurry up, Fred, with the rest of it; there
must be a romance somewhere."

"Probably there is, but so far I haven't seen anything of it."

"Fred, you are most unsatisfactory. Here are
mother and I just dying to know all about this distinguished stranger, and you just drop a word or two
like a stingy farmer feeding corn to his chickens."

"Some evening I may bring him down here to see
mother—an evening when you are detained at the
store."

"Fred Sauvier! if you do anything so mean I
will disown you; I will disinherit you; I will leave
my estates to an institution for Distressed and Afflicted Sisters. No, sir! No store for me the evening
when the 'paragon' is here. And even if I take
half of my department 'home on approval' I will
be arrayed as Solomon never dreamed of. Meantime won't you tell us his name?"

"His name is Disney, John Disney. He said his
father was a doctor, uptown somewhere. But what
ails mother? Oberta, quick!" but without waiting
for Oberta Fred sprang to his mother's side, only
in time to save her from falling to the floor. In
an instant he had carried her to the lounge, where
Oberta bathed her forehead, also sprinkling her face
with water. After a time she returned to consciousness, opening her eyes in a dazed, bewildered way.
Fred knew nothing of the former attack when Sister
Nora mentioned Dr. Disney's name, but Oberta

remembered and wondered what it meant. But she was careful not to say anything to Fred, for naturally he was anxious about his mother. Oberta put him off with such replies as came to her, finally retiring earlier than usual, that she might keep closer watch over Mrs. Sauvier, who had fallen into a heavy but restless sleep.

It was a dismal ending to an evening which started so well.

CHAPTER XXX.
Madge Visits the Mission.

TOTAL depravity is the totality of nonsense. Because some men are bad, therefore all men are bad, is the insanity of logic. That a man who has weaknesses and failings is incapable of real good is more than a fallacy—it is a lie. Gold is not mined in chunks. The best of grain has wrappings of chaff. Apples grow on trees, and the trees are nearly always scraggy, scrawny, miserable affairs. Hugh Dunbar was finding out these very things, deriving, too, much hope and comfort in the discovery. Men whom he approached with the desire of securing their cooperation in his work did not all turn away with the indifference of Mark Brompton. Far from it. Some of them gave generously of their means; nor were they content with this, but gave something of much greater value—their sympathy and presence. Women who stood high in the social world were glad to have a share in the work of Sister Nora. There is something in nearly everyone which admires heroism and self-sacrifice. When it became known, then, that Hugh Dunbar, for the sake of the neglected thousands on the East Side, had voluntarily resigned a life of ease, actually making his home among the people whom he served, there was a generous recognition of his fidelity to duty. There were many who thought that the sacrifice was needless, that his conscience was overstrained, and his sense of duty too serious by far. Still, no one could question his motives or doubt the principles under which he acted.

Sister Nora retained her elegant home on Fifth Avenue, for she had by no means withdrawn from society, but a great deal of her time was given to the Mission. Several of her intimate friends entered heartily into many of her plans, sharing sympathetically in her enthusiasm.

The result of all this was quickly felt in the Mission itself, for while there was no parade or display of wealth there was an ability to meet the growing needs of the work. A large Mission house was built and fitted up with generous care. Quarters were provided for reading rooms, children's play rooms, drill rooms, gymnasiums, bathing rooms, halls for general entertainment, and the great building was occupied in every part.

Hugh Dunbar had no use for mere temperance harangues—idle denunciations of the saloon, but providing nothing by way of counter attraction.

Once he said to John Disney, who was discussing the matter with him: "The rich man drinks in his club; the poor man drinks in the saloon. The one gets drunk on wine; the other gets drunk on whisky. The one makes a beast of himself where the floors are covered with carpet; the other where the floor is covered with sawdust. The only difference is that the club keeps open on Sunday, while the saloon is supposed to be closed."

" But the evil of the one does not justify the evil of the other," John very properly replied.

" Then remove the evil from both, leaving in each case that which is good. But let there be no discrimination in favor of the rich man's club as against the poor man's saloon."

On this principle Dunbar proceeded, so that a part of the Mission building became in reality a working-men's club. The experiment amply justified itself, for scores, even hundreds, of men of the Silas Smithers type spent many of their spare evenings in this club.

Dunbar was just as radical on the subject of amusements. He had too generous an appreciation of life to imagine that young people would content themselves with twirling their thumbs all evening, after a hard, grinding day in some noisy shop or crowded workroom. Such puritanic notions were not to his mind. They might be safe, certainly they were silly ; anyhow they belonged to a past age. Hence he went ahead with his own plans.

Of course he was criticised—sharply, bitterly, unkindly. All manner of things were said about him. Dear little men, pious little men, even good little men, would condole with each other, every time they met, over the daring irreligiousness of this frank revolutionist. But Mr. Dunbar went on just the same. When a clergyman is young, handsome, and rich—particularly rich—he can afford himself a large measure of independence. Hugh Dunbar could afford this luxury ; but, better still, he lived up to the utmost extent of his privilege.

One bright Sunday morning—and when New York undertakes to furnish a bright Sunday morn-

ing it supplies the genuine article. The air may not
be quite so clear as at Eastwich. The blue in the
sky may not be as deep, nor reach away so far before the wandering eye. In Eastwich one can hear
the lowing of the cattle in the meadows, the song of
the birds in the trees, the hum of life which rises
out of the ground, the rustle of the leaves as they are
played upon by the myriad-fingered wind, and yet
amid all a Sabbath stillness rests upon everything.
The stream which throws itself over the rocks down
by the paper mill is less noisy than on other days.
The horses in the mill stables stand in their stalls
with the solemnity of a Scottish kirk elder of the
olden time. The bell from the white-painted church
with the Corinthian columns sends out its mellow
notes far across the listening hills, only adding to the
holy quiet of the place. The cemetery, so beautifully
calm on other days, now seems to be resting under
the hush of eternity.

But while in New York we cannot have this expressive stillness, for there are too many of us to be
all quiet at the same time, yet there are Sunday
mornings when even this great city seems under a
spell of rest and peace.

It was on one of these mornings John Disney said
to Madge :

" Suppose this morning we go to the Mission, then
after service take lunch with Dunbar. You know
we have been promising this for a long time."

By this time we have all discovered that Madge
Disney was a fairly easy and self-possessed young
lady ; not so stately as Ethel Brompton, not so ter-

ribly frank as Janet, not so cold as Anita Von der Plonk, but as well balanced as any of them.

How, then, happened it that the simple mention of Hugh Dunbar's name affected her as it did? We admit that the effect was felt more than seen, reminding one of an inward and spiritual grace rather than an outward and visible sign. An onlooker, after John had made his suggestion, might have seen her eyes shine; but it must be remembered that her eyes were always bright. A little bit of color might also be noticed; but anyone's color may heighten at times.

But there was something the onlooker could not see—a peculiar heart throb; a quick, keen sense of delicious pain; a soul tumult, as if the spirit, like a bird, was frightened in its cage and was fluttering helplessly against the imprisoning wires.

Up to the time of her first meeting with Hugh Dunbar, on that eventful Saturday afternoon nearly a year ago, it was tacitly understood between the Brompton and the Disney households that Madge and Percy in due time would arrive at an understanding mutually agreeable.

In many respects Percy Brompton would have been an admirable husband for Madge. Under her guidance and with her ambitions as an incentive Percy might have developed into something really worthy. But it is always unfortunate when a woman cannot look up to a man as a lover, for she rarely ever can look up to the same man as a husband. The woman who is conscious of her superiority at the start seldom loses that consciousness. Now this in

itself may be a pleasant feeling, but it is not love in
anything like its highest form. Love is a passion, a
splendid passion, honoring the one to whom it gives
itself. It carries that one to the mountain heights of
the soul; the sky of the heart is flooded with trans-
figuring light, and in that light the loved one lives
with a glory almost divine. But Madge could not
do this with Percy Brompton. And now that Hugh
Dunbar had come into her life, to think of Percy
as more than a mere friend was impossible, for
there was something singularly attractive about
Hugh Dunbar. He was unlike—altogether unlike—
the other young men of her acquaintance. His unselfishness, his devotion to his work, his fearlessness,
his strength of character, she could not but recognize,
so that he had come to be a very prominent figure in
her thoughts.

Still, though she admired him, confessing to herself the extraordinary influence which he exercised
over her, yet her mind was by no means clear.
Madge was an ambitious young woman, with leanings
to social prestige as well as social enjoyment. The
life to which Hugh Dunbar had devoted himself was
not the one she would have chosen for him. With
his conceded abilities and social rank he might easily
attain the highest dignity in the Church. Had she
expressed her real wish she would have preferred a
political career for him, but now that the matter was
decided she could see a vast difference between a
clergyman in a wealthy city parish and one working
over in the slums among all sorts of people. And
already she was aware that this work of his was

not taken up for a time, but one to which he had given his life. Madge was quite worldly in her way. She was a thorough Gothamite. She enjoyed the week of the Horse Show; she was partial to smart gowns and becoming hats; she liked going out to balls and receptions and parties. It was an article in her creed to see the best there was at the theaters and hear the best there was of the operas. She was by no means either romantic or sentimental. She admitted, of course, that poor people had claims, and that it was beautiful of Mr. Dunbar to espouse their cause as he did. Still, so far, no sense of personal duty had come to her.

But as she stood there in the hall waiting for John—she was ready first, an unusual circumstance, in all truth—she did not show any marks of inward disturbance, looking rather like a picture of womanly peace and feminine contentment.

With that instinctive sense of the proprieties which is common to every genuine woman, her costume was very unobtrusive. So far as apparel was concerned no one would have taken her as belonging to the smartest set in the city. Still there was something in her face and bearing which removed her quite a distance from Mrs. Silas Smithers. A brisk walk of about ten minutes brought them over to Second Avenue, where they took the "Elevated," which rapidly carried them downtown. Going to a mission church in the lower part of the city on a Sunday morning was a new experience with Madge. It was almost as novel as that Coney Island trip. Indeed, the feeling was very much the same. Looking out of the car window, she noticed the immense numbers of people on the avenue and side streets. She saw also that most of the small stores were open and that Sunday had but scant recognition. As they went farther down she could not fail but observe conditions of life which she had never imagined in her native city.

With her Sunday was usually a very quiet day. In the morning she went to church with her mother. In the afternoon she read a little, but wrote more, as this was a good chance to catch up with her correspondence. In the evening a few friends dropped in, so that the time was taken up some way. Sunday, however, was not a red-letter day in the Disney household. It was therefore a great surprise for Madge to see how the day was spent on the East Side.

"John," she asked, with a more serious face than she usually wore, "are there no churches in this part of the city?"

"A few," answered John, "but very few."

"And yet the other evening Dr. Bland said there were too many churches in New York."

"Too many in certain parts of New York, but certainly not too many over here."

"How, then, about libraries and schools, and things of that sort?"

"They are no more numerous than the churches. There are serious conditions over here. Dunbar is on the right track. But what can one man do in such multitudes as these?"

Madge said nothing, but looked out of the car window with even deeper interest than before. John's mention of Dunbar's name once more heightened her color and gave a clearer light to her eyes.

In due season they reached the Mission church, where Madge saw a very different people from those with whom she was wont to meet on Sunday morning. And yet that difference was in raiment only, not in heart. They were the same people after all— the same sins, the same struggles, the same temptations, the same sorrows. In his way Silas Smithers was living the same life as Mark Brompton; Mrs. Smithers the same as Mrs. Von der Plonk. But Madge this morning did not think much of either gowns or bonnets. Far more serious matters had taken possession of her. This service had other meanings than an aisle march, with a rivalry of texture and color.

19

CHAPTER XXXI.

Dixon Faber: Boy and Man.

MISS POLLOK yet remained in that splendid
altitude of soul which enabled her to continue her attentions to the piano of Mrs.
Gubbins, making it her heart confidant and friend.
Nor could she have chosen a friend more ready or
responsive. It is true that Miss Pollok had deserted
the piano for months, ignoring its very existence,
yet with that royalty of forgiveness for which all
great natures are noted, pianos especially, it most generously pardoned this unkind neglect. Yea, it went
far beyond the limits of mere pardon, for in its intense
desire to share the heart yearnings of Miss Pollok it
strained even to breaking some of the most sensitive
cords of its being. Hence there were notes in the
keyboard of its sympathies whose feelings were too
deep for utterance. And then, as if to show how its
whole nature was affected, the poor, broken wires lay
prone and helpless across such other wires as yet
remained in place, transmitting to them tones of vary-
ing mystery and cadence. Under these sympathetic
relations Miss Pollok could not but pour out of her
strong, heroic soul chords and harmonies expressive
of the profoundest emotions.

The artist, going up stairs one evening, ventured to
remark to Mr. Wright, who was also going up stairs,
that the piano was "a little off color." As an artist,

his use of this expression was quite natural. The reply of Mr. Wright, however, cannot be so easily explained : "'A little off color' is good." He contrived, though, in some way, a stage trick most likely, to make his meaning clear, for Mr. Singleton, Mr. Faber, and Edward Vaughen, who heard both the remark and the reply, smiled in a large, opulent way. At that moment Miss Pollok warbled, "In the gloaming, O my darling," when another smile of even more ample dimensions was distributed among the group, Edward's share occupying his undivided energies all the way to his room.

Edward had just received a letter from his mother. As he reads it, with his permission, we will peep over his shoulder :

"EASTWICH, Jan. 28, 189-.

... "You are a good boy to write so regularly and at such length, but then you surely know how much your letters are to me. I am here all alone, but not alone in any morbid sense, for I have you even more constantly in my thought than when you were here in the home. The miles may separate us in body, but spirit life knows no separations.

"Then in you and through you I am having my part in the joy as well as the strife of the great world. My larger life is now being lived by you. When you are true I am true ; when you are worthy and upright I am the same. The life that you are living is my life, only in another form. The mother never dies so long as her children live. ...

"Coming so soon after your conversation with your Uncle Mark, it was singular that you should have

gone to the office that night. These impressions of
ours are strange things. Often I find myself wondering how far we are influenced by forces which are
purely spiritual.

"Two things, however, occur to me as to Dr.
Disney being in the office that night. It may be
that he was there in the interest of a patient who had
intrusted some confidential matters to his care—not
an uncommon thing ; or it may be that he had some
business affairs of his own, for which he could not
find any other time. Still, I confess—"

"May I come in ?" It was Mr. Faber who spoke,
nor did he wait for any formal reply. The young
men by this time had established the most friendly
relations, coming in and going out of each other's
rooms with scant ceremony.

"Singleton gone out?" Faber queried, but not
before he had filled his pipe out of Edward's jar, tilting his chair back to a satisfactory angle, making
himself as comfortable as timid, modest, unobtrusive
reporters care to do.

"Yes ; he said he had a ward meeting to attend."

"Singleton has been going out a good deal this
winter," Faber observed, in a contemplative sort of
way. "Is he much in politics?"

"I think he is chairman or secretary of some committee, though I don't know just what."

"Anything in my line, I wonder? You know all
is grist that comes to my mill."

"Why don't you ask him? Singleton's a good
fellow, and will help you if he can."

"For that matter, all politicians are good fellows. Politics, though, is only a game, and the politician plays it—heads I win, tails you lose."

Faber smiled softly, but not innocently, for he was a reporter on the *Trombone*, which implies that he knew better than to always come in when it rained, but to stay out sometimes and hear what the raindrops were saying.

"But, my dear fellow, what has Singleton to gain? So far as I can see, he is giving his service without recompense or even hope of reward."

"Vaughen, there are times when I have wished for a lawnmower which could be applied to individuals. The superfluous verdancy with which some people are burdened is something remarkable. According to your notions, Singleton is a patriot. He is working solely in the interests of his country. His one thought is the welfare of this city. This is beautiful; it is noble. Singleton should have a monument. All of which proves that if that lawnmower was within reach I could use it to advantage."

"'Superfluous verdancy' in the vernacular is 'uncommonly green,'" laughed Edward. "Still, you must admit that luxurious, succulent grass is much better than wizened, dried-up herbage, for that is useless to either man or beast."

"O, if you mean to consider yourself as pasturage for sheep to nibble or cows to munch, undoubtedly. Remember, though, that the nibbling and the munching come out of you. Now, in New York a man who is green enough for pasturage is a good deal of a curiosity, but he never lasts longer than one season.

Your sentiments are worthy of that mighty city of Eastwich, with its vast population of nearly a thousand people, with its noble Board of Selectmen, who at times have the soul-absorbing problem of a new handle for the town pump or a larger lock for the pound gate. In this town the politician is simply a man with a scheme. That is all there is of it. But won't you please pass the jar? When a weary man undertakes the sublime task of enlightening such benighted creatures as you are he might be asked to take a pipe of tobacco."

Mr. Faber proceeded to renew his pipe in the inner man. He liked Edward's tobacco, and said that "for a country coot Vaughen put up quite a mixture."

Faber's father died when Dixon was a little bit of a fellow, leaving a heart-broken widow with three small children, Dixon being the eldest. It was a sad, desolate house to which Mrs. Faber returned on the afternoon of her husband's funeral. A few of the neighbors had thoughtfully prepared supper, remaining also a little while, so as to break up the evening; but after they had gone the burden of Mrs. Faber's grief came upon her in all its force. Mr. Faber, a steady, industrious mechanic, had been sick for some time, so that the little savings were entirely exhausted. There was nothing left; even the funeral expenses had yet to be met.

Dixon did not say much that evening, but somehow there came to him the feeling that he was now, in part, at any rate, the head of the house. The very next day he was at the ferry, for the Fabers lived in

Brooklyn, and before supper time had sold two good-sized bundles of papers. Early on the following morning he started out to build up a paper route, calling mostly upon those who knew his father and mother. He was more successful than he had hoped, but then the poor are always the best friends of the poor. Every morning, from this time on, Dixon, though not quite ten years old, went around with his papers, having a route that took fully two hours to cover. Then in the afternoon he had his stand at the ferry house, where his bright, cheery face soon became familiar. As people came to know him and something of what he was doing, he acquired a line of steady patronage, so that he could almost depend upon a regular income. The men who distributed the papers took quite an interest in the little fellow, putting certain favors in his way, which helped him materially.

At first his mother went out by the day, doing such work as she could find, but this was a most inconvenient arrangement, for it left Tim and Mab at home by themselves. The other people who lived in the house, especially Hans Christian's wife, did what they could for the little ones, yet it was agreed on all sides that they were too young to be left in this way. Dixon determined, therefore, to open a little store, with his mother in charge, adding to the store such things as might find a ready sale.

The newspaper men, hearing of this, took the matter up, subscribing various amounts, so that one day the managing editor of the *Bassoon* called the boy into the office, and in behalf of his staff presented him with a cash capital of twenty dollars to start the concern. With this goodly sum in hand, as well as a line of credit, which he was careful not to abuse, the little store was opened under very favorable auspices. The lad prospered, so that in due time he put an extra boy on his morning paper route, then another, finally having half a dozen of them. Business kept on increasing; he therefore gave up his place at the ferry, though supplying it through another boy, he finding it more profitable to remain at the store, where he prepared the papers for the afternoon and evening delivery.

By this time Tim had grown to be quite a boy, just as Mab had grown to be quite a girl, so he gradually worked them into the business, which they soon learned to manage very nicely.

Then he went to the foreman of the *Bassoon*, applying for a place in the printing department. Not long after he was chosen for the high and honorable position of " printer's devil," from which elevation he descended, however, to a place at case work.

The store now supported the family, for Mrs. Faber was a most thrifty, prudent woman ; hence what Dixon earned, after paying his share of the home expenses, he laid aside for the purpose of a college course in the years to come.

Meantime he took up a line of home studies, working even harder than when he first started on his paper route. One of the reporters, a Columbia man, and a whole-hearted, noble fellow, took quite an interest in Dixon, coaching him most generously, so that when he was about eighteen, perhaps nineteen, he entered the New York University. While here he wrote two or three bright things for the *Trombone*, whereupon the city editor dropped him a line with a request to call. This he did, but not without a letter from his good friend, the managing editor of the *Bassoon*. The interview was satisfactory, and Dixon became not only college correspondent, but a regular contributor as well.

As a further result of this interview he was brought into relations with some out-of-town papers, so that he was able substantially to pay his way in college. This allowed his savings to go to an increase of the business at the store, for that now had become quite a concern. He retained his position on the *Trombone*, and at the time of our first meeting him was one of the most trusted writers on the staff. He boarded at the house of Mrs. Gubbins, as it was important for him to be in the city most of the time. Still he made regular and frequent visits to his Brooklyn home. He was a bright, wide-awake fellow, able to give "pointers" to even Wall Street men; while he knew more in five minutes of city affairs than most of the politicians would know in five years.

Having relighted as well as refilled his pipe, he proceeded :

" Now, Singleton is doing one of two things—either turning the grindstone for some one or having some one turn the grindstone for him. What men are after in this town is not honor, but shekels. The average politician is ready to lie, cheat, bribe, make

promises, sell out his friends, commit almost any
crime short of murder, so as to get what he wants.
The more I know of politics the more I am reminded
of that scene on the mountain where the tempter
says to the Man, 'All these will I give thee if thou
wilt fall down and worship me.' Now, that may be
poetry; some people think it is. It may be an
oriental parable; some people think it is; but it is
New York life nevertheless. Why, I have known
men for the sake of such kingdoms of the world as
are represented by a seat in Congress or the Senate
or an ambassadorship, all the way down to some petty
office in the city, sell out everything that was good
in themselves, and simply grovel at the feet of the
one who had these prizes to dispose of."

We would be doing Mr. Faber an injustice if we
did not say that this lengthy speech of his was not
given as it appears in print. Here it is in solid,
unpicturesque type, whereas in speaking to Edward
he puffed it out with mouthfuls of smoke. He
jerked it out in oracular fragments. He pulled it
out in lengths as parlor magicians do narrow strips
of paper. Mr. Faber was not an orator. He was
versatile, though.

"By the way, Vaughen, Mr. Mark Brompton is
your uncle?"

"He is."

"Keen & Sharp, your employers, are his agents
and brokers?"

"They are."

"Well, they are now at work on a scheme to get
control of a railroad in which Mr. Brompton is

heavily interested. If they are successful they will make it lively for your worthy uncle."

" How did you hear of this ?" Edward asked, with an excitement which he made no attempt to conceal.

" The question is not how did I hear of it, but has Mr. Brompton heard of it ? The best thing for you to do is to go right uptown, see Mr. Brompton, find out if he knows anything of it; if not, put him on his guard."

It was not long before Edward was on his way to Mark Brompton's, taking the " Elevated " at Eighth Street station. To his great relief, when he arrived he learned that his uncle was at home and in the library.

" And so they thought to catch me napping," he said, after Edward had told him what he had heard. " Tell Mr. Faber I am very much obliged to him. I have known of this, however, for some time."

Edward thought this a favorable opportunity to speak of the evening when he went downtown and saw Dr. Disney in the office with Keen & Sharp. Mr. Brompton listened with the deepest interest, questioning Edward closely as to the date and his certainty that it was really Dr. Disney. No amount of questioning, however, could shake his statement, for he was so certain as to leave no room for doubt.

"I am sorry if Keen & Sharp have led Dr. Disney into this affair, for he can't afford to lose much money, which Keen & Sharp know just as well as I do."

Edward looked surprised.

" Dr. Disney is by no means as well off as people

imagine. He has a large practice, and he deserves
it, for he is a splendid physician ; but, poor fellow,
he is dabbling in stocks all the time. Within the
last two years he must have been all cleaned out.
Two or three times the market went dead against
him. I don't really know how he pulled through."

"Is he aware that you know of his speculations ?"

"O no! He will sometimes, after taking my pulse
and putting his ear down to my heart, tell me that
Wall Street is too much for me, while at the same
time he is under a far heavier strain than I am. I
cannot but admire his pluck. Fine fellow his son
John is."

Edward launched out, young man fashion, on the
various good qualities of John Disney, a theme upon
which he could always be eloquent.

"What does he mean by clerking in the rolling
mills ?" Mr. Brompton asked.

"I think he intends to go into the business himself. This will give him a chance to learn something of it."

"You believe, then, he is serious in this move ?"

"Most assuredly. He told me you were interested
in the concern, one of the directors."

"That is true."

"Well, my dear uncle, let me just say that in three
months' time John Disney will know more about the
Hematite Rolling Mills and Tubal-Cain Iron Works'
than all the directors on the board, excepting yourself, of course."

"You needn't except me, and even then he
wouldn't know much. I attend a directors' meeting

once a month. It lasts an hour. During that hour we listen to some reports, pass on some bills, transact some formal business, then adjourn. I know nothing about the concern, nor do I wish to know. All I care to have out of it is a good fat dividend."

Mr. Brompton, as he spoke, went over to his desk, which gave Edward a chance to leave.

Mr. Brompton then renewed his thanks to Mr. Faber, which Edward promised to convey, and the young man was soon on his way to the home of Mrs. Gubbins.

CHAPTER XXXII.

Ethel Brompton's Choice.

HENDRIK VON DER PLONK has not, so far, been a prominent figure in these pages. Indeed, his name has been mentioned only once, and then in but an incidental way. This, however, was not with the intent of keeping Mr. Von der Plonk within permanent shadow of the "wings," while others held the center of the stage. The fact is, the time had not yet come for him to take his place close up to the footlights, where he could be seen and heard by all in the house. Thus far, therefore, he has been very much in the background, only a sort of stage dummy, just to fill in what otherwise would be a blank space. Stage dummies, however, are useful in their way. What chances, too, they have of seeing things and saying things as they stand in little knots and groups on different parts of the stage !

For some time, even before the opening of our story, Hendrik Von der Plonk had been quite marked in his attentions to Ethel Brompton. So definite and pointed were these attentions that it was generally understood among the Gothamites that there would be a wedding in the course of time.

He had met her at a charity ball, where she looked uncommonly well in what was anything but a charity gown. She wore diamonds on her neck and in her hair, which were not bought at a charity bureau, and

she disported herself in a way which would not suggest a heart breaking with sympathy for the poor.
Nevertheless it was a charity ball, for the proceeds,
after certain expenses were paid, were given to some
deserving cause.   " Cause " in these instances should
always be put either in capitals or italics.

It would be a vulgar impertinence for anyone to
ask what the net proceeds were, or what special fund
was enriched by such offerings.   The idea of making
common, sordid, commercial inquiries in matters of
this sort is simply preposterous.   Rather let us think
of the comfort that the mere fact in itself brings to
the poor.   Just to know that Ethel Brompton, with
scores, perhaps hundreds, of her class, spent a whole
night dancing any number of times, eating any number of ices, having supper somewhere between midnight and morning, wearing a gown that cost a little
fortune in itself, and doing all this for the sake of
sweet charity, is surely enough, without going into
such vulgar details as to how much money was made
or who got it.   What if there is no money made ?—
which is often the case.   The charity ball has been
given, and the upper-class Gothamites have met all
the proper demands.

Mr. Von der Plonk was not an eminent success as
a dancing man.   Even his best friends said so; but
what was still more singular, he said so himself.
This simple circumstance in itself, not the fact that
he could not dance well, but that he knew it and
acknowledged it, at once gave him high rank.
Indeed, there were those who spoke of him as an extraordinary man.

Nor was he a special success as a society man.
Here again his best friends said so, but here he dif-
fered with them out and out. The difference of opinion, however, was merely one of standpoint. Some
people think that to achieve social success one needs
to be bright, witty, say sharp things, do smart things,
thus compelling a certain measure of attention. This
was not Mr. Von der Plonk's idea at all. He thought
when he went to a dinner and ate heartily, hardly
even speaking to his neighbors on either side, when
he made the round of "afternoons" and "evenings,"
putting in just so much time in each place, that he
had done his whole duty. He therefore regarded
himself as a bright and shining light in the social
world.

But most assuredly he was not a literary man.
Once at Fitz Noodle's he took in to dinner a Boston
girl. She was on familiar terms with Browning,
knew Longfellow by heart, could quote Whittier in
yard lengths, regarded the "Autocrat" of Holmes
as another gospel, and simply reveled in Emerson.
O the hopeless look on that girl's face long before
Mrs. Fitz Noodle gave the retiring signal!

But we are not to infer that there was anything
the matter with Von der Plonk. He ate well; he
slept well; he had a big, strong, healthy body; his
habits were fairly good; indeed, in many respects he
was to be envied. Mammas having daughters on
hand regarded him with favor. Daughters, old
enough to get along without mammas, thought kindly
of him. Widows, upon whose once sorrow-stricken
hearts time had wrought its consoling miracle, looked

upon him with yearning approval. The mere incident that he was clay all the way from his feet to his head—dull, heavy, opaque clay; clay without anything of soul or spirit, absolutely void of real life—did not seem to affect his social prestige in the least.

Of course he had money—much money, a great deal of money—which possibly had something to do with his general popularity.

"Ethel," said Janet, one night, as they were languidly laying aside the robes with which in the early evening they had gone forth from conquering to conquer, "what are you going to do with Von der Plonk?"

The disrobing process had reached that stage when Ethel might sit down in comparative ease. Ethel possessed much of her mother's stateliness, for she was tall and of fine figure. Handsome gowns were becoming to her, which is not the case with everyone. Ethel liked handsome gowns just as well as they liked her. Still, when one has been on dress parade for several hours under inspection by staff officers, both male and female, an easy chair in one's bedroom has much in its favor. So she sat down, and deliberately, Janet meantime waiting for an answer to her question.

"I hardly know what you mean," she was beginning, in her cold, distinct way, when Janet interrupted her with:

"You know very well what I mean, Ethel, and there isn't any use in your fencing and quibbling."

" Supposing I do ; is that any reason for either your asking such a question or my answering it?"

20

Ethel's face had now the same set, stern look which might often be seen on her father's.

"Now, Ethel, see here. You and I are sisters, and while we often have our little bickerings and differences, yet we are very fond of each other. You know just as well as that you are sitting in that chair that Hendrik Von der Plonk means one of these days to ask you to marry him. My question is, what are you going to say in reply?"

"I wish, Janet, you would let my affairs alone; besides, it will be time enough when Mr. Von der Plonk has spoken."

Ethel now turned her face to the fire, looking sadly and earnestly at some pictures which she saw in the blazing coals.

"And I should like to know why I should not trouble myself with your affairs," was the quick reply of Janet, though without the least anger or impatience. "You are my only sister. You are the closest and best friend I have in the world. I am interested in you, just as you are in me, and in a matter of this kind a nice sister I would be if I was not concerned."

"Then if Mr. Von der Plonk asks me the question you suggest there is but one answer which I can give," said Ethel, speaking in a low, sad tone, still looking into the fire, but keeping her face partly hidden from Janet.

Neither of the girls spoke for some time—Ethel busy with her fire pictures, Janet turning over the pages of a magazine which she had taken from the table. But though they sat opposite each other by the cheerful fire, their chairs but a few feet apart, neither one was really there.

Through the blaze and glow, as gateways of flame, Ethel's thoughts had gone thousands of miles. Through the pictures on the page, as mysterious doors, Janet's thoughts had gone thousands of miles. Their thoughts, however, had not gone in opposite directions, but like "homing" pigeons set free from a ship in midocean, each had flown in line with the other, each coming to the same destination.

"Won't you wait for me, Ethel?" pleaded David Stanley, as fine a young fellow as one would ask to see.

In some way, through Percy, Stanley had met Ethel, and at once fell in love with her. He was a great-natured, generous fellow, not shrewd, perhaps, with less unscrupulous ambition, possibly, than many, but just the kind of a young man to whom a girl's pure heart would go out with all its wealth of affection. Ethel became deeply interested in David, allowing matters to go so far that David finally asked her to wait for him, when he would be ready to offer her a home. There was no pledge, no form of engagement; she would not allow him to speak to her father or even make a confidant of Percy. So far as either of them was concerned there was nothing but a vague understanding. David went to South America to take charge of some matters in which the firm with which he was connected had important interests, where he expected to remain for two or three years. Nothing was said as to what might happen when he returned; still, there were certain hopes in his heart

which made the thought of coming back very pleasant to him.

Mrs. Brompton saw more of what was going on
than anyone imagined, but she was far too shrewd to
attempt anything by way of opposition. Unless one
is prepared by sheer strength of wind to blow a fire
right out the best thing is not to blow it at all. At
certain stages even a breath will fan the smoldering
embers, kindling into new life that which was surely
dying. Hence Mrs. Brompton spoke pleasantly of
David Stanley. She even sympathized with the poverty of his prospects, regretting that there was so
little chance of his ever getting on. After a time she
went so far as to pity him, intimating that Mr.
Brompton had a poor opinion of his business ability ;
that the probabilities were against him ever rising
higher than a clerkship, and that he would most
likely remain in South America.

Mrs. Brompton's method of putting out the fire
was to throw on a large quantity of hard coal, which
weighted down the little life below so that it could
not find any outlet. Then, when she was perfectly
certain of the results, she raked and poked until even
the hot ashes fell through, leaving nothing but the
cold, shining coal to fill up the grate.

Then in that delicate, motherly way of hers she
spoke of young Von der Plonk, but she was careful
not to throw him at Ethel's head.

Mrs. Brompton probably knew nothing of the
mysteries of chess, or the importance of seeming to
play the game on one part of the board when in
reality the game is on another part. But this was

just what she was doing. Using Von der Plonk as the "king," she showed how strong was the attack of certain of Ethel's friends : how Miss Fitz Noodle smirked and smiled when his name was linked with hers ; how Mrs. Harlem, a heartless widow, though not yet twenty-five, was making a dead set for him. In this way and in others she led Ethel to that side of the board, calling her off from the real point of the game. Chess, whether played with boxwood pieces or things of flesh and blood, is capable of fine strategy, though, after all, the game usually comes to the one who makes the fewest mistakes. Mrs. Brompton may not have been either brilliant or daring in her play, but she seldom made mistakes.

The result was that Hendrik Von der Plonk had been practically accepted by Ethel. Only the formalities remained.

"And what will you do with David Stanley?" Janet said, after a long pause.

"What have I to do with David Stanley?" Ethel questioned, in turn, now turning her face from the fire and looking almost angrily at Janet.

"He may think that you have something to do with him. You know better far than I do that he has a right to think so."

Janet answered with frank fearlessness ; perhaps indignation would be a better term, for she was angry with Ethel.

The sisters soon parted for the night—Janet going to her room much troubled about her sister, still able to sleep a sweet, pure, healthy sleep, rising in the morning with clear eyes and light heart ; Ethel going to her room not to sleep at all, only to spend the night in tearless agony.

Mr. Faber, had he known as much of the Brompton household as he did of politics, could easily have added to his chapter on " The Kingdoms of the World " and the crowds who worship at the altar of ambition. For here was Ethel Brompton deliberately putting aside the love of a good, true man to obtain simply a wealth upon which her soul was set.

The next morning when Ethel came down to breakfast she was very pale and had heavy rings under her eyes. Her mouth, though, was firmly set, and the determined look was on her face.

That evening Hendrik Von der Plonk asked her to marry him, and she consented to do so.

CHAPTER XXXIII.

John Disney Hits Hard.

JOHN DISNEY'S scheme, though well meant, was, after all, more romantic than practical. What could he really learn of the hard, narrow life of the average workman by the plan he proposed? Suppose he did get up early in the morning, being at his office in time to see the men begin the work of the day. Suppose he did remain at his post until the last workman had left the premises and the place was put in charge of the night watchman. Suppose he did try in every possible way to bring himself into close touch with all classes of the men and make his life almost a part of theirs. What was gained? Nothing of any moment. John Disney was not required, when his day's work was done, to trudge wearily to some cheap tenement of two or three small rooms in some crowded, common neighborhood, where the evening and the night would be spent under the most barren conditions. Neither could he put himself in the place of some of these men who would go home to a sick wife or a sick child, remaining all night at the bedside of the poor sufferer, snatching now and then a few minutes of disjointed sleep, then on the morrow weary and jaded begin the work of another day.

Nor was he compelled when Saturday came to distribute his wages over the wants of a household, so much for rent, so much for coal, so much for food, so much for clothing, only to find that with the utmost care many things were unprovided for.

Nor did any inexorable law demand that he—in hot weather or cold weather, in dark winter's morning or glare of summer noon, whether sick or well, whether glad or broken-hearted—should answer the merciless call of the steam whistle; then, having answered the call, work all day long, just as one of the machines in the mill. The monotony, the dull, wearisome routine, the drudgery, the sense of a labor from which there is no escape, the terrible hopelessness of it all—these were the things John Disney could not know.

Still, in himself certain good was being done. He was acquiring a broader humanity. His sympathies were deepening as well as becoming more genuine. A truer sense of brotherhood was being developed. The hundreds of men who came in and out every day were creatures of flesh and blood, each the center of a little world of his own.

The first one to attract him especially was Fred Sauvier. This, however, was only natural, seeing they were in the same office, and their work brought them into familiar contact. Fred had charge of the "time" of the men—no small matter in an establishment so large as this one. The "time" was taken from the books of the foremen in the several departments, every hour on or off meaning just so much in the wages of the men.

Evan Evans was a hard-working fellow, who could ill afford to lose that half day when he overslept him-

self because he had been up nearly all the night before with his sick boy. But when Saturday came the
half day was gone from his pay, leaving the little
family with so much less to live on.

Dennis Doolin must needs attend the funeral of
Michael Muldoon, for was not the late Mr. Muldoon
"the broth av a bhoy" as well as "all the way from
Galway?" Grief, though, is an expensive luxury, for
when Dennis received his wages on the following
pay day a whole day was gone, much to the regret
of Mrs. Doolin.

Pietro Farino is so eminently religious that quite
frequently a saint's day demands his pious recognition. His absence, though regretted, is carefully remembered. He therefore eats less onions and mac-
aroni for some days to come.

Tommy Jones thinks the sun rises but rarely
sets on Belinda Smith. He is saving up his extra
earnings with which to buy an imposing bracelet for
her birthday. The two hours overtime which he put
in every evening for a week is charged faithfully to
his credit. His name, then, on the next pay day, if
written according to his feelings, would be Thomas
Jones, Esq.

To keep the "time" was a work of much responsibility. Such a man could easily be dishonest. He
might secure for himself favor with the men. To
go shares would not be a difficult arrangement, mark-
ing men "in" when they were "out;" for such things
have been done not only in mills and machine shops,
but in other places as well.

But Fred Sauvier was of the rigidly honest type.

He would put a mark against himself with even less
hesitation than against Dennis Doolin or Pietro Farino. Consequently there was a little handful of
men who looked upon him in the light of a mortal
enemy ; for there are some who believe that corporations have no souls, and may be robbed without breach
of any known commandment.

John Disney found Sauvier to be an active, intelligent, and fairly ambitious young fellow. Sauvier
had no definite idea as to who John Disney really
was, for though it was through Mark Brompton his
place in the office had been secured, yet that meant
nothing, as it was always by the influence of some of
the directors that the clerks were engaged.

They were about closing up the work for the day,
and had a few minutes of comparatively idle time.
They chatted, therefore, as young men will.

"I have been here several years," Sauvier said, in
reply to a question of John. "I got in as an errand
boy ; after some time I was put in the office, so gradually I have crept along."

"You have seen a good many changes since you
came in ? "

" Yes, a good many."

" For the better ? "

"No, I can't say that. When I first came here
this was an individual concern. Mr. Mallable was
the owner—a fine, generous-hearted man who had
worked his way up from 'puddling.' He knew
every man in the place, could call them by name and
was interested in them. They say that there wasn't
a strike or any kind of a disagreement for the whole

thirty years that he ran the concern. His daughter, the only child he had, married a Mr. Bessemer, who, at Mr. Mallable's death, about five years ago, succeeded to the business. Shortly after Mr. Bessemer turned the concern into a stock company. Since then things haven't been the same."

"In what way? I should have thought that a stock company bringing in fresh capital would have built up the business."

"One would think so at first, but you see Mr. Bessemer sold out at a very high valuation, so dividends had then to be made on the whole amount."

"I am afraid I don't quite get your meaning."

"Then let me explain. Mr. Mallable regarded the concern—machinery, buildings, trade, good-will, the whole plant in short—as worth about half a million. When he made anything like a fair profit on that amount he was perfectly satisfied. Now, Mr. Bessemer sold the concern to the new company for a million. Consequently it had to make twice as much as before so as to keep up the old rate of profits."

"O, I see. If the old concern after paying expenses made, say, thirty thousand a year, the new concern had to make sixty thousand out of the same actual capital."

"Exactly; which meant all kinds of economies, scaling down wages, scrimping in work, using all sorts of odds and ends, and not turning out anything like the quality of stuff as in Mr. Mallable's time."

"The concern, though, is running full time?"

"Yes, but it is not the kind of work that really pays."

" You mean, then, that the outlook for this concern is not very good?"

" Well, I hardly know just how to put it. You see, now that the concern is a corporation, there is no individual responsibility one way or the other. What the directors care for is dividends. What the men care for is wages. Each is thinking of himself; neither is thinking of the others. When orders are coming in with a rush the men strike for higher wages. When trade slacks off the directors cut the wages down. There is no such thing in this establishment as master and man. The master is simply a calculating machine, the man a working machine."

" But in these days business has taken on such larger forms that we require the corporation."

" I don't know about that," replied Sauvier, gathering up some books that were on his desk, preparatory to putting them in the office safe; " there is usually some one man at the head of every concern, whether it be a corporation or not. But the fact is when a man has a nice business he is not content with a fair living. He turns it into a stock company. He makes himself president, his eldest son vice-president, and so on down the list on both sides of the house. The result is that the men's wages are cut down to meet the big salaries of a lot of officials."

" Then you don't like the present condition of things," said John Disney, turning from the wash-bowl in the corner of the office where he had been washing his hands, and was now drying them off on a coarse towel.

" Frankly, I do not," Sauvier responded. " The

only people who do are the officials and their
friends."

The office which Fred Sauvier and John Disney
occupied was, perhaps, as much of a gatehouse as
an office, the main office being quite a pretentious
affair.

The chief clerks in the main office were very important individuals. Mr. Falcon, the head book-
keeper, condescended to appear every morning about
ten o'clock, then remaining with more or less regularity until two or even three. This was very kind of
Mr. Falcon, seeing that he was married to a sister of
one of the directors. Mr. Stubbs, the cashier, was
equally as gracious, and as he was the nephew of the
president of the company the very fact that he came
to the office at all was an act of the most extreme
courtesy. Mr. Stafford, to whom was intrusted
most of the general correspondence, and whose signature at the foot of a typewritten document was
magnificently illegible, enjoyed the distinction of
being the son-in-law of the vice-president. Mr.
Stafford's duties were not arduous ; his salary,
though, was based on the general principle in such
cases—the less work the more pay. All told, there
were ten of them in the main office. Under these
was a little army of junior clerks, typewriters, down
to office boys.

"That Disney fellow is rather airy, is he not?"
said Mr. Stubbs to Mr. Falcon, as he somewhat
languidly laid down the morning paper, though not
before he had read the racing and theatrical news, for
Mr. Stubbs had sporting tendencies.

"You mean the Pill Box over there in the gate-house?" replied Mr. Falcon, who had heard in an incidental way that John Disney's father was a doctor. He assumed that the practice was limited and that the new clerk was eking out the family income. "For a ten-dollar craft he carries altogether too much sail."

Mr. Falcon was the owner of a tenth in a cat-boat. His use of nautical terms was, therefore, quite natural, as well as proper.

"I should say so!" said Mr. Stafford, looking up from a letter which he was writing, said letter, how-ever, having no reference to the business of the firm, being a crushing and masterly reply to his tailor, who had the impudence to ask him for payment of a bill when it was only two years due. "I went in to that cubby-hole yesterday to get him to do an errand for me, and the fellow refused point-blank. Indeed, he even suggested in the most lordly way that he was not hired to do that kind of work. A hint to the V. P. will—"

Mr. Stafford did not say what the hint would bring forth, but resumed his writing. Mr. Stubbs once more took up the morning paper, this time giving his undivided energies to the baseball column. Mr. Falcon proceeded to draw a rough sketch of a proposed boathouse which he intended to submit to the Cutty Hunk Yacht Club. Thus went on the hard, grinding work of these sons of toil, who were also sons-in-law of directors and shareholders.

John Disney, remarkable as it may seem, was not affected by the haughty bearing of these august and imposing personages, but went on with a serenity which they could not understand.

On this particular evening after Fred Sauvier had set the safe "combination," and the office generally had been put to rights, it was about time for the night watchman to come.

"How careful Wilkins is not to arrive a minute before his time!" John said, somewhat impatiently. He had an engagement that evening to go out with Madge, so was anxious to get away.

"No more careful than we are not to remain a minute after our time," was the smiling response of Sauvier. "You see how this illustrates our conversation."

"You have had your innings so far," said John, who was a very Scotchman in his love of an argument. "Every question has two sides. The other side has yet to bat."

Just then Wilkins came in, and the two clerks were soon on their way home.

Though the days had lengthened quite perceptibly since that night, a few weeks before, when Edward Vaughen walked down Broadway, afterward seeing Dr. Disney in the office of Keen & Sharp, still it was comparatively dark as they made their way to the corner where they usually bade each other good night. Hence neither of them noticed a gang of rough-looking men who had followed them all the way from the office, though at such a distance that even had they noticed them no suspicions would have been aroused.

In this part of the city there is not much regard

for the niceties of the law. The man whose business takes him to this neighborhood, once night has
set in, needs to be very careful. In the daytime
there is usually so much traffic and travel of one kind
and another that the streets are comparatively safe,
but at night the dark gateways, the deserted store-
houses, the high buildings, in which there is no
light whatever, easily make possible almost any
form of crime.

On reaching the corner, the young men parted.
John starting out in his usual brisk way, walking
across to where he would get a car, but he had only
gone a short distance when he heard the noise of
angry voices, then a loud cry for help, and then almost instantly, "Disney! Disney!"

It at once flashed upon him that the voice was that
of Sauvier. Like a deer he ran to the place from
where the cries came, to find Sauvier surrounded by
some half dozen burly ruffians, against whom he was
bravely defending himself. It was not long before
John was at the side of Sauvier, dealing a tremen-
dous blow at one fellow who had Fred by the throat,
which caused him to let go his hold and stagger to
the ground.

But this only infuriated the others, who rushed
at John like so many mad bulls. John, however,
had his wits all about him, and already had backed up
against the wall, so as not to be struck from behind.

Now, in the very first chapter of these most accu-
rate and trustworthy chronicles it is stated with great
clearness that John Disney could "don the gloves,"
an accomplishment which some people regard with

disfavor.. At this particular time the skill thus acquired was of more value to him than all the rest of his college work, for he was able to parry and strike with an ease and a force which under the circumstances were highly desirable. Even in fighting, the scientific method has points of advantage which count very materially. The man who knows just where to hit and how to hit is usually able to give a good account of himself.

But two against six, for the first man had now resumed his place among the combatants, means that in the end the six are likely to prevail, unless the two in some way are reinforced, or special means taken to dispose of the six. As there was no Blücher anywhere in sight, and as Sauvier was not holding his own against his proportion of the enemy, John determined to assume the offensive, and that in a most vigorous way. Watching his chance, he threw himself with all his might against the most vicious of his opponents; then, before the fellow had recovered from the shock, quick as lightning he had his arms around his waist, locked one hand over the other, and gave the ruffian a squeeze which caused him to leap almost a foot in the air, crying out for very pain, and fall helpless on the ground.

John was now in a splendid rage, just in that mood when he would kill without mercy, for when he was angered to the full he had the remorseless spirit of a gladiator. With the same passion, therefore, he flung himself upon another man, performing the same feat as before, his strength only seeming to increase with his rage.

21

The others, seeing the mighty wrath of this young Goliath, fell back a few paces, but John rushed upon them with terrible fury, hitting one fellow with such force that he fell crashing over some crates and empty boxes which littered that part of the street. The other three now slunk away, though not until one of them came behind Fred Sauvier, who for the moment was off his guard, and striking him on the head knocked him almost senseless.

Just now a policeman came running up, who at once whistled for help, when another officer soon appeared. The two men with whom John had been so righteously unmerciful had crawled into the shadow of a gateway, but they were soon discovered. The other one was gathered out of the crates and boxes, and the precious trio were marched to the police station. Other policemen, meantime, had arrived, two of whom took Fred Sauvier, one by each arm, for poor Fred was pretty well used up. At the police station, however, he recovered sufficiently to give a general account of the proceedings. After the usual course in such cases—identification and lodging formal complaint against the prisoners—a carriage was called to take Fred and John home. At that particular moment John Disney was, so far as appearance goes, a most disreputable-looking young man. His coat and vest were nearly torn to pieces. His face was all scratched and battered. Spatterings of blood and daubings of mud were plentifully distributed all over him. The spick-span dapper fellow who left his home that morning would now not be recognized by even his own mother. Fred Sauvier had not fared quite so badly by way of wounds and scratches. His real injuries, however, were more serious.

It was late when they reached the Sauviers', for some time had been spent in the police station. Mrs. Sauvier and Oberta were both beginning to think that something must have happened, when in Fred walked, closely followed by John. There was the usual little shrieking and "oh-ing," but the Sauviers were sensible people and soon recovered from their fright.

In a few minutes John got up to go home, when Fred took him by the arm and, turning to his mother, said:

"Mother, you have Mr. Disney to thank for my being here at all. He saved my life at the risk of his own."

Mrs. Sauvier looked at John in a dazed, bewildered way, sinking faint and helpless into a chair. John very naturally thought that the fright and excitement of the past half hour were too much for her. Even Oberta, quick-witted as she was, did not associate her mother's strange condition with the mention of the name of Disney.

CHAPTER XXXIV.

An Evening at Mr. Keen's.

WHAT story in all literature has caused more heart throbbings or awakened such profound interest as that of a certain ancient dame whose progeny was so numerous as to disturb her peace by day, while at night she pillowed her distracted head under a leathern roof? What pathetic pictures have come to our minds when we have thought of this sorely troubled mother, whose offspring gave her such painful anxiety! It is possible that had she not chosen such a singular place of abode, but contented herself with a home of the regular order, her children might not have been either so restless or unruly. But, be that as it may, the fact remained, embalmed even in poetry, that this woman "did not know what to do." In the thrilling but pathetic narrative we learn that she was forced finally to adopt a treatment which was at once both drastic and heroic. There the story ends. To stop at the right time is more than art—it is genius.

It would hardly be true to say that Mrs. Vaughen was in anything like the plight of the much-harassed female referred to. She was troubled, though, about Edward—troubled, too, in a way that gave her serious concern. Knowing that he was high-spirited to a degree which might be considered romantic, with a sort of honor of the ancient knighthood type ; fully aware of his obligations to Mark Brompton; conscious also of the duty which he owed to his employers; deeply in love with Rhea Keen—his position, when all these things are borne in mind, was one of much complexity.

Like a wise young man, he wrote to his mother, fully stating the case. Like a wise mother, she wrote back almost at once, refusing anything in the way of positive advice. To refrain from giving advice shows great strength of mind. If people are ever to be worth their salt in this world—or any other—they must learn to work out their own salvation. Edward was now of age. He was on the ground. It was his life in which the battle had to be fought. Mrs. Vaughen therefore left with him the responsibility of deciding. At first he was tempted to give up his position in the office of Keen & Sharp. But this would surely offend his Uncle Mark. Then he thought of making a confidant of Mr. Singleton. But this would be treachery to Mr. Faber. And all the while there was his love for Miss Keen, only adding to the difficulty of the situation.

What, then, could he do? He was like a man flung into the sea, with a life-preserver fastened so around him that he could not drown, but with his hands and feet bound, making swimming impossible. All he could do was float and drift with the tide.

The only thing which surprised Mark Brompton in his conversation with Edward Vaughen was to learn definitely that Keen & Sharp were the parties who had charge of the "deal" by which he would be forced into a losing game.

For some years Mr. Brompton had recognized the feasibility of a great railroad system in the West and South, connecting a number of roads which were now in opposition. Without acquainting anyone of his purpose he began buying up large blocks of these various stocks. This buying had been going on for some time, so that his holdings were enormous. Virtually he had the market in his hand. To perfect the system one short connection was necessary. It was therefore of the utmost importance that this be secured. For years that stock was practically valueless. It had not paid any dividends for a long time, and the chances were that it would never pay any. Mr. Brompton had his agents on the lookout among the farmers and country people for such of this stock as could be found. Quiet, innocent-looking men these agents were. Some of them were so demure and pious-looking that they seemed more like Bible distributers or Tract Society visitors than anything else.

"Ah calcurlate that er money is just as good as found," old Jake Heymough said to his wife, after Mr. Brompton's agent had gone and he was counting over the roll of bills which the agent had given him in exchange for his stock.

"'Tisn't quite writ in the Book about a fool an' his money bein' soon parted; it's true, though," said Deacon Swingsyth, after he had disposed of what to him was only a useless piece of paper. Deacon Swingsyth did not make this remark in the presence of Mr. Brompton's agent, a mild, soft-voiced young man.

"For 'sperimentin', I s'pose?" questioned Squire Bredstock. "Good, nice road; well built—just the road for 'speriments." The squire could speak feelingly with regard to "'speriments." His stock in the X., Y. & Z. had not, though, been quite the success he so confidently expected.

So the buying went on, every little while another certificate coming in to Mr. Brompton. One thing certain—he had enough of that stock quietly laid away to give him control. Keen & Sharp never dreamed of what Mark Brompton had done. They knew, however, that there was a "big deal" on hand. They knew also that the purpose of this deal was to give Mark Brompton a squeeze to which the hug of a Russian bear would be only a gentle embrace.

"Young Brompton was in the office this morning. He seems quite intimate with Vaughen. They went out together at lunch time."

Mr. Keen made these remarks to Rhea one evening, not, however, looking up from the paper which he was scanning with some care.

"That is only natural, seeing they are cousins," Miss Keen answered, rising from her chair as she spoke, and going over to another part of the room where her face would be more in the shadow.

"Now that your mother is so much better," he went on, after a short pause, still looking at the paper, "you ought to have a little gathering of your friends sometime soon."

"Would it not be better to wait so that mamma can take her usual place? Two or three of her affairs have been postponed."

"O, I don't mean anything formal. Just a few of
your own friends—the young people of the Bromptons, and the Disneys, and two or three others.
Of course you will have to invite Von der Plonk,
also that radical parson, Dunbar, who means to con-
vert the East Side into a public park and have mechanics ride about in carriages. When a parson sets
out to be a fool he usually makes a big success of it.
Vaughen, I suppose, had better come."

Though Mr. Keen was very much absorbed in
business, giving his entire time almost to the special
matters which were now on hand, yet he had noticed
that Rhea looked anxious and careworn. This he
attributed to the illness of her mother; for sickness,
when long continued, always depresses and exhausts
the household. Hence he proposed some little break
in the monotony of Rhea's life, with the hope of
arousing her to her former brightness and vigor.

But there was another motive at work. Now that
Madge Disney was accepting the evident attentions
of Hugh Dunbar, there was no reason why Percy
Brompton should not become in good time a member
of the Keen household. If his present plans resulted
successfully Mr. Keen would make considerable
money. But what to him was of even more consequence than the money, he would have an assured position as the leader of new and important movements.
The fact that both the money and the leadership
would be at Mark Brompton's expense had no weight
with him. His understanding of life was simply
every man for himself.

Then, on the other hand, if by any means his plans

failed—though he could not imagine such a thing possible—the engagement, perhaps marriage, of his daughter to Percy Brompton would be as an anchor to the windward, so that he could easily outride the storm.

If anyone had told Mr. Keen that he was now on that awful mountain top where the most terrible temptations of life are experienced he would have turned away with an incredulous smile, or even laughed outright at the mediæval suggestion. And yet he was on that mountain top. To gratify his ambitions he had cast aside almost everything of honesty. He was working treacherously against the man who had befriended him. Yea, he would actually sell his daughter to that man's son, counting out as of no moment whatever the possibilities of her lifelong misery !

"O, you should have seen John !" said Madge Disney, in her lively, impetuous way—a way which not infrequently resulted in a certain colloquial form of expression which, while it was vivid and picturesque, was not up to the high standard of her elegant father. "When I came home that evening from a *musicale* at the Savoy—you remember that *musicale*, Janet, where the new tenor, Gamutino, sang so divinely—I inquired the moment I got into the house for my illustrious brother. Going to his room, I found him anything but an ideal of manly beauty. He was plastered and bandaged like some old Pharisee, with a phylactery of vast proportions on his head, two or three smaller ones on his hands, and with wounds and bruises all over him."

"Are you not putting it rather strong, or is it that poetic gift of yours which confuses fact with fancy?" John suggested, meantime smiling at the picture which Madge had just sketched with that nimble tongue of hers.

"Truth, my dear brother, is always stranger than fiction. Nor could any poet or romancer of this generation do justice to the crushed, broken, helpless warrior who looked out despairingly from under his burden of bandages in response to my agonized appeal."

John offered no further protest, so Madge went on with her flamingo-colored account of her brother's condition as she found him on the night when he went to the rescue of Fred Sauvier.

It will be seen that Miss Keen had accepted her father's suggestion, and it will also be seen that the young people were having a very lively time. Even Hendrik Von der Plonk said "Gad" at least twice during Madge's recital, which showed a high condition of mental activity on his part. Ethel Brompton could hardly believe her ears when she heard the second exclamation from Hendrik—turning to look at him with more interest than at any time since their engagement.

As for Hugh Dunbar, he gave full proof that evening of his membership in the Church militant, for when John, in sheer self-defense, was forced to tell the story from the beginning Dunbar rubbed his hands in a way which was not at all saintly. There was also a certain gleam in his eye, not to speak of a peculiar look on his face, which gave the distinct impression that he would have enjoyed being in the fight.

There may be those who can explain it—for there are people who have an explanation for everything —still it is singular, to say the least, that when Madge caught Dunbar unconsciously making fisti- cuff gestures she actually liked him all the better for it!

Janet Brompton asked in a kindly way about Fred Sauvier, for John was so modest as to be barely truthful. But the rarity of such a sin is so great as to make it self-forgiving.

Madge recalled the day when Ethel, Janet, and herself went to the store of Linsey & Woolsey, there meeting Miss Sauvier, whereupon Janet declared that she would go to Linsey & Woolsey's the very next day to congratulate Miss Sauvier on having such an heroic brother.

It should be said just here—though why it should be said either here or anywhere else is not quite clear—that from the day Madge made the acquaint- ance of Miss Sauvier, every time she was in the store of Linsey & Woolsey she went upstairs to "cloaks and wraps" and had a little chat with Oberta. And it should also be said here—though for what reason goodness only knows—in that little chat the name of Dunbar was sure of being mentioned.

"Your mother lives in Eastwich, you say?" Miss Keen said to Edward Vaughen, as they sat some lit- tle distance from the general group, talking in low tones. "And are you her only son?"

"Only son, and, for that matter, only child. My

mother and I are very dear to each other. I hope sometime to have her with me in New York."

"Then you expect to remain here permanently?"

"Yes. When I first came I was not quite certain. I am now."

"Of course in the beginning you were lonely. Everything was so new and strange that you could not be expected to feel like 'settling down,' as we call it. But after a time that feeling wears off."

"Yes, that may be. The cause, though, is not what you think it is. The reason—" Here Edward raised his eyes; at the same moment Miss Keen raised her eyes, with the result that their eyes met in one of those long, strange, mysterious looks when hearts reveal themselves to each other.

Now both of these young people were very foolish. We might go so far as to say they were inexcusably foolish. Miss Keen knew that her father would angrily refuse any proposal which Edward Vaughen might make. She also knew that he was poor; that he would be poor for many years to come, and that she would not consent to share a poor man's home.

Edward knew that as matters now stood it was the veriest folly for him to even think of Miss Keen; that he would not have a home worthy of her for years, if ever.

And yet they had looked into each other's eyes, each hoping to find the secret of the other. But now that the secret had been revealed, each sat still and frightened, not knowing just what to do.

Rhea was the first to recover herself, so with a few

commonplace words she managed to turn the conversation away from that unfinished sentence of Edward's. In a few moments she joined the group in the other part of the room. Before Edward had an opportunity to supply the missing words—in case he so desired—the company broke up for the evening.

CHAPTER XXXV.

A Black Eye.

OF course it was impossible to keep that affair
of John Disney and Fred Sauvier out of the
papers. Police news reporters, when they
once get hold of such a sensational affair, attend to
it in their own lurid and characteristic way. So
there were startling headlines, heavy type summa-
ries, any quantity of vivid description, interspersed
with photographs and sketches. The photographs
were taken out of that marvelous collection which
every city newspaper keeps on hand, answering
equally well for preachers and pugilists, authors or
anarchists, though usually with no more relation to
what they are supposed to stand for than the man
in the moon has to Angelo's " Moses."

The sketches were made by "our own reporter,"
who was probably not within five miles of the place
at the time of the struggle, but who gathered up all
the news from the police.

Then there were biographies of the principal
characters going back not only to their childhood,
but to their ancestors of remote generations.

The name of "Sauvier" was proven to be distinctly French, easily traced to the time of William
of Normandy. The courage, therefore, which the
young man showed was only natural to one whose
ancestors had fought at the battle of Hastings.

Of "Disney" it was established beyond all peradventure as belonging to a branch of an old Border clan, which had made common cause with Sir William Wallace. This easily explained his daring and unconquerable spirit. Every item in the history of each family was gathered up with greater care than Ruth gleaned in the fields of Boaz, so that by the time the reporters had got through with the case every uncle, aunt, cousin, and grandmother had been thoroughly exploited.

For days, in type an inch long and correspondingly broad, one might read: "Murderous Attack!" "The Son of a Distinguished Physician Proves Himself a Hero!" "Damon and Pythias in New York." As the men under arrest were identified as laborers and yard men in the Tubal-Cain Iron Works, whose wages were not attractively high, some of the papers worked off rampant editorials on "Labor Conditions in New York." Others hinted at "Startling Revelations" to be made at the forthcoming trial.

Though the work was not in the line of Mr. Faber's wishes, yet it fell to his lot to report it for the *Trombone*. He called, therefore, on the Sauviers, getting from Fred a full account of the trouble from beginning to end. Mr. Faber never had a case to which he gave such close, direct, and personal attention. If Fred Sauvier, at the coming trial, was going to be the defendant, with Mr. Faber as his counsel in chief, Dixon could not have gone with more minuteness into every detail and circumstance. And what was even more singular, he seemed as fully satisfied with the information which he got from Oberta as that given him by Fred! Even after the papers had given up special mention of the affair—for there is no such thing as a nine-days' wonder in New York—he still continued his attentions to the Sauvier home. Fred enjoyed Faber's bright, breezy way, and urged him to come in as often as he could spare the time.

Just how he happened to know that Oberta was no longer at home in the early part of the day—for after the first week she had gone back to Linsey & Woolseys'—we cannot tell. Anyhow the "dropping in" was always in the evenings. And it was remarkable how much of his work brought him to that part of the city!

When Fred Sauvier was able to go back to his place in the office Faber had to call to inquire if there was likely to be any more trouble with the men. Then he had to call an evening or two later to ask something about John Disney. Another time he wanted special information on some matter connected with the iron interests, of which he knew more in his little finger than Fred did in his whole body.

After this he had tickets, usually only two, to some specially fine entertainments. Fred couldn't go, Mrs. Sauvier had to remain at home with Fred. The burden of using the tickets therefore fell upon Oberta and himself. So it went on, "as it was in the beginning, is now, and ever shall be."

John Disney, being partial to athletics and having played football on the college team, did not attach much importance to the cuts and scratches which he received on that eventful evening. Still, for some days he remained at home in a seclusion which no one outside the immediate family was permitted to invade.

For one thing he had a black eye; not such a black eye as may be acquired by accident, but one which proves that the bearer thereof has been in a regular scrimmage.

And what an obstinate, obdurate, obtrusive, objectionable object a black optic is! It has an evil look. It glares at you in a way that is diabolical. It cuts off all, relationship with the other eye. It refuses absolutely and positively to withdraw itself from publicity. A green patch doesn't help matters. Blue goggles only make things worse. For the time a black eye is monarch of all it surveys. It was surely one which suggested "great eye and little you."

Not far from the black eye was a swollen nose. "Not far" is written advisedly, for while as a general thing the eye and the nose are seldom far apart, yet there is a recognized distance arranged for by nature. But in John's case the nose insisted upon humping itself most aggressively, occupying more facial territory than was ever written in the bond. And so the black eye glared down at the humped nose. The humped nose defiantly lifted itself before the black eye. Each, of course, had its friends, so John's face was in general warfare.

Now, one would think when a poor fellow was in such plight as this that at least the members of his own household would pity him profoundly.

22

It is true Madge would begin, "You dear, poor boy!" but then she would smile, the smile ending off in a laugh, giggle and snicker, just half and half.

Then she would apologize, but the apology usually ended where the smile did.

"Some people are very easily amused," John took occasion to say once by way of rebuke, but catching a glimpse of his face just then in a mirror opposite he laughed himself, much to the annoyance of his upper lip, upon which a piece of court-plaster was exercising squatters' rights.

Even Mrs. Disney, gentle and motherly as she was, could not forbear a smile when the black eye would try to make an exception in her favor and not look quite so malignant.

Dr. Disney, having had "accident ward" practice in his time, was accustomed to seeing young men very much in the condition of John. He was not, therefore, alarmed, and poked some fun at John now and then.

One evening when they were by themselves John gave his father all of the particulars of the fight and what led up to it. Dr. Disney being a very busy man, exceptionally so just then, had not troubled himself with newspaper reports, so that all he knew was that John and another clerk in the iron works had been attacked by some disappointed employees.

John began at the beginning, going on without interruption until he mentioned the name of Sauvier, when the doctor started, but instantly checked himself. His face, though, became deathly pale, and had that haunted, frightened look which at times came

upon him. As the room was comparatively dark—
for John's eye became more painful in the light—Dr.
Disney's agitation was not noticed. Being a man of
superb self-control, he soon mastered his feelings, so
that by the time John had finished he was able to
take his part in the conversation.

"What sort of a young man is this Sauvier?" he
asked.

"A first-rate fellow, though, of course, I don't know
much about him except what I have seen in the office."

" Are his people living in the city?"

John did not dream of the intense anxiety with
which Dr. Disney waited for his reply. After all,
the name, though uncommon, might be only a coincidence, or at most a remote connection of the Sauviers
with whom he was related.

"I have heard him speak of a mother and sister.
I take it that the father is dead."

" You say there is a sister?" the doctor went on,
putting his hand to his face as though to smooth it
down, a favorite gesture of his, but in this case to
account for a palpable unevenness in his voice.

" Yes, and once or twice when speaking of her he
mentioned her name—Oberta, if I remember cor-
rectly."

Dr. Disney said no more just then, but sat with
his hand so shading his face that even had the light
been good John could not have seen how troubled
and distressed it was. There was now hardly the
possibility of a doubt that Bertha Sauvier was in
New York. He had tried to find out where she had
gone; for when Fred Sauvier went to prison, and

her home was broken up in disgrace, she went away, no one could tell where.

He did not know that on every visiting day a sad-faced woman came to the prison, waiting at the door for the moment to arrive when she would be admitted. Neither did he know that when Fred Sauvier died broken-hearted, years before his sentence was even half completed, she took the poor, emaciated body and gave it holy burial. He did not know either that the grave in which that body slept was lovingly cared for by the woman whom he had so foully wronged, not even the pitiless winter interfering with her pilgrimage to that little hillock, lying so pathetically under the snow. Still less did he know that when he had gone to the place of burial, but a few miles distant from his present home, with some of his friends who had entered the realm of mystery and silence, he had seen the poor, lone woman, standing pitifully at this very grave, sometimes bending over it as a mother over a sleeping child.

"I know," said John, speaking after a long pause, for he had been waiting on his father to resume the conversation, "how your time is taken up. Still I wish you could manage to call on Fred Sauvier. He has been very kind to me in the office, and the poor fellow was pretty well used up before I got to him."

"I hardly know just how I can manage it, for the present at any rate," the doctor replied, speaking as calmly as he could; but his voice, at least to himself, sounded strange and forced, almost as if it came from another man.

John said no more, but his silence only added to the pain and distress of his father, for Dr. Disney knew that John was disappointed in the refusal of his very natural request. But how could he call upon the Sauviers? How could he meet the woman whose life he had ruined and whose terrible curse was ever ringing in his ears. Of physical cowardice he knew nothing whatever. He had faced death in almost every form. Without a moment's hesitation he had gone into homes laden with the most malignant disease, where every breath was poison, and with a courage which would have made him a hero on the battlefield accepted the chances such as they were.

He could face death without flinching, fighting with supreme daring for his patient amid the most reeking and dangerous conditions; still he dare not meet Bertha Sauvier!

Yet of what crime had he been guilty? Where was the one who could point to a single law upon the statute book which he had broken? Who could show cause against him in any one particular, or produce the slightest shred of evidence upon which he might be condemned? What if Mrs. Sauvier did denounce him? Would not her charges be taken as the ravings of a demented woman, whose husband, while under sentence for forgery, had died in prison?

But, while Dr. Disney could dispose of the criminal code, he could not dispose of conscience. For the code he cared very little, but for conscience he cared a great deal, because conscience was implacable. With all the strength of his imperious will he had tried to forget that sin of so many years ago, but it sternly refused to be forgotten.

One thing, however, he was determined on—he would not see the Sauviers. He would temporize with John, for appearance' sake make conditional promises, but he would so arrange his work as to make the visit an impossibility. As a last resort he would even leave the city for the time being. Meet Mrs. Sauvier he would not. Upon that he was fully resolved.

"There is no immediate hurry," he said to John, as he rose up and was preparing to go out, "in this matter of calling upon these people. Perhaps in a day or two I may be able to manage it."

"No hurry at all," answered John, much gratified at his father's response. "But it would greatly please me, and I am sure it would gratify the Sauviers."

That night Dr. Disney slept badly. Not even the drug which we have seen him take once before was powerful enough to induce dreamless unconsciousness.

CHAPTER XXXVI.

Concerning Mrs. Smithers.

RS. SILAS SMITHERS was by no means an extraordinary woman, but there was one thing she could do, and do it well—make an attractive, winsome, comfortable home. The armchair in which Silas sat, when after his day's work he read the evening paper and smoked his stubby brierwood pipe, was an illustration of her genius and skill. This chair she had found in a secondhand furniture store on the avenue, a short distance from her home. The dealer was glad to sell it for almost anything she would give, for it took up considerable room, and he was afraid would have to be broken up for firewood. She saw possibilities in the chair, and bought it. Silas had work just then which took him out of town for a week, so she spent most of that week in fixing up the chair. A few yards of cheap cretonne of an agreeable pattern were used in making new cushions for the back and seat, as well as re-covering the arms. Then with Jamie's help she put in new casters and about a score of large-head brass nails to keep in place some braid which she used for binding. When Silas got home the chair was wheeled up beside a little table upon which a lamp was burning and where the paper was ready for his perusal.

Silas could hardly take time that evening to eat

his supper, he was so anxious to get into the arm-chair. How comfortable he looked as he sat in it! What nice things he said about his Mollie!

It wasn't every week that Mrs. Smithers could indulge in such a luxury as this, though all told it did not cost as much as a pair of Madge Disney's street gloves. But she picked up sundry odds and ends, setting each off to the best advantage. There were two or three little ornaments on the mantelpiece; one of them was more than an ornament, for it was a clock which kept excellent time. At Christmas she would allow Silas to make her a present of a picture of some kind, usually a chromo, for she was partial to colors. Her own attempts at fancywork were not either beautiful or fine, but they were effective, which, after all, is the main thing. She therefore worked a mat for the lamp and covers for the two little tables which stood in the windows. A few pennies judiciously expended in Japanese fans supplemented the chromos, so that the room—parlor, sitting room, and dining room, all in one—gave the appearance of being quite pleasantly furnished. So long as Silas had steady work Mrs. Smithers was able to keep her home in good running order, even adding a trifle almost every month to their account in the savings bank; but when work fell off one third, then one half, then down to stray jobs of a day or two, with some weeks not even that, the Smithers household felt the pinch very severely.

And then—for misfortunes are never solitary things which, like milestones, we pass one at a time—little Jamie was forced to give up carving, as he could no

longer do any work. The fight that boy made was
worthy of the Victoria Cross. But there came a time
when the poor, frail body was not able to sit even in
his own chair, but was forced to lie helpless on the
bed.

And now it was Mrs. Smithers's turn to earn the
bread for the family. Silas could not find work anywhere. Their little savings were entirely exhausted.
No money whatever was coming in, and there were
five of them to be provided for. Mrs. Smithers accordingly went to the manufacturers of certain arti-
cles of apparel, such as cheap, common shirts for
men and the rougher, coarser kind of boys' clothing, who gave out work which might be done at
home. By working at her sewing machine all day,
sometimes well on into the night, she was able to
earn hardly more than would pay the rent.

What could they do? Where would they go?
The city had nothing for them but a poorhouse, and
the poorhouse is the last refuge of honest poverty,
for, after all, it is not much better than the common
jail.

In sheer despair Mrs. Smithers made application
to a charity bureau, where she received about the
same treatment as that described by Mr. Sterling to
Hugh Dunbar. The next day, or possibly a few
days after, an agent made his appearance in the
Smithers home. He saw a little bit of carpet on the
floor, two or three little pictures on the walls, the big
armchair which had been rescued from the woodpile,
the sewing machine at which Mrs. Smithers was able
to earn three cents an hour, whereupon he turned

on his heel with the remark, " People with carpets on their floors and pictures on their walls, and a house furnished with armchairs and sewing machines, have no business to make application for help." With this he went out, leaving them more hopeless than when he came in. He did not see a boy almost dying for lack of proper nourishment and medical care; he did not see a woman who had worked all day without hardly a morsel of food crossing her lips; he did not see a man who was on the verge of despair through lack of work and anxiety for his family; he did not see a fire which was dying in the stove, with not a handful of coal to keep it living; he did not see a larder which was absolutely empty, and that these people were actually suffering with hunger— O, the number of things which that agent did not see!

Now, if Silas Smithers, under the stress of hunger, or the still greater woe of seeing hunger in his house which he could not relieve, should become a phrenetic, and in a moment of wild, hopeless passion murderously attack the members of his family, instantly he will be taken care of by the State. His cell in the prison will be crowded with eager visitors; charitable women will vie with each other in their attentions to the distinguished criminal; nothing will be left undone that would promote his peace and well-being; the commonwealth will spend thousands of dollars upon his trial; his name will appear in every newspaper in the country, making him as widely known as if he had been a hero or benefactor of national celebrity. But as an honest mechanic, out of work and hungry, Silas Smithers may starve to death !

Sister Nora had been absent from the city for some weeks. When she returned almost her first inquiry was for Jamie Smithers. Mr. Sterling gave her to understand that things were not going well with Jamie nor with the Smithers family. The very next day she went to see them.

" What! gone to bed !" she said to Jamie, as she took the little fellow by the hand, feeling instantly the fever which was throbbing in his blood. " And I have a friend who must have a whole lot of your carvings. So anxious is he to get his work done first that he insisted upon payment in advance." With that she took out two five-dollar bills, laying them down on the little table beside the bed.

The boy's eyes sparkled with pleasure, and his poor, wasted face lit up at her sweet, grateful words. Then she laid her cool, strong hand upon his hot forehead, giving him a strange sense of comfort and relief. And was there ever anything quite so delicious as that spoonful or two of jelly which she made him take, or those few sips of cooling drink? Already Jamie felt better—at least he thought so, and his face had a more grateful, contented look than for several days.

" Do you think Mr. Smithers could find time to do some work in a house over on Fifth Avenue?" she asked Mrs. Smithers, not once intimating that Silas was out of employment. "I know of a house in which a carpenter is sadly needed, for there are a lot of things to be done."

The house was her own, but she did not say so ; neither did she intend that Silas Smithers should know.   Her one thought was to get him something to do, as it was work, and not charity, which he was in need of.

By this time Jamie was fast asleep, of which Sister Nora took advantage to slip out, but not until she had given Mrs. Smithers the address to which Silas would go in the morning, where she would meet him and arrange for the work of which she had spoken.

Poor Silas came in soon after utterly exhausted, having tramped about all day looking for work, only to meet with the same discouraging reply.   But he had not even crossed the threshold before Mollie had her arms about his neck and with tears of joy stream- ing down her face told him of the visit of Sister Nora and of the work which awaited him on the morrow.

Then Silas broke down and sobbed like a child. For weeks he had borne up as best he could.   No man could have made a braver fight.   But when he saw his patient " Mollie " working all day over the sewing machine, not eating enough to keep her alive ; when he saw his poor wee Jamie actually dying be- fore his eyes ; when he knew that Effie and Bob were hungry and that he had no means of buying bread, he was tempted to give up in despair.   And so he went all to pieces.   His big, rugged frame quivered, and he wept as a man weeps but few times in his life.

What an evening that was for all of them !   Mrs. Smithers, now that Silas was going to work on the

morrow, " borrowed " some of Jamie's carving money,
going out to the store and coming in with a big bas-
ketful of things. In a time so short as to be almost
magical something was simmering on the kitchen
stove which diffused a grateful odor all through the
little apartment. Effie was busy helping her mother
to set the table in a way not very common of late.
Bob was going in and out on all kinds of errands, and
doing it, too, with great cheerfulness. A fire was
kindled in the " sitting " room stove. The lamp was
filled and set in its old place. The big armchair was
wheeled over near to the lamp. Mrs. Smithers
(" Bless her dear heart! " Silas said), in the midst of
the multitude of her cares that evening, had not forgotten her husband's one luxury; so the old brierwood
pipe came to the fore again, for she had bought him
a paper of tobacco. Jamie was carried from his bed
to the room where they all were, at first sitting with
his father in the big chair; then, when the table
was cleared away and everything was put to rights,
he crept into his mother's arms, where after a little
while he fell asleep.

That same evening John Disney had been at the
Mission to see the opening of another department,
for Hugh Dunbar was constantly adding something or other. After the more formal exercises
John went in with Hugh to a little private room
which Dunbar called his "snuggery." John dropped
contentedly into a big easy chair, while Dunbar took
another of much the same order.

" O, I am making discoveries all the time! " Dunbar said, in reply to a question of John. " One of

my latest is that the deepest poverty is not the result
of strong drink."

" That would have surprised me a year ago," answered John, " but it does not surprise me now."

" I used to accept as gospel the things that men
said about pauperism and drink," Dunbar went on;
" but I know better now."

" Suppose you let in a little of your superfluous
light on me. In a chair so comfortable as this one
could almost endure a sermon."

" Then here goes. In my opinion, the crime of our
city—that is, the common, coarse, brutal crime—is
largely traceable to strong drink; and so, also, is
much of the poverty; but it is a low, vulgar kind of
poverty, which may be relieved by charity. Now, the
real, deep poverty has causes of an altogether different nature."

" So far the sermon is fairly interesting, but with
more assertion than argument."

" Then let me bring forward the proofs. You have
heard me speak of Silas Smithers ? "

John nodded.

" Well, Smithers is a carpenter—a house carpenter, one of the most steady, industrious men in New
York. Now, Smithers is out of work; but what is
far worse, he can't get work; and there are thousands
of men like him with nothing to do and with no
prospect of anything to do."

" You mean to tell me that there are thousands of
house carpenters in this city out of work ? " John
questioned, with an incredulous air.

" It is very evident that you are yet ' in the gall of

bitterness and in the bond of iniquity ' so far as the industrial problem is concerned. Do you not know that one trade is so related to another that no one can suffer without the others feeling it almost if not quite as much ? "

" No, I do not know it ; and what is more, I doubt if you do either."

" Then listen, you incorrigible doubter. Because the stone masons are not at work, the bricklayers are idle ; because the bricklayers are idle, the carpenters have nothing to do; because the carpenters have nothing to do, the plasterers, slaters, painters, plumbers, paperhangers are all unemployed. Hence the furniture men close their factories, the carpet men shut down their mills, and the result is widespread poverty."

" The sermon is interesting, but rather lengthy," John remarked.

" The end is coming ; have patience. Now, when the question of poverty has come up I used to content myself by saying, ' The poor are themselves to blame ; they waste their wages in drink ; they are unthrifty ; they are careless and extravagant.' But I know better now. The question that troubles me is not concerning the poor, miserable wretch who wastes his money in a pothouse, but the problem of this great army of honest, sober men of whom Silas Smithers is a fair type."

" The sermon nears the end. Now put in the application."

John was far more serious than he pretended to be. Dunbar, however, knew this.

"The application is this: These silly dreamers and 'press-the-button' philosophers, who think they can change things by petty legislation and cheap reforms, are so far gone in their delusions that there is no hope for them. As for the working people, with their strikes and brotherhoods, they are as helpless as Canute at the incoming of the sea. The only cure is the development of a principle which has been in the world for nearly two thousand years. That principle is simply the Christianization of business. Any man, therefore, who will really solve the problem of the age must Christianize his business. He must apply the Golden Rule in his workshop and counting house. In time this spirit will prevail with the workmen, and the question will be settled for all time to come. But the sermon is ended. It is time you were going home."

It was late that night, very late, when John got home, but Madge was waiting up for him. Knowing that he had been at the Mission, she was anxious to hear how everything passed off. She was now quite interested in the Mission, though not, it must be admitted, to the same extent that she was in Hugh Dunbar.

After John had lighted his pipe (he always smoked the last thing at night—a most reprehensible and unhealthy thing to do) he reached over to the chair where Madge was sitting and, laying his hand lovingly upon hers, said:

"Madge, Hugh Dunbar is a noble fellow. Unless you mean 'playing for keeps,' to use an expression of our childhood, you ought to give him a hint. I am very fond of him and would feel badly if he got hurt."

"It is all right, John," Madge answered, in a low tone. "This time it is 'playing for keeps,' and not much playing either."

Whereupon John kissed her, and they parted for the night.

23

CHAPTER XXXVII.

Ethel Brompton's Wedding.

OF course Ethel Brompton got married, and of course there was a wedding of becoming pomp and circumstance.

For weeks preceding the august event the usual preparations had been going on, involving any number of visits to dressmakers and milliners and drygoods stores, for it was of the utmost importance that Ethel be not only handsomely gowned on the day when she became Mrs. Von der Plonk, but that she enter upon her new life with such an array of gowns as would entitle her to distinguished consideration.

These were busy days in the Brompton mansion. The house was in a regular bustle. Every few minutes a wagon of some kind stopped at the door with a bundle or a package. Messenger boys brought cardboard boxes of all shapes and dimensions. Ethel's rooms, though carefully arranged every morning, were all littered up before night. Janet was having about the same experience. So was Mrs. Brompton. Even Mr. Brompton had to surrender the library for the time being.

Later on the wedding presents began to come in, which only added to the confusion and excitement. On the principle which is never more fully illustrated than at weddings—" to him that hath shall be given "—the presents were both numerous and costly.

—any quantity of fine cut glass, delicate china, exquisite bronze, bric-a-brac of every imaginable description, dainty little water colors, paintings in oil,
fans, clocks, silver by the bushel, dinner services,
crates of Royal Worcester, of Limoges, of Dresden,
of Beleek, rare old lace, shawls from Cashmere, rugs
from Persia, furs from Russia, everything, in fact,
that money could buy, with everything repeated over
and over again.

Meanwhile Mr. Coke, of the eminent legal firm
Coke & Littleton, and Mr. Blackstone, of the equally
eminent firm Erskine & Blackstone, the one representing Mark Brompton, the other representing
Hendrik Von der Plonk, had charge of the marriage
settlements. What a singular thing it is that when a
rich man's daughter is going to be married to a rich
man's son a lawyer has to stand guard over the settlements lest the one in some way obtains an advantage
over the other !

But the one person of all others who enjoyed these
days was Mrs. Brompton. Never was she quite so
stately as now, nor more thoroughly appreciated the
honors of her situation. This marriage of Ethel with
young Von der Plonk was the realization of her most
fondly cherished hopes. Unlike Hugh Dunbar, she
did not possess a grandfather, either living or dead.
Neither did her husband. He did not even possess a
father, for it was known everywhere that Mark
Brompton came to New York as a poor boy, from
which lowly condition he had worked himself up.
Time and again she had gone over her family tree,
hoping to find something of Norman blood, but try

as she would she could reach nothing more noble than tailors or weavers or shoemakers. Finally when she ran out her branch on the tree to Jed Snipkins, who married Nancy Ann Bilks, she gave up her genealogical studies.

But now, through Ethel's marriage, she will have kinship with people who have any number of grandfathers, for the Von der Plonks were here long before Columbus! If that worthy had only known enough to sail his caravels into New York harbor the Von der Plonks would have met him at the wharf and extended the hospitalities of the city.

In the various shopping expeditions which Ethel was required to make Mrs. Brompton nearly always accompanied her; giving her judgment on carpets, furniture, hangings, on all of the requisites for the new home, with the superb dignity of a duchess whose pedigree was four yards long.

But while she was so delightfully absorbed she did not forget the possibilities of a letter from South America. By this time David Stanley would probably have heard of what was going on. The young man had friends in New York who could not keep back an event of such importance. If he wrote to Ethel, his letter, containing reproaches and regrets, as it surely would, could do nothing but harm.

She therefore left word with the footman to have all foreign letters put aside and given to her privately. Right glad was she of this arrangement, for one afternoon the dreaded letter came. For a few moments she held it in her hand, not knowing just what to do with it. Mrs. Brompton knew that under the

law that letter should have been given to Ethel.
Ethel had a right to it, for she was its lawful owner.
But Mrs. Brompton reasoned that she was Ethel's
mother; that this letter was dangerous, and if given
up might seriously affect Ethel's future.   Mrs. Brompton was too honorable to read it, but not too honorable
to steal it.   She was too high-minded to open it, but
her high-mindedness did not prevent her from bribing
the footman to purloin it.

And so she stood there undecided.   What a pity
that Mrs. Brompton had never learned that honesty
is the best policy!   The giving of that letter to Ethel
would most assuredly have broken off her approaching
marriage to Von der Plonk, but Mrs. Brompton herself
would have been the first to counsel this very thing.

And Mrs. Brompton would have held her head
higher than ever, glorying even in the broken engagement, for this is what the letter contained:

"MY DEAR ETHEL : The most extraordinary thing
has happened.   Through a succession of deaths, two
of them accidental, and all of them entirely unexpected, the estates and duchy of Paddington now fall
to me.   Last Saturday I heard from the lawyers who
have the estates in charge, and with whom I have
been in cable communication almost every hour since.
There is now not a doubt as to the fact that I am the
next of kin.   I would have telegraphed you, but I
did not wish to say anything until I was certain.   Besides, telegrams are not only unsatisfactory things,
but they soon become public property.   This I was
anxious to avoid, preferring the matter to remain
quiet for the present—our secret, yours and mine.

"I start to-day for England, sailing direct from here. If you write within a day or two after receiving this it will reach me as soon as I land. Direct to me at Bank of England.

"Now, my darling, I can offer you a home and a name which are worthy of you. Our weary waiting will soon end. Forgive me for not writing at greater length, but you can easily imagine how anxious and excited I am. (Another cable despatch delivered just this moment; it is addressed to the Duke of Paddington!) Think of my Ethel as a duchess! Ah! she is more than a duchess to me. She is my queen! God bless you and keep you till I come for you. Ever your   DAVID."

Mrs. Brompton stood with the unopened letter in her hand. She turned it over, looking one time at the address, which seemed to be very plain and large, then at the postmarks, some of which were not distinct. She weighted it on her fingers, all the time wondering just what was best to do. Once she wished the footman had not given it to her, or that Ethel had seen it somehow. Then she lit a match, held the letter to the flame, and when it had burned more than half way down, she carried it to the grate, for she had been in her own sitting-room all this time, where she watched it char through in every part. Then she carefully washed her hands, and after a time began to dress for dinner. The embers crisped and crackled in the grate, as burnt letters always do, and with each crackle Mrs. Brompton's conscience troubled her. She now began to wish that she had not been so precipitate. Certainly she should not have burned it. So she went over to the grate with the hope that a part of the letter might have escaped. But nothing remained only the black, flaky embers which crumbled at her touch.

It was a very brilliant wedding. The church was filled long before the time appointed for the ceremony. Though there was something of a restraint upon conversation, because of a recognized church propriety, still there was a fair amount of decorous whispering.

"I don't see what Hendrik Von der Plonk could find in Ethel Brompton," Miss McSwoodle said to Miss Bronx. "She always seemed to me a snippy, conceited thing, with airs enough, goodness knows."

Miss McSwoodle and Miss Bronx, having been school-girl friends of Ethel, were seated well up front among the special guests.

"I have often wondered at that very same thing," Miss Bronx sweetly replied. "But then you know love is blind."

"All the love that is in this affair would be lost in my thimble," Miss McSwoodle responded, in a very delicate whisper. This led Miss Bronx to smile a dim, religious smile, for she remembered that she was in a church where smiles only of Gothic architecture are permissible.

Then they both gazed seraphically at a stained-glass window through which the noon sun was shining, making very vivid the inscription, "My little children, let us not love in word, neither in tongue; but in deed and in truth."

"I hear that the settlements are very generous,"

said Mrs. Gramercy, turning around in such a way
that she was able to speak to her friend, Mrs. Stuyvesant, who sat in the pew immediately behind.

"More than generous," responded Mrs. Stuyvesant.
"Von der Plonk has been liberal to a fault."

Neither of them knew the first thing about the
settlements. Outside the lawyers and the principals
concerned, not a soul in New York had the faintest
inkling of how the marriage papers read. This, however, did not prevent Mrs. Gramercy and Mrs.
Stuyvesant from having a whispered discussion on
the subject, even going into sundry details.

"I suppose Mrs. Brompton will be more uppish
than ever, now that her family is related to the Von
der Plonks," said Mrs. Bayridge to Mrs. Stapleton,
both out-of-towners, and both very intimate friends
of Mrs. Brompton.

"She may feel a little more uppish, but just how
she can act more uppish I cannot imagine," was the
sweet response of Mrs. Stapleton, spoken, too, with
such softness and tenderness that one would think
she was repeating the Litany.

And so it went on all over the church—whisperings in the gallery, whisperings under the gallery,
whisperings in the front pews, whisperings in the back
pews, whisperings everywhere.

And still the people came flocking in, so that the
ushers had much trouble to find places for them.
Many a stout dowager who had settled down comfortably was forced to move along in the pew to
make room for some other stout dowager. Many a
brave gown got badly crumpled. Many a dainty

costume had small chance to display itself. It is to
be feared that, church though it was, angry frowns
were exchanged more than once among these wedding guests.

For some little time the organ had been giving the
order of music customary on these occasions—part
opera, part oratorio, part organist—when all at once
the strains of the familiar march were heard. Everyone then knew that the bridal party had arrived.

At this moment the Rev. Dr. Bland, in full ca-
nonicals, appeared in his place, while from a door
near the chancel Hendrik Von der Plonk came forward, attended by Percy Brompton.

And now comes Ethel Brompton, leaning on the
arm of her father, with her sister Janet and Miss Von
der Plonk as bridesmaids.

Ethel was pale, but cool and collected, responding
in clear, distinct tones, while in kneeling to receive
the nuptial benediction she was sufficiently conscious
to droop gracefully, something which cannot be said of
Hendrik, for he bumped down, evidently not having
calculated the distance from his knees to the cushions.

There was no need whatever for Hendrik to look
so flushed and hot as he went down the aisle with
Ethel on his arm, or to nearly trip once or twice before he reached the church door, or to give almost a
gasp of relief when he got fairly into the carriage.

Ethel walked down that aisle with calm graceful-
ness. Her face was neither hot nor flushed. When
Hendrik handed her into the carriage she took time
to so adjust her gown that it would not be crushed
or wrinkled.

And so they were married.

With the breakfast provided by the famous caterer Chaufrappi, to which he gave personal attention—a rare thing for him to do; with the toasts and responses; the departure of Hendrik and Ethel; the trip to Europe and the return, we have nothing now to say. It ought, though, to be mentioned that the notice of the marriage was cabled across the Atlantic for the benefit of the American colony in London, and the still larger colony in Paris, which notice appeared in the *Times* of both cities.

On the day after the wedding David Stanley, now Duke of Paddington, reached London, going immediately to the Bank of England with the hope of receiving letters from Ethel. His steamer had been longer making the run than he had planned for, so Ethel could easily reply to his hurried note, perhaps add others on her own account. He was greatly disappointed at not hearing from her. He was also lonely and homesick, for, though he had come to enter upon the inheritance of his fathers, he was in a land of strangers.

He had telegraphed his lawyers, Court & Deeds, from Liverpool, making an appointment for the following day. So he went back to the hotel, wondering how he would get through a long, dull, lonely evening. After dinner in the coffee room he picked up the *Times* with the hope of finding some American news. By the merest chance he turned to the marriage column, and he smiled pleasantly when he thought that in a few months his name would be in that list. He therefore read on, going over one and then another, but as he came to the end he saw something which struck him as with a deathly chill; the paper trembled in his hand; his eyes strained painfully in their sockets, and for the moment were covered with a hot mist. But, instantly assuring himself that there must be a mistake, he compelled his eyes to steady themselves upon the page, when he read:

"VON DER PLONK—BROMPTON. On Wednesday, May 1, at the Church of St. Ezekiel's, New York, U. S., by the Rev. Horatio M. Bland, D.D., Ethel, daughter of Mr. Mark Brompton, to Hendrik Von der Plonk, son of the late Hendrik Von der Plonk."

Poor David Stanley! And he had called her his queen! He had filled his heart all the way across the sea with pictures of her as Duchess of Paddington! This, then, was the end of his dreams.

"You remember that David Stanley who used to come here quite frequently?" said Mark Brompton to Mrs. Brompton and Janet one evening about a week after the wedding, as they were sitting in the library.

"Yes," was the eager reply of both women— one reply prompted by a vivid remembrance of a letter which had been stolen and burned, the other by an equally vivid remembrance of Ethel's tears and despair, but final surrender to pride and ambition.

"Well, you know he was in South America acting as the agent of a New York house. I have a correspondent in the city where Stanley was, from whom I heard this morning. He writes me that Stanley, in the most unexpected way, has come into possession of a large estate in England, and the fellow is actually a duke."

" A duke!" and again the two women answered in the same breath, looking at Mr. Brompton with an interest for which he could not account.

" Yes, a duke! The Duke of Paddington is now his title, one of the most honorable in the English peerage." With this Mr. Brompton resumed the reading of his paper.

Neither Mrs. Brompton nor Janet made any reply, but they were both doing some unpleasant thinking.

" She might have been a duchess!" thought Janet, going back rapidly to some of the times when Ethel was almost on the point of breaking with Von der Plonk and taking her chances with David Stanley.

"She might have been a duchess!" thought Mrs. Brompton, as she recalled the letter which she had kept back from Ethel, for in that letter David Stanley had undoubtedly written of his good fortune.

In a few minutes Mrs. Brompton and Janet retired, each going to her own room to think over what Mr. Brompton had told them.

No sooner was Janet alone than she burst into tears, and with the cry, " My poor Ethel!" she threw herself upon the bed, sobbing as if her heart would break.

No sooner was Mrs. Brompton alone than she locked her fingers together and walked to and fro in her room like one demented. Her face became livid with passion. Her eyes fairly blazed in anger. She bit her lips until they were stained with blood. She cursed herself when she remembered that it was her doing that Ethel was not a duchess. The bitterness, the shame, the agony of that hour! It was simply maddening, and she had only herself to blame. With lightning-like rapidity but awful vividness the events connected with David Stanley and his love for Ethel passed before her. She saw with what remorselessness she had kept them apart. How implacable she had been! And now he was Duke of Paddington, and Ethel might have been a duchess! It was infuriating. It was more than flesh and blood could stand. So she stormed and raved, clenching her hands until her nails made deep, livid marks in the burning palm.

And is this the stately Mrs. Brompton, the woman of superb self-control, whose ease and dignity we have so often admired?

To gratify her ambition Mrs. Brompton had stooped to dishonor. That dishonor had gained a Von der Plonk, but lost a dukedom.

There was no sleep for Mrs. Brompton that night. " She might have been a duchess ! " in letters of fire was written on her soul.

CHAPTER XXXVIII.

Dr. Bland of St. Ezekiel's.

IT was not to be expected that the Rev. Dr. Bland would permit Madge and John Disney " to absent themselves from their accustomed place in the sanctuary " (using here his own words) without at least ascertaining the reason.

The Disney pew was a prominent one, and, though Dr. Disney was not often present, Mrs. Disney and Madge—John also when he was not away from home—had been quite regular in their attendance.

But for some time past Mrs. Disney was the only member of the family upon whom any dependence could be placed. That pew, therefore, now comparatively empty, gave the worthy clergyman much concern.

There are those who might be disposed to think that if the Disney pew had been in a less conspicuous place, or the Disney family been of less prominence, the pastor would not have been so quick to notice their absence nor so prompt in his efforts to secure their return. But any such suggestion is unjust to Dr. Bland. A more conscientious man could not be found anywhere, nor one who labored more earnestly for the people over whom he was placed. That he was exclusive, perhaps narrow, all who knew him would concede. Some went so far as to call him bigoted. This, though, was hardly just. His father

was a man of high scholarly attainments, a professor
in a leading university. Nor was he altogether dependent upon his income from the university, having
a fair property in his own right. Thus he was able
to gratify many of his tastes, which were mainly in
the line of the fine arts. He bought some nice
pictures at times. He had a few rare bits of
statuary. He was fond of books with dainty bindings. His home had choice bric-a-brac which he had
picked up when abroad. Then he had married into
one of the oldest and most aristocratic families in
Boston, his wife having no difficulty in tracing her
pedigree to William Bradford, one of the *May-
flower* passengers, afterward the first governor of the
Plymouth Colony. Brought up in such a home as
this, the only child too, what could Horatio know
of the rough, brawling world? Of that life in which
men fight for mastery; in which hunger and pride
and ambition, like chisels of steel, cut their terrible
marks upon human souls; in which avarice and desire, as vultures, swoop down upon the helpless and
the dying; in which thousands trample upon each
other in their mad strife for bread—of such a life Dr.
Bland knew nothing whatever.

Of the world in which common people live, the
world of injustice, of tyranny, of fraud, of heartless,
selfish cruelty, he did not even dream. It was not
priestly sanctity which allowed him to pass unheed-
ing the poor fellow who lay crushed and bleeding on
the Jericho road, but rather the rapt, ecstatic character of his faith. Utterly unworldly, gentle-hearted,
pure-minded, his was more the life of a mediæval

saint than of a man of this generation. He was far more familiar with the life of Corinth or Antioch or Ephesus than with the city in which he lived.

To his thought the Church was a magnificent ideal of spiritual desire; a sublime memorial of religious aspiration; a venerable institution hallowed by the centuries out of which it had come. Never once had it occurred to him that the Church, like leaven entering the meal, like salt arresting the process of decay, like light in the midst of darkness, was to take a part in the common affairs of life. With him the Church was a mighty edifice of steeples and towers reaching into the measureless sky, with no relations to the earth except as a mere resting place, from which it would ascend heavenward.

That the Church was to be a refuge for the tempted and tried; that it was to be the resolute, abiding friend of the downtrodden and the poor; that it was to stand as a mighty defense between the oppressor and the oppressed; that in everything pertaining to the real progress of the world it was to be the stalwart leader, were all things of which this good man had not the faintest idea. But how could he? He had never met with poverty, nor with crime, nor with coarse, brutal sin in any form.

" You will excuse me, Miss Disney, but, not having seen you at church for a Sunday or two, may I ask if you have been ill or out of town? "

The tone was grave, the look kindly, the inquiry sincere.

Madge was just a little troubled as to what to say.

She had not been ill. She had not been out of town. These time-honored and most convenient excuses could not, therefore, be brought forward. To confess that she had been going to the Mission with John, and also that she had become deeply interested in the Mission, might possibly annoy Dr. Bland. This she did not wish to do, as for years he had been an intimate friend in the Disney home.

Mrs. Disney, however, came to her relief.

"The fact is, Dr. Bland, a college friend of John's, and a very dear friend of the family as well"—here just the daintiest bit of color crept up in Madge's face, and Dr. Bland, though he was devoted to the Ante-Nicene fathers, thought Madge was looking most sweet and winsome—"has gone over to the East Side to engage in some kind of mission work, and Madge and John have been doing duty as assistants. I have told them that one of these days they must explain matters to you, as you would be sure to notice their absence from church."

Mrs. Disney smiled in a good-humored way at Madge. She did not altogether approve of this mission business, but she approved very thoroughly of Hugh Dunbar. Dunbar dropped in quite frequently now, not always to consult with John, nor even to have a friendly chat with Mrs. Disney. It is hardly worth while to mention that Madge was nearly always at home when he called.

Mrs. Disney's frank statement of the case opened the way for a general discussion of the Mission. This, of course, led to the mention of Hugh Dunbar, when Dr. Bland said:

24

"I have heard something of this young man. He must be a noble fellow."

Again that dainty color stole in Madge's face, and again Dr. Bland forgot for a moment or two the Ante-Nicene fathers.

The result of the conversation was that Dr. Bland remained to dinner, after dinner going over to the Mission with Madge and John.

When the dear man got over to the East Side, into the swarming, living streets, where he saw such strangeness and variety of life, he was almost frightened. His fears, however, were not for himself, but for Madge; but when he saw how fearlessly she walked at the side of John his anxiety gradually disappeared. After this he began to enjoy the novelty and excitement.

Here was a life unlike anything he had ever seen. Here were all these thousands of people of whose existence he had never been really conscious—men, women, young, old, street Arabs, peddlers, fakirs, factory girls, newsboys, sweatshop workers, mechanics, laborers, stevedores, draymen, marketmen—united to him in bonds of human relationship, but as much strangers as if they had come from a distant planet. From one he heard Italian, from another Spanish. One jabbered in Polish, another in Russian. Here he listened to the gutturals of the German, there to the brogue of the Irish. One spoke Parisian, another cockney English.

What an infinite distance lay between the parish occupied by the Mission and that of St. Ezekiel's! For the third time that day he forgot about the

Ante-Nicene fathers, but for the first time that day, or even in his whole life, he began to see the real meaning of the parable of the Good Samaritan.

The Mission House was a revelation to him. Mr. Dunbar took him all through it. He saw sewing rooms, where girls—little girls some of them—were taught dressmaking, shirtmaking, garment-making of all kinds. He saw boys' tradesrooms, where instruction was given to boys who otherwise would never be anything but common laborers. He saw gymnasiums, where young men were taking courses in physical training, the value of which would make life stronger and better for all the years to come. He saw reading rooms, where scores of men were reading books— some on mechanics, some on chemistry, some lighter, such as history or fiction. He saw play rooms, where groups of light-hearted young people forgot about the drudgery of the shop and were enjoying themselves wholesomely. He saw many things in that tour of inspection. Several times he coughed suspiciously, as if there was a sob in his throat. More than once he wiped his eyes, as if the dust troubled him. But there wasn't any dust.

Somehow there came upon him the feeling that he had thought too much about the Ante-Nicene fathers and not enough about the fathers of this generation. St. Ezekiel's seemed like a church in the sky, but this Mission was a church on the ground. His had been a Gospel of spires and minarets, whereas it should have been a Gospel of pavements and cobblestones. A remark of Hugh Dunbar wonderfully impressed him:

"If we will but allow Christianity to be thoroughly Christianized the whole problem will be solved."

It was later than usual that night when Dr. Bland returned to his home. Nor did he retire even then, late as it was. For hours he sat in his room pondering over the things he had seen and heard. The crowds at length died away, the voices ceased to beat upon his ear, but somehow in his sleep there came to him the vision of the Macedonian standing helpless and entreating, and he could hear his pitiful cry, "Come over and help us!"

On the next Sunday Dr. Bland made no reference to the Ante-Nicene fathers, nor even to the heresies of the church at Colosse. He preached on the "Good Samaritan," saying some plain things about the priest and the Levite.

The sermon gave rise to considerable discussion. Mark Brompton didn't like it at all. Some of the Von der Plonks were indignant. Mr. Keen was angry. Madge and John, who were at St. Ezekiel's that morning, could not but associate the sermon with Dr. Bland's visit to the Mission. Mr. Dunbar, when he heard of it, smiled in that grateful but suggestive way of his and said, "The leaven is at work."

CHAPTER XXXIX.

Edward Vaughen's Sad Discovery.

IN that mysterious, elusive, but singularly effective way which women have, Miss Keen gave Edward Vaughen to understand that for the future their ways must be more apart than they had been. At first Edward was completely mystified. He would look at her when they met (which, of course, they did quite often) in a pained, perplexed way, wondering what it all meant. Sometimes, when he would take her by surprise, he found a sad, almost hopeless, expression on her face; but the moment she saw that he had noticed her the expression would change, so that she would appear as when he first became acquainted with her.

He was fully aware of the fact that for the present he had nothing to offer her save the strong, honest love of his eager heart. But he was hopeful. He was ambitious. Other men had made their way; he would make his. He was resolved, though, that his way would be made honestly. But the world of business was a very different thing from what he had imagined in his college days. Most of his dreams and theories had been rudely dispelled. Long since he had parted with his hobby of the " unearned increment," though Madge, in her talks with John, still used that name for him. He no longer spoke of " the poor sheep huddling on the bleak mountain side." He saw the conduct of Gallio in a new light. His pet notions concerning the redistribution of property he had abandoned as foolish to the last degree. The meaningless socialism which he once had held he now saw as a foolish dream. Gradually it had dawned upon him that capital and labor were merely relative terms.

"John," he said one night, as the two cronies were talking after the manner of their college days, "what arrant nonsense we used to get off in the old times!"

"Speak for yourself, Edward Vaughen," John answered, in his dry way. "Say 'we' at your peril. You evidently fail to remember the valuable advice which I wasted on you when you would fill my room with the bleating of your lost sheep, or make the air blue with angry denunciations of that Gallio who had the good sense to mind his own business and wanted other people to mind theirs. Was there anything ever so soul-distressing as that 'sad undertone of the toiling millions' which you used to wail out with such fervor? Edward Vaughen, son of Thomas, if you say 'we' again, my wrath will descend upon you with the force and precision of a pile driver. When I think of the stuff you used to throw at my defenseless head—the 'unearned increment,' the 'evasion of responsibility,' and all the rest of it—it makes me marvel at my patience. What a Job I would have made! The only drawback is Mrs. Job. I never could have got along with that woman. But this 'we' of yours is the coolest thing I ever heard of. Icebergs are burning volcanoes in comparison with it."

There were few weeks in which the young men did not spend at least one evening with each other, one time Edward going up to the Disney home, another time John coming down to the Gubbins mansion.

"Slight rift in the lute," John remarked one evening as Miss Pollok pathetically warbled, " When: other lips and other hearts."

" Her 'tales of love' have flounces, or ruffles, by the way she lengthens them out," he said, as the next line, in quivering installments, came up stairs.

"Disney, the soul of music is not in you ; it never was. Miss Pollok shall no longer waste her dulcet strains on you."

With this Edward closed the door. At the same moment the artist closed his. Likewise Mr. Wright. Likewise Mr. Singleton. Miss Dawdledom, a new boarder, did not close hers. Miss Dawdledom was almost totally deaf.

The time came when Edward opened his heart to John about Miss Keen, for he was in sore need of just such help as John could give. He told him of his hopes, of the way in which they used to look for each other, of the tender, sympathetic relations they had sustained for now almost a year. He also spoke of that evening in Miss Keen's home, then adding in a brave but pathetic way :

" Old fellow, I am hard hit, and I won't get over it for a good while."

" You mustn't be too hard on Miss Keen," John said, sympathetically, for he was awfully sorry at the turn which affairs had taken. But he had expected this to come sooner or later. "Mr. Keen is one of the most ambitious men in the city. He has been anxious for a long time to get himself well placed with leading business men. His plan all along was to marry his daughter to Percy Brompton."

"Percy Brompton! my cousin!" Edward exclaimed, incredulously.

"Yes, Percy Brompton, your cousin. Your worthy uncle, however, saw through Mr. Keen's nice little plan. This may explain why Percy was sent South on some railroad matters at the time when Miss Keen's regard for you seemed to decline, and when Percy was quite a frequent guest at the Keen domicile. It was Madge who called my attention to this. Since she spoke of it I have been keeping track of things."

Now that the matter was brought to Edward's mind, he recalled several circumstances which seemed to favor John's putting of the case. But with instinctive chivalry he refused to think that Miss Keen was a party to these proceedings.

"An unwilling party, I grant, but a party, nevertheless," John insisted. Now that the matter was up, the truest kindness to Edward would be to open his eyes to the facts just as they were. It was anything but a pleasant task. John was just as chivalrous as Edward Vaughen. With such a mother and sister as he had he could not but have a high ideal of womanhood. To reflect on Miss Keen, so as to lower her in the thought of Edward, seemed a cruel thing to do. So he began:

"We must not be too severe with Miss Keen. She has not only her father's blood in her veins, but all her life has been under his influence. If you were Mark Brompton's son instead of his nephew she would gladly share your lot. But she has the same ambitions as her father. Then she has been accustomed all her life to put everything on a money basis. Percy is rich; you are poor. She is sorry that you are poor. She doubtless wishes that you were rich and Percy poor. That, however, will not affect her. We have known the Keens a long time, and these things which surprise you are no surprise to me."

What a night that was for Edward Vaughen! The poor fellow sat in that old rocker by the window watching the clouds bank and mass themselves in the sky. The moon was hidden behind these sky mountains—Alpine ranges of cloud and darkness. Then the wind came up strong and fierce from the sea, blowing a very tempest which swept through the streets in mad passion. After weary hours of darkness and storm the pale stars came out from their hiding-place. The clouds gradually disappeared. Once again the moon broke upon the mystery of the night. And still Edward sat at the window, looking out upon the parable of passion and despair in the earth and in the sky.

Then the morning came—gray, cheerless, barren; after this the sun; but the sun did not shine upon the same world as yesterday. The poetry was gone. The romance was gone. The very joy of life was gone. But, worst of all, his noble ideal of womanhood was gone. The woman to whose feet he would have gladly brought all the hopes and desires of his heart had only trifled with him. She was heartless and mercenary. To gratify a mere sentiment she had taken advantage of his unfamiliarity with the world, but when it came to a test she put him utterly aside. He watched the stars fade away, the gray light open out into morning radiance, the new day come upon the city.

He was very quiet as he sat at the breakfast table that morning. His face was pale, and there was a stricken look upon him which no one had ever seen there before. Faber noticed it, but said nothing. Mr. Singleton also noticed it, but he said nothing either. The people who say nothing are the wisest and truest in their sympathies. Any brook can babble.

Mrs. Gubbins, being a very practical woman, expressed her sympathy through a cup of most excellent coffee and the nicest chop she could find. She did not speak of the matter at the table, but afterward said to Jemima:

"That poor, dear Mr. Vaughen was in some kind of trouble, and looked real sick."

.   .   .   .   .   .

In the numerous expeditions which Ethel Brompton, now Mrs. Von der Plonk, was called upon to make in the weeks preceding her marriage, the dry-goods house of Linsey & Woolsey received due patronage. This led to a number of meetings with Oberta Sauvier. Janet, who often accompanied her sister on these very interesting pilgrimages, would

sometimes remain in "cloaks and wraps" while Ethel
went to another part of the store to study carpets or
furniture under the leadership of Mrs. Brompton.
Janet found Miss Sauvier very much of a lady.
After a time they chatted quite pleasantly, and when
Janet spoke of her sister's approaching marriage
Oberta, of course, was much interested, for have we
not high authority for the statement that "the whole
world loves a lover?" And does not the right kind
of a lover usually mean a wedding? Oberta having
exquisite taste, as well as considerable experience,
was able to suggest certain arrangements and combinations which met the approval of the Brompton
contingent. Indeed, Mrs. Brompton was once heard
to remark that "that young person in Linsey &
Woolsey's was a most capable saleswoman."

After the wedding there was quite a little interval
when Janet did not go to the store; but one day she
went alone. She had no special need to visit Oberta's
department; nevertheless she went up stairs to
"cloaks and wraps." When she saw Oberta, in the
most cordial, kindly way she held out her hand,
greeting her as she would any of her friends. They
talked for a few moments, Oberta asking about Mrs.
Von der Plonk, and saying with what interest she
had read of the wedding. Just then a young man
came over from the elevator, but seeing Oberta
engaged with a lady, whom he took to be a customer,
he waited quietly, standing somewhat in the background. As soon as Oberta saw him she impul-
sively said, "Why, here is my brother!" upon which
Fred at once came forward. But in a moment the

situation became embarrassing. Oberta could not introduce Fred to Miss Brompton. Without Miss
Brompton's permission such a thing could not be
done, and if done would be rudeness unpardonable.
But when a keen-witted, good-hearted woman undertakes to lead anyone out of a difficulty she soon finds
a way.

"Miss Sauvier, will you kindly introduce me to
your brother?" said Janet, reaching out her hand at
the same moment to Fred, for she never did anything
by halves. "Mr. John Disney, a dear friend of
ours, has spoken so often of Mr. Sauvier that we all
feel acquainted with him."

Then she remained for a couple of minutes, chatting in the most cordial way.

"Miss Brompton," Fred repeated, after she had
gone; "any relation, I wonder, of Mr. Mark Brompton, one of our directors?"

"His daughter," answered Oberta, not, either,
without pride, for it was a source of much gratifica-
tion to her that people of the social rank of the
Disneys and the Bromptons gave her a place in their
regard.

How the leaven of Hugh Dunbar's ministry was
spreading! And with what amazing energy it was
doing its work!

The next day in the office Fred spoke to John
Disney of having met Miss Brompton, upon which
John declared that "Janet Brompton was one of the
nicest girls in New York." To this remark Fred
Sauvier took no exception, either then or ever after-
ward.

CHAPTER XL.

Mr. Blinks and Mr. Winks.

HERE we have a question in casuistry. Mr. Blinks and Mr. Winks at one time were most intimate friends. So cordial were their relations that when they moved from the city to the suburbs they had their houses built on adjoining lots, without any fence between. But for some reason Mr. Blinks changed in his feelings toward Mr. Winks. So complete was this change that he began to consider Mr. Winks as the personification of all villainies. Feeding his anger with highly inflammable material, he soon had a heart which almost breathed out threatenings and slaughter. He determined, therefore, to dispose of Mr. Winks. After thinking the matter over Mr. Blinks concluded that a bomb of the right size, properly located under the house of Mr. Winks, would answer his purpose. In short, to put it in the plainest terms, Mr. Blinks resolved that Mr. Winks should be blown up "sky high."

Accordingly he procured a bomb, connected it with an electric battery which he had concealed in his own room, watched his opportunity to carry the bomb to his neighbor's house, after which, Wellington-like, he wished for night.

Mr. Winks, for some reason, came home earlier than usual that evening. Having never outgrown

his passionate love for a lawn mower, he went down
to his cellar, that he might gaze with rapture upon a
new one which he was anxious to use. While in the
cellar he saw the bomb. At first he did not know
just what to do with it, for bombs are quick-tempered,
and fly off on the least provocation. Seeing a wire
attached to this bomb, he traced that wire to the
next house. Being a very honest man, he at once
decided that the bomb belonged to the next house,
and that it had strayed out from its proper home.
With all the tenderness of a shepherd with a poor,
sick lamb he carried the bomb back to its fold. The
strained relations between these once good friends
prevented Mr. Winks from informing Mr. Blinks of
what he had done. Besides being honest, Mr.
Winks was modest, for he even waited for the early
night before carrying the bomb home. And so no
one saw the kindly thing which he had done.

Sometime in the night he was aroused from his
peaceful slumbers by a terrific explosion, upon which
he rushed to the window, just in time to see Mr.
Blinks taking a skyward excursion, moving upward
with such rapidity that he must soon land somewhere in the moon. Now for the question : Of
what crime was Mr. Blinks guilty? or of what crime
was Mr. Winks guilty?

This affecting anecdote is explanatory of the relations between Keen & Sharp and Mark Brompton.
Keen & Sharp procured the bomb, set the battery,
and arranged for the time when the button would
be pressed. Mr. Brompton cautiously removed the
bomb from his premises, carried it over to the prem-

ises of Keen & Sharp, and when Mr. Keen gave the sign for Mr. Sharp to push the button Mr. Brompton was standing at the window to see them go flying in the air.

That was a terrible day in Wall Street. It opened like the battle of Waterloo. There was firing all along the line. For hours it raged, fortunes going down, like the Old Guard, into the terrible ravine. Men who were rich that morning when they left their homes went back bankrupt. Friends of Keen & Sharp charged upon the friends of Mark Brompton, as the French upon the Château de Hougomont. But Mark Brompton knew how the battle would end. In his strong box he held stock for which Keen & Sharp would gladly have paid a hundred times its value. At the right moment he gave the sign, and Keen & Sharp were hopelessly ruined.

It meant utter bankruptcy for Mr. Keen. He was well aware that once his treachery became known on the "Street" he might just as well leave New York forever. Wall Street admires pluck, grit, gigantic schemes, combinations that reach all around the world. When a man is beaten down by misfortune, if he has made a fair fight, Wall Street will help him to his feet again. But when a man has acted dishonorably, when the broker goes back on his client, Wall Street rises in its wrath, and such a one is cast out of the financial synagogue. This was what Keen & Sharp had done, and when that terrible day closed they knew that the end had come.

It is impossible not to pity Mr. Keen. He had

played for high stakes, and he had lost. The ambitions of his whole life centered upon the results of this day. But he was beaten. And the worst of it was that he deserved to be beaten. He had played his game dishonestly. He has listened to the voice, " All these will I give thee," but the voice lied.

That night he gathered up such things as he could, leaving the city on the midnight train. The next day, when the newspapers were announcing his failure, he was on his way to Rio Janeiro, where he remained for the rest of his life.

Mrs. Keen was not left quite destitute, as some years before Mr. Keen made over to her a little property intended just for " pin money," but now it was all she had. She and Rhea left New York as soon as they could conveniently get away. They did not go to Rio Janeiro, but to some little place in Maine, where Mrs. Keen had distant relations.

One thing here should be said of Rhea. Edward Vaughen wrote her in the most tender and sympathetic way, which, had she been disposed to take advantage of, might easily have led to a return of the conditions once existing between them. But she merely acknowledged his letter, taking care in her reply to obviate the necessity of his writing again.

He then called, but a formal " not at home " was the only result. Not content with this, he called again, but Mrs. Keen and Rhea had left town.

On the evening of that eventful day when Keen & Sharp met with such an overwhelming defeat Dr. Disney looked anxious and troubled. As it was known in the family that he had two or three very serious cases on his list which were unusually severe, his anxiety gave no special concern. But he was, if anything, even more gracious and considerate than for weeks past. In the course of the evening Mr. Dunbar came in and spent a little while with Mrs. Disney and Madge, afterward going to the doctor's sitting room, saying he wished to see him alone. After Mr. Dunbar had left the parlor Mrs. Disney looked inquiringly at Madge, upon which Madge looked answeringly at Mrs. Disney. Then Mrs. Disney got up from her chair, Madge at the same instant getting up from hers. In another moment Mrs. Disney had Madge in her arms, and they were kissing and smiling and shedding tears all at once.

Then Dr. Disney came in with Hugh Dunbar, and taking Madge by the hand, gave her to Dunbar, saying, "She is worthy of all the love that you can give her."

As he spoke he tenderly kissed her on the lips and on the forehead, and stroked her head in that gentle, loving way of his. He shook hands cordially with Dunbar, and in Mrs. Disney's behalf as well as his own gave him hearty welcome to their household. But he was very grave, and his voice seemed full of tears. He soon went back to his sitting room, where he remained alone.

Later on John came in, and he had quite a long talk with his father, John going over some plans which he had partly formed about starting in business for himself.

"That clerking of mine in the Tubal-Cain Iron Works has given me both information and experi-

25

ence," John said. "But now that I have decided upon going into regular business the sooner I get at it the better."

To this Dr. Disney assented, at the same time asking John if any definite plan had occurred to him. John then went on to speak of Mr. Brompton, who, he said, had a large interest in the Tubal-Cain Works, but who might be disposed to make some arrangement in the matter. Indeed, he had spoken of it himself, "not so much on my account," John said, with a frank smile, "as to make an opening for Percy. Mr. Brompton has made the discovery that Percy is much better off when he has something to do. That was why he sent him South on that railroad business. You have seen the evening papers, of course? Terrible affair that of Keen & Sharp! But they should have known better than run up against Mark Brompton. Dad, you are not looking well. As you sometimes say, 'been rather overdoing of late.' Why not let up on things?"

"I am going to write to Mr. Brompton perhaps to-night," the doctor said. "I have a matter upon which I desire his judgment. If you wish I will refer to what you have said."

"O, thank you! A word from you will have great weight with Mr. Brompton," John answered.

So they talked on for some little time longer. Then with, "Good night, my boy!" "Good night, dad!" they parted.

Mrs. Disney had retired when the doctor went to her room, but was not asleep, so he went over to the bed, kissed her, bade her good night, saying that he had some letters to write which would detain him in his office for perhaps an hour. Then he turned down the light, arranged the shade so that even the faint glimmer would not disturb Mrs. Disney, looked about the room to see that everything was all right, after which he went out, closing the door gently behind him.

On going to his office, he went to the little safe, taking from it a box in which he kept his private papers. He went over these papers carefully, selecting first one, and then another, until he had perhaps a dozen, all told, which he put in a large, heavy envelope, securing it with rubber bands. The others he burned, careful even to stir up the light crisp remains, so that no one looking at the fireplace would suspect anything of what had been done.

Then he wrote a long letter to Mark Brompton, inclosing with it the large, heavy envelope, the contents of which he had so carefully arranged. This he weighed on his " postal scale," affixing the necessary stamps. Everyone now being in bed, he took the letter himself to the mail box, which was on the corner of the next street, going out and coming in so quietly· as not to disturb Mrs. Disney, who was a very light sleeper.

When he came back he did not go up stairs to his room, but returned to the office, sitting down in a big chair, where he watched the fire slowly dying in the grate.

And this was how they found him in the morning. But his eyes were closed never to be opened again, and his face was still in death !

That night when Fred Sauvier came home from

the office he told his mother and Oberta of the awfully sudden death of Dr. Disney. Oberta, glancing
swiftly at her mother, saw that her face was like
marble. But Mrs. Sauvier said nothing. She soon,
however, went to her room, where she remained for
the rest of the evening. In response to the inquiries
of Oberta she complained of not feeling well, but
hoped to be better in the morning. In the morning
she was at the breakfast table in her usual place, but
her face was almost as gray and deathly as that of
the dead man who had been found in his office chair.

Mark Brompton was at home when the morning
mail brought him Dr. Disney's letter, but, seeing that
it was marked " Personal," he did not open it at the
breakfast table with his other letters. On going into
the library, from the weight and size of the envelope
he thought it must be a lengthy communication. He
therefore sat down, but before he had read the letter
half through he hastily rose from his chair, and, calling the footman, ordered the carriage to be brought
immediately. While waiting for the carriage he
finished reading the letter, which he then folded up,
carefully replacing it in the envelope with the other
papers, locking them all up in his private desk.

A stern, pitiless face Mark Brompton had as he
stepped into his carriage. As a man of iron he had
gone through the battle of the previous day. Without a quiver or an emotion of pity he had driven
Keen & Sharp to a ruin from which escape was hopeless. Nor had even this contented him, but with a
spirit that was remorseless he had brought ruin upon
many who had taken sides with them. The taste of

blood was upon his lips. His face was therefore implacable as his carriage stopped at theDisney home.

But on coming to the door, to his amazement, he
saw the fatal flowers against a background of dark
ribbon, tied to the bell handle. He knew then that
death was in the house—most likely Mrs. Disney, he
thought. When John gave him the terrible news his
anger died within him, for who can be angry in the
awful presence of death? He remained for some
time, comforting as best he could the sorely afflicted
home, and before he left, when they took him to the
room where the poor dead body lay, he could not
restrain the tears, and broke down helplessly.

On going back to his home, which he did as soon
as he left the Disneys, he took out Dr. Disney's letter once more, this time, however, not to read it, but
to destroy it, as well as all the other papers with
which it came.

Twenty-five years before Dr. Disney had tempted
Fred Sauvier to dishonor and crime, for it was at his
suggestion that the forgery was committed. But
now the same sins are upon his own soul, for he
has forged, using Mark Brompton's name on notes
given by him to Keen & Sharp. Discovery is now
inevitable. The same horror and disgrace which fell
upon Fred Sauvier will now fall upon him. " What-
soever a man soweth, that shall he also reap." ,

But Mark Brompton never told. So the world
never knew of the awful secret which was buried in
Dr. Disney's grave.

Hunger has slain its hundreds, pride its thousands,
ambition its tens of thousands.

EPILOGUE.

HOWEVER strenuously Edward Vaughen might object to a preface, there is surely no reason for him to question the propriety of an epilogue, for one cannot leave a story as he would a play—with the stage full of people to go scampering off as they please when the curtain drops. Neither can we let go in this abrupt way the friends with whom we have enjoyed such a lengthy companionship. For instance, there is Jamie Smithers. We surely ought to know how it fared with him. Well, he recovered from that sickness of his, for all the boy required was rest and nourishment. These Sister Nora took care of. He still carves, but he has gone far beyond salad sets, or "them Swiss frames." His work is now eagerly sought for. Indeed, there are decorating establishments, well known to wealthy Gothamites, who are glad to have Jamie do special carvings for them. His face is not so white nor so thin as it once was; he has grown quite a little, still he is not too big for his mother to take him on her knee; so she croons to him and sings to him as she ever did, and most likely ever will until he goes back to his home among the angels.

As for Silas Smithers, his days of trouble ended just as soon as he found steady work. This Sister Nora also took care of. Nor was it a very difficult matter, once he got a fair start; hence through Sister

Nora's influence his way opened from one place to another, so that his business steadily increased; he has now a little shop of his own and is doing nicely; he enjoys his armchair just as well as he ever did—also the old stubby pipe. Last Christmas "Mollie" was fairly extravagant, buying him a handsome brier with a genuine amber tip, but he only uses it on state occasions.

Ethel Von der Plonk could not but hear in due time of David Stanley's good fortune; but whatever regret she may have felt she was sufficiently wise to keep her own counsel. Once Janet alluded to it, then rather thoughtlessly, when she said:

"Ethel, you came very near being a duchess."

"Yes," answered Ethel, "but perhaps it is just as well as it is."

The reply was quiet, but so conclusive that the matter was not spoken of again.

Mrs. Brompton did not realize all the happiness she had expected from her alliance with the Von der Plonks. Ethel was accepted as inevitable, but that acceptance did not include Mrs. Brompton. Then she had the bitter memory of the stolen letter, and with it the still more bitter reflection that but for her Ethel might now be a duchess, hobnobbing with royalty, in which exalted honors Mrs. Brompton herself would have had a share. As David Stanley, now Duke of Paddington, was too much of a gentleman to write or make any inquiries, Mrs. Brompton is the only one who knows just how near Ethel came to wearing a coronet.

The Keens never came back to New York. Mr.

Keen died within a short time after reaching Rio Janeiro. It was rumored, though, that Rhea was going to marry a wealthy lumber merchant quite a little older than herself ; how much truth was in the rumor no one could say.

Edward Vaughen, after some years of experience in office work, started in business for himself. Mr. Brompton was his backer to a substantial amount, all of which Edward repaid. Mr. Singleton has an interest in the new firm, besides being confidant and manager. Edward is not making money "hand over fist," but he is making a good income, one which would have enabled him to give a pleasant home to Rhea Keen, had she only waited for him. His mother lives with him the greater part of the year, but she spends her summers at Eastwich, keeping tender watch of that grave in the village churchyard.

Mr. Faber in due time was promoted to one of the editorial desks on the *Trombone*. Not long after this promotion Oberta left "cloaks and wraps," much to the regret of Linsey & Woolsey, Hugh Dunbar performing the ceremony which changed her name to Mrs. Dixon Faber.

Janet Brompton, when she heard of this wedding possibility, actually asked, in just about so many words, to be Oberta's bridesmaid! Mrs. Brompton was indignant, but Janet appealed to her father, who decidedly said :

"Certainly, if Miss Sauvier wishes it."

A great change had come over Mark Brompton since the death of Dr. Disney. He withdrew almost entirely from speculation, giving his time to other interests. He carried out a number of Janet's notions in Bromptonville, where his mills and factories are. Comfortable dwellings are now provided for the ' operatives; the scale of wages has been carefully revised; a fund has been set apart to secure pensions for such as are no longer able to work; the principle of cooperation has been recognized, not formally, for that Mr. Brompton did not consider expedient, but in spirit, which, after all, is of more importance. When he goes to Bromptonville a regular ovation is given him. As for Janet, the people simply worship her.

John Disney had no difficulty in arranging with Mr. Brompton for control of the Tubal-Cain Iron Works. Neither had Mr. Brompton any special, trouble with the other stockholders, for when he made a thorough investigation he found that the concern had actually been losing money for some time, though paying dividends all the while! Mr. Brompton placed no reliance whatever upon the time-honored remark, "Figures won't lie." He knew that when properly juggled figures are the biggest kind of liars. So these dividends had been taken out of the plant, out of the quality of the goods, out of everything there was.

The concern was therefore virtually bankrupt. In his curt, decisive way he gave the other stockholders to understand that they must "either buy or sell," else he would ask for the appointment of a receiver. Being children of this generation, therefore wise as regards "the mammon of unrighteousness," they sold out to Mr. Brompton. He in turn sold out to his son Percy and John Disney. Our distinguished friends, Mr. Falcon, Mr. Stubbs, and Mr. Stafford, were very much aggrieved at the turn of affairs, particularly as it turned them out upon a cold, inhospitable world. Fred Sauvier is, at this writing, general manager.

The concern is now Disney & Brompton, Mr. Brompton insisting that John's name should have the first place.

John Disney is no dreamer, no Arabian Nights reformer, no Utopian philosopher; on the contrary, he is one of the coolest, shrewdest business men in the city. But he recognizes that his men have rights which he is bound to respect. He thinks there is a "Golden Rule" somewhere which ought to be applied in business. Hence he tries to do as "he would be done by." Once in a while he "strikes a snag" among the workmen, but they talk it over, finally adjusting it to mutual satisfaction.

The removal of both Edward Vaughen and Dixon Faber from the kindly care of Mrs. Gubbins was a great grief to that good-hearted woman. Their commendable promptness in paying their board bills, not to speak of certain other good qualities, had secured for them a deep place in the affection of Mrs. Gubbins. She therefore viewed their departure in the light not only of a personal bereavement, but also a household calamity.

"Prompter pay I never had from anyone," she said to Mr. Wright, an expression which served two purposes, for it was both an appreciation and a reminder. It could not truthfully be said of Mr. Wright that he was enthusiastically prompt. Neither was the humorist. The artist was. So was Miss Pollok.

It was with a feeling of downright regret that Edward left his "third floor, hall back." Still, he could not forbear a quiet smile when, on coming down the stairs, he heard Miss Pollok warble, in tones that were distinctly tremulous, "No one to love, none to caress," the piano responding with all the power of which it was capable.

Mrs. Sauvier now makes her home with Oberta, for the time came when Fred had his home in the suburbs. A sweet, pleasant home it is, presided over by our good friend Janet Brompton! This was about the last drop in Mrs. Brompton's cup of bitterness. When she saw the growing intimacy of the young people she appealed to Ethel. Ethel looked sternly at her mother out of those sharp eyes of hers—at times Ethel strongly resembled her father—and said:

"I should think that you ought to know by this time the sin of interfering in matters like these."

It was not a sweet remark, hardly even a proper one, but there were some things which Ethel could not forget. Mrs. Brompton turned very pale when Ethel made this remark. For the moment she was almost certain that Ethel knew of the stolen letter.

Mrs. Sauvier has lost not only from her face but from her heart the old bitterness. Indeed, so completely is the past forgiven that she visits frequently at the Disney home. Madge she loves dearly. But then every one loves Madge.

At first the congregation of St. Ezekiel's listened with amazement as Dr. Bland discoursed on the problems of city life, taking them up one after the other in his dignified but earnest way. He made no reference whatever to the Nestorian theories, and the extremes to which they led in the Eutychian heresies. He even omitted to give his reasons for taking exception to the chronology of Archbishop Usher in some matter concerning the Hittites. As for the Ante-Nicene fathers, they were ignored altogether. But after a time St. Ezekiel's entered into the spirit of Dr. Bland, so much so that if the labor delegate to whom Hugh Dunbar gave serious attention one Sunday afternoon should ever visit St. Ezekiel's he will receive as cordial a welcome as he can desire.

The death of Dr. Disney did not involve any marked change in the public life of the family. Mrs. Disney's income, supplemented by that of Madge, enabled them to live very much as they had done. It was a matter of some surprise, though, that Dr. Disney left almost nothing in the way of money or personal property.

"Dr. Disney made some very unfortunate investments," Mark Brompton said to Mrs. Disney; for it was known that Dr. Disney had written Mr. Brompton the night before he died. Indeed, Mr. Brompton had spoken of this himself. "He arranged with me, however, concerning an interest in the Tubal-Cain Iron Works, in case I could manage it for him. You will have an income from that one of these days."

The simple fact was that Dr. Disney had appealed on behalf of John in that letter, earnestly pleading that for the sake of "his boy" Mr. Brompton would not have recourse to the law. This was what Mark Brompton called an "arrangement." But it gave him an opportunity to do a kindly, generous thing for both Mrs. Disney and John, and while some people might question the truthfulness of his statement no one could question the purpose of his heart.

Madge allowed nothing to interfere with her work at the Mission. Though her heart was almost broken when her father died, yet she went on bravely in the divine service of comforting and helping others. Her bright face, her kindly ways, her quick, eager, earnest sympathy, have endeared her to scores and hundreds of the laboring and heavy laden.

Hugh Dunbar is going on just as we saw him in the beginning. He startles people every little while, but that does not distress him. Men say that he is a "radical," which, he says, means "progressive." Others say that he is a "revolutionist," which, he says, means "turning things right side up." Some of his ministerial friends say that he preaches nothing but "humanity," upon which he smiles and replies: "So far I have met only human beings in my ministry. Please send on your angels." His one theory for everything is "the Christianization of Christianity."

Of Sister Nora it need hardly be said that she remembers with the most tender fidelity her mother's holy legacy. Her wealth she administers as a sacred trust. Her womanhood she has consecrated to the cause of the poor and the forsaken. Her noble life is a benediction to all who come within its reach.

We read that after that terrible conflict in the wilderness, when the tempted One was worn out with hunger and weakness, angels came and ministered unto Him. That mighty parable is repeated in the life of to-day. Sister Nora may not have the wings of an angel, but she has the heart of an angel. Among the angels there may be fairer faces, but no more earnest or loving soul. But among all the women of Gotham there is none more tender, more kind, or more pitiful than Sister Nora.